Intellectual Property Rights in Pharmaceutical Test Data

Adam Buick

Intellectual Property Rights in Pharmaceutical Test Data

Origins, Globalisation and Impact

Springer

Adam Buick
School of Law
Ulster University
Belfast, UK

ISBN 978-3-031-29435-8 ISBN 978-3-031-29436-5 (eBook)
https://doi.org/10.1007/978-3-031-29436-5

This Springer imprint is published by the registered company Springer Nature Switzerland AG
The registered company address is: Gewerbestrasse 11, 6330 Cham, Switzerland

Acknowledgements

As with any project, this book would have been a great deal more difficult and significantly less enjoyable without the input and support of many people who, as with any project, are too numerous to list here in full. However, I must specifically acknowledge the contributions of Professor Graham Dutfield, Dr César Ramírez-Montes, Professor Peter Drahos, and Dr Subhajit Basu as especially important.

In addition, I am grateful to the support of all of my friends and family, especially my wife, Cécile, and my parents, Brian and Lynn.

Contents

Abbreviations

AIDS	Acquired Immunodeficiency Syndrome
ARV	Antiretroviral
ANDA	Abbreviated New Drug Application
AGCM	*Autorità Garante della Concorrenza e del Mercato* (Authority for Competition and Market; Italian Competition Agency)
BIO	Biotechnology Industry Organisation
BLA	Biologic License Application
BPCIA	Biologic Price Competition and Innovation Act
CAFTA-DR	Central American Free Trade Agreement—Dominican Republic
CETA	EU-Canada Comprehensive Economic and Trade Agreement
COVID-19	Coronavirus disease 2019
CPTPP	Comprehensive and Progressive Agreement for Trans-Pacific Partnership
DSB	Dispute Settlement Body
EC	European Communities
EEA	European Economic Area
EFPIA	European Federation of Pharmaceutical Industries and Associations
EFTA	European Free Trade Association
EGA	European Generic Medicines Association
EMA	European Medicines Agency
EMEA	European Medicines Evaluation Agency
EPA	US Environmental Protection Agency
EPO	European Patent Office
EU	European Union
FDA	Food and Drug Administration
FDCA	Food, Drugs, and Cosmetics Act
FTA	Free Trade Agreement
GATT	General Agreement on Tariffs and Trade
HIV	Human Immunodeficiency Virus
HWA	Hatch-Waxman Act
ICTSD	International Centre for Trade and Sustainable Development

IFPMA	International Federation of Pharmaceutical Manufacturers and Associations
KEI	Knowledge Ecology International
LDC	Least Developed Country
MFN	Most Favoured Nation
MPAA	Motion Picture Association of America
MSD	Merck, Sharp & Dohme
MSF	*Médecins Sans Frontières* (Doctors Without Borders)
NAFTA	North American Free Trade Agreement
NCE	New Chemical Entity
NCI	New Chemical Indication
NDA	New Drug Application
NG11	Negotiating Group 11
NIH	National Institutes of Health
NME	New Molecular Entity
NTP	New Trade Policy
OECD	Organisation for Economic Co-operation and Development
PCT	Patent Cooperation Treaty
PhRMA	Pharmaceutical Research and Manufacturers of America
R&D	Research and Development
TPA	Trade Promotion Agreement
TPP	Trans-Pacific Partnership
TRIPS	Agreement on Trade-Related Aspects of Intellectual Property Rights
UNCTAD	United Nations Conference on Trade and Development
US(A)	United States (of America)
USC	United States Code
USD	United States Dollars
USMCA	United States–Mexico–Canada Agreement
USTR	Office of the United States Trade Representative
UK	United Kingdom
VCLT	Vienna Convention on the Law of Treaties
WHO	World Health Organisation
WIPO	World Intellectual Property Organisation
WTO	World Trade Organisation

List of Figures

List of Tables

Chapter 1
Introduction

Abstract This introductory chapter sets out the basic issue under discussion in this book (intellectual property rights in submitted pharmaceutical test data), as well as the theoretical framework, scope, aims and methodology of the book.

1.1 Introduction

The process of drug development is a long and costly one. Estimates of the true cost of drug development are controversial and vary widely,[1] but it is certainly the case that the process is extremely expensive—not least because the large majority of potential pharmaceutical products fail to make it to market. As a result, only a relatively small number of pharmaceutical companies, often referred to as 'research-based' pharmaceutical companies, take part in this process. These firms are willing to spend such large sums developing new drugs because by obtaining patents over a new pharmaceutical product they can earn considerable returns on their investments. Freed from direct competition, patent holders may set a price for their pharmaceutical products far in excess of the cost of manufacturing those drugs. Given that obtaining these products could very well be a matter of life or death for some, purchasers—whether individuals or healthcare providers—may be prepared to pay extremely high prices.

The purpose of patents is not, of course, simply to raise the price of medicines. Patents are intended to incentivise the development of new inventions, including medicines, by permitting right holders to earn a profit during the patent term, as well as to incentivise the dissemination of those inventions by requiring the inventor to disclose how to work their invention in the patent application. When a patent over a pharmaceutical product ends, other pharmaceutical companies, often referred to as 'generic' firms, will therefore seek to enter the market with 'generic' versions of the original pharmaceutical. As these generic drugs are chemically identical to the

[1] A controversial paper by DiMasi et al in 2016 put the cost of bringing a new drug to market, accounting for the cost of the many drugs which fail to reach market, at $2.6 billion USD. However, this figure has been the subject of a number of criticisms; see Narcyz Ghinea et al. (2016), p. 1284.

A. Buick, *Intellectual Property Rights in Pharmaceutical Test Data*,
https://doi.org/10.1007/978-3-031-29436-5_1

original product, the price for the drug in question will thus rapidly decrease as purchasers seek the cheapest seller—a phenomenon sometimes referred to as the 'patent cliff.'[2]

A significant cost of bringing a new pharmaceutical product to market is the fact that in virtually all jurisdictions, evidence of the safety and efficacy of a pharmaceutical product must be submitted to regulators before the product can be marketed.[3] The cost of generating this evidence is significant; some have put the figure at 60% of the total costs of developing a new drug.[4] Manufacturers of generic drugs must also demonstrate the safety and efficacy of their product, but doing so by conducting their own extensive clinical trial is not a viable option because it will not be possible for them to obtain patent protection. In order to enable generic pharmaceuticals to enter the market, most jurisdictions therefore provide an 'abridged' or 'abbreviated' drug approval pathway for generic products; when applying for market authorisation through such a pathway, a sponsor for a generic need only establish that their drug is 'bioequivalent' (identical for practical purposes) to the originator product, and may therefore be approved on the basis that the data submitted by the originator firm has already established the safety and efficacy of the drug in question.[5] Bioequivalence studies can be conducted quickly, and typically only involve a few dozen healthy subjects; as a result, the cost of gaining marketing approval for generic drugs is significantly lower than for originator products.

Research-based pharmaceutical firms deeply resent that the very data they produce at such expense is subsequently used to enable their competitors to enter the market. As a result, in the 1980s research-based pharmaceutical firms in the US successfully pushed for measures to protect the data submitted to regulators from use by competitors for a time-limited period. This protection is now widely recognised as a *sui generis* form of intellectual property in submitted test data known as 'test data exclusivity', sometimes also referred to as 'data exclusivity',[6] 'data protection'[7] or 'regulatory data protection.'[8] From the beginning, critics have charged it has never been demonstrated that test data exclusivity leads to greater pharmaceutical innovation, and that test data exclusivity rights unnecessarily inflate the price of medicines by further delaying the market entry of generic products.[9] Against this, proponents of test data exclusivity argue that these rights are an important

[2] Song and Han (2016), p. 692.
[3] Dutfield (2008), p. 118.
[4] Grabowski (2002), p. 95.
[5] See further Food and Drug Administration (2003).
[6] Spina Alì (2018), p. 201.
[7] Meitinger (2005), p. 123.
[8] Wadlow (2008) p. 355.
[9] See further Engelberg (1999).

component in ensuring that the development of new drugs remains financially viable, in particular in situations in which patent protection is for some reason unavailable.[10]

During the Uruguay Round of General Agreement on Trade and Tariff (GATT) negotiations which eventually led to the establishment of the World Trade Organisation (WTO), the US, EC and Switzerland pushed for the inclusion of a requirement to provide test data exclusivity in what would become the Agreement on Trade-Related Aspects of Intellectual Property Rights (TRIPS Agreement). This was opposed by developing countries, and an explicit requirement for test data exclusivity was ultimately rejected from the Agreement. However, the final version of TRIPS did require some protection for submitted test data; Article 39.3 of TRIPS states that members must protect 'undisclosed test or other data' submitted as a condition for approving the marketing of 'pharmaceutical or of agricultural chemical products which utilize new chemical entities' against 'unfair commercial use.'[11] What is meant by 'unfair commercial use' and what members of the WTO must do to protect against it remains unclear almost three decades after the TRIPS Agreement came into force. Despite this, test data exclusivity provisions are now found in many national legal systems. Much of this globalisation has occurred through trade agreements negotiated by the US, EU and European Free Trade Association (EFTA), as have other 'TRIPS-plus' intellectual property rights. However, test data exclusivity has become significantly more widely globalised than other TRIPS-plus measures such as patent-linkage provisions and patent term extensions. Since the advent of test data exclusivity for pharmaceuticals in the US in 1984, over 50 countries, virtually none of which have a significant domestic research-based pharmaceutical industry, have adopted test data exclusivity laws of some kind.[12]

1.2 Regulation and Globalisation

Like other forms of intellectual property, test data exclusivity rights are a form of regulation. All regulation imposes costs on society; while ideally the benefits to the public interest of a particular form of regulation outweigh these costs, this outcome is not guaranteed. As James Boyle has observed, in the case of intellectual property rights, these costs and benefits are closely linked. Intellectual property rights provide incentives because they also provide monopolies; if the public domain is undervalued and intellectual property rights are too many in number or too

[10] The International Federation of Pharmaceutical Manufacturers and Associations (IFPMA), a pharmaceutical trade body, argues that the availability of test data exclusivity 'can be a key consideration in the business decision to introduce new innovative drugs into a market.' See further IFPMA (2011), p. 5.

[11] Agreement on Trade-Related Aspects of Intellectual Property Rights (1994) (TRIPS) Article 39.3.

[12] Shaikh (2016), p. 231.

expansive in scope, such state-backed monopolies will provide established players with an anticompetitive advantage.[13]

In addition to the risk that regulation may be poorly designed and through unintended consequences harm the overall good, regulation may also be 'captured' and intentionally designed to serve the interests of a small group of actors at the expense of the public interest. This is possible even in a democratic society because, as highlighted by the economist Mancur Olson, the logic of collective action means that small but organised groups have an advantage over large but diffused groups with regard to influencing the regulatory process because they face lower barriers to organising and because the actors involved stand to gain a larger share of the benefit created.[14] These risks are especially relevant regarding intellectual property rights; these impose very obvious costs (such as the increased prices consumers must bear for patented pharmaceuticals), advantage a small and often powerful class of rightsholders (such as the pharmaceutical companies to whom this wealth is transferred) and confer benefits which are often difficult to quantify (such as the incentivisation of innovation). This book therefore proceeds from the assumption that there is such a thing as 'too much' intellectual property.

As the title suggests, this book is also concerned with the globalisation of intellectual property rights in submitted pharmaceutical test data. As Susan Sell observes, given that most countries are consumers and importers of pharmaceutical intellectual property rather than producers and exporters, we might reasonably ask why they would choose to enact measures creating intellectual property rights such as test data exclusivity that necessitate a transfer of wealth from their economies to the countries in which the rightsholders are based.[15] In understanding how test data exclusivity has globalised, this book draws on the framework set out by John Braithwaite and Peter Drahos in *Global Business Regulation*.[16] Drawing on over a dozen case studies examining the globalisation of regulation in different business areas (including intellectual property), Braithwaite and Drahos describe of globalisation of regulation as a process in which a variety of different categories of *actors* use various *mechanisms* to push for or against various *principles*, with detailed rule-making following the principles which have been established over time.[17]

The chief categories of actors involved in the process of globalisation highlighted in *Global Business Regulation* are states, organisations of states, business organisations, corporations, non-governmental organisations (NGOs), mass publics and epistemic communities.[18] Braithwaite and Drahos define principles as abstract prescriptions that precede rule complexity,[19] and note that negotiation between actors

---

[13] Boyle (1996), p. 179.

[14] Olson (1965), p. 9.

[15] Sell (2003), p. 9.

[16] Braithwaite and Drahos (2000).

[17] Ibid p. 9.

[18] Ibid p. 25.

[19] Ibid p. 15.

mostly occurs at the level of principles, particularly in trade negotiations, because it would be too complex to negotiate over the details of every set of rules.[20] Some principles have achieved extreme importance as a result of their codification in international treaties; for example, the principles of national treatment, the prescription that states should treat both foreigners and nationals equally and under the same set of rules, and most favoured nation, the prescription that any benefit granted to citizens or firms of one nation by a state should be accorded to citizens or firms of other nations, are both entrenched in the treaties of the WTO.[21]

Mechanisms, on the other hand, are the processes (whether social, economic or political) that are used to increase the extent to which regulatory conditions in one state resemble those of other states.[22] Seven mechanisms in particular are highlighted in *Global Business Regulation* as important in the globalisation of regulations—military coercion; economic coercion; the modelling of the actions of other regulatory actors; systems of rewards (the use of systematic means of increasing the expected value of compliance with globalising forces); reciprocal adjustment (non-coercive negotiation in which parties mutually agree to modify the rules they follow); non-reciprocal coordination (the movement of parties towards a common set of rules without all parties believing they share a common interest in this movement), and capacity building (aiding other actors in acquiring technical competence to satisfy global standards).[23] While principles set the direction of regulatory change, mechanisms are necessary to make principles concrete at the regulatory level.[24] The mechanisms of economic (and to a lesser extent, military) coercion, modelling, and non-reciprocal coordination are especially important for the purposes of this book.

A classic example of globalisation, the inclusion of higher standards of intellectual property rights in an FTA between the US and a developing country, illustrates this framework. Business organisations such as the Pharmaceutical Research and Manufacturers of America (PhMRA) and corporations such as Pfizer enrol the US negotiators to push for higher intellectual standards based on the principle of strategic trade. The US negotiators advocate US intellectual property rights as the world's best standard, while the developed country negotiators resist with reference to the principle of national sovereignty. The fact that the trade agreement deals with many areas means that the developing country negotiators may be incentivised to take the loss over intellectual property rights in exchange for a concession in another area (the mechanism of non-reciprocal adjustment), and the US may attempt to

---

[20] Ibid p. 527.

[21] Ibid p. 25. National treatment clauses can be found at General Agreement on Tariffs and Trade (1947) Article 3, General Agreement on Trade in Services (1994) (GATS) Article 17 and TRIPS Article 3; most favoured nation clauses can be found at GATT Article 1, GATS Article 2 and TRIPS Article 4.

[22] Ibid p. 530.

[23] Ibid p. 26.

[24] Ibid p. 530.

economically coerce the developing country into agreement by threatening economic sanctions under Section 301 of the US Trade Act 1974 if the country does not increase intellectual property standards. If the developing country is a member of the WTO, the principles of most favoured nation and national treatment embedded in the WTO agreements mean that nationals of other WTO members will also be able to take advantage of the higher standards of intellectual property rights within the developing country.

In should be borne in mind that, as Braithwaite and Drahos conclude, globalisation of regulation is never due to any single mechanism, category of actors, or principle. Instead, many actors deploy many mechanisms to push for or against many principles in complex webs of influence.[25] Realist conceptions of international relations, which focus only on the actions of states (a single type of actor) and their pursuit of self-interest (a single abstract mechanism) thus fail to explain globalisation.[26] While this book often speaks in terms of the actions of states and organisations of states for reasons of simplicity, it must be understood that these actors also act as agents for others, in particular business organisations, corporations and epistemic communities. The actions of 'the US' at trade negotiations often reflects the actions of business organisations or corporations that have successfully enrolled the support of the United States Trade Representative (USTR). Similarly, the actions of 'China' regarding internal reforms of its law on the protection of submitted test data may be the result of the actions of an epistemic community within the Chinese regulatory bureaucracy pushing for a reform which flatters their view of the world and China's role within it.[27]

In addition, it should also be noted that the globalisation of regulation can create regulatory 'ratchets' which drive the standards of regulation up (in the case of a positive ratchet) or down (in the case of a negative ratchet). For such ratchets to come into existence, a minimum standard of some kind must become entrenched, a principle which encourages regulatory innovation must be established and a feedback loop must be created which means that each new innovation causes the minimum standard to go up or down.[28] The global intellectual property framework created by TRIPS and subsequent bilateral trade agreements, which establish minimum but not maximum standards for intellectual property rights, have formally embedded a positive intellectual property ratchet; this ratcheting process also extends to test data exclusivity.[29]

[25] Ibid p. 480.

[26] Ibid p. 480.

[27] See further Yu (2020).

[28] Braithwaite and Drahos (2000), p. 519.

[29] Ibid p. 521.

1.3 Scope and Aims of This Book

This book is concerned with the origins, globalisation and impact of intellectual property rights in submitted pharmaceutical test data, with a particular emphasis on test data exclusivity rights. Test data exclusivity rights are of relatively recent origin, first appearing in 1984,[30] and this book seeks to better understand the rationale behind the creation of these rights in the US, as well as their adoption soon afterwards by the EC.

Despite this recent origin, test data exclusivity's globalisation has been rapid; Reichman suggested in 2009 that test data exclusivity rights had become so widespread that they might be permanently recognised at the international level.[31] This book is also concerned with how this globalisation has occurred. While authors such as Carlos Correa,[32] G. Lee Skillington and Eric M. Solovy,[33] Ingo Meitinger,[34] and Gabriele Spina Alì[35] have written at length about the highly contested meaning of Article 39.3, its role in the globalisation of test data exclusivity remains unclear; this book seeks to further understand the relationship between Article 39.3 of TRIPS and the globalisation of test data exclusivity. This book also investigates other means by which test data exclusivity has globalised. Much has also been written on the development of the test data exclusivity terms in trade agreements negotiated since TRIPS;[36] while this book is concerned with the role of trade agreements in the spread of test data exclusivity, it also seeks to understand the role of other mechanisms such as the role of negotiations around accession to the WTO and the role of coercion.

While there is universal acknowledgement that approaches to the protection of submitted test data vary significantly between jurisdictions, understanding of what these approaches entail is more limited. Owais Shaikh's 2016 study examined the test data exclusivity provisions of those jurisdictions which had signed free trade agreements, with this analysis focussing largely on assessing how 'pro-access to medicines' these national test data exclusivity laws are in comparison to the trade agreements they implement.[37] This book takes a more general approach to understanding the ways in which submitted pharmaceutical test data is protected, including in jurisdictions that do not provide test data exclusivity.

[30] Weiswasser and Danzis (2003).

[31] Reichman (2009).

[32] Correa (2002).

[33] Skillington and Solovy (2003).

[34] Meitinger (2005).

[35] Spina Alì (2018).

[36] Owais Shaikh's book *Access to Medicine Versus Test Data Exclusivity* is an illuminating account of how the test data exclusivity terms of a number of trade agreements have developed over time from an access to medicines perspective; Shaikh (2016).

[37] Shaikh determined that, perhaps surprisingly, many national laws are considerably less 'pro-access' than the FTA provisions which they implemented. Ibid p. 199.

The question of what impact intellectual property rights in submitted pharmaceutical test data have in practice is clearly a critical issue. A full overview of the impact of test data exclusivity, however, obviously impossible. Existing research has analysed different aspects of the impact of test data exclusivity in a number of jurisdictions; for example, a 2007 study by Oxfam found that pharmaceutical prices in Jordan had increased by 20% following the introduction of test data exclusivity,[38] a 2009 study by Ellen Schaffer and Joseph Brenner focusing on test data exclusivity in Guatemala found that several drugs would continue to be protected by test data exclusivity even after the drugs became open for generic competition in the US,[39] and a 2014 study by Mike Palmedo concluded that there was no relationship between investment by the pharmaceutical industry and whether or not a country has passed test data exclusivity protection provisions.[40] This book aims to shed further light on the impact of test data exclusivity on the market entry of generic products through an analysis of generic product approvals in the US, as well as the relationship between test data exclusivity and measures designed to promote public health such as compulsory licensing, particularly in the context of the response to the COVID-19 pandemic.

The answers to these questions lead this book to advance the argument that while the globalisation of test data exclusivity is part of the wider phenomenon of the globalisation and ratcheting up of intellectual property rights from the 1980s onwards, it has also been the product of a number of more specific circumstances. Article 39.3 has played an important role in globalising test data exclusivity despite its rejection from TRIPS. Test data exclusivity laws are surprisingly similar across jurisdictions—a fact which the ambiguity of Article 39.3 may, paradoxically, have contributed to. These textually similar provisions are likely to have very different impacts in practice as a result of the diversity of conditions (economic, social, political and epidemiological) present in these jurisdictions. As a result, test data exclusivity rights may therefore be poorly adapted to the needs of many of the jurisdictions in which they are found.

1.4 Methodology

For the most part, this book takes a doctrinal approach to the treaties and national laws under discussion, supplemented with reference to their historical, political and economic contexts. An empirical approach to assessing the impact of test data exclusivity on the market approval of generic competitors for new chemical entities approved in the US between 1999 and 2009 is taken in Chap. 7; the full methodology for this approach is set out at 7.32. These methodologies provide a strong basis for

38 Malpani (2009).

39 Shaffer and Brenner (2009).

40 Palmedo (2012) p. 8.

furthering the aim of this book, i.e. to examine and analyse the origins, globalisation and impact of intellectual property rights in submitted pharmaceutical test data.

The analysis of TRIPS and other treaties with provisions related to the protection of submitted test data is guided by the general principles of international law, with particular reference to the interpretive principles of the Vienna Convention on the Law of Treaties (VCLT).[41] Article 31 of the VCLT states that treaties should 'be interpreted in good faith in accordance with the ordinary meaning to be given to the terms of the treaty in their context and in the light of its object and purpose',[42] while Article 32 states that recourse may be made to the *travaux préparatoires* of the treaty in order to confirm Article 31 or when applying Article 31 leaves the meaning ambiguous or obscure or leads to a conclusion that is manifestly absurd.[43]

1.5 Structure of This Book

The structure of the rest of this book is as follows. Chapter 2 sets out an overview of the pharmaceutical industry and the issues surrounding the protection of submitted test data. Chapter 3 then discusses the origins of test data exclusivity for pharmaceuticals in the US in the 1980s as well as the adoption of test data exclusivity laws by the EC and parallel developments relevant to the protection of submitted test data in Japan. Chapter 4 considers the history of test data exclusivity in the GATT Uruguay Round negotiations which lead to the TRIPS Agreement, as well as the meaning of the Article 39.3 of TRIPS. Chapter 5 looks at how test data exclusivity has globalised since the 1990s, chiefly focusing on the negotiation of trade agreements and the process of accession to the WTO, although other means of globalisation are also discussed. Chapter 6 examines how the protection of submitted pharmaceutical test data has developed at the national level. Chapter 7 considers the impact of test data exclusivity on the market entry of generic pharmaceuticals in the US, while Chap. 8 considers the impact of test data exclusivity on measures intended to protect public health such as compulsory licensing. Chapter 9 provides the conclusion to this book.

References

Boyle J (1996) Shamans, software and spleens: law and the construction of the information society. Harvard University Press, Cambridge

Braithwaite J, Drahos P (2000) Global business regulation. Cambridge University Press, Cambridge

---

[41] Vienna Convention on the Law of Treaties (1969).

[42] Ibid Article 31(1).

[43] Ibid Article 32.

Correa C (2002) Protection of data submitted for the registration of pharmaceuticals: implementing the standards of the TRIPS agreement. South Centre, Geneva
Dutfield G (2008) Delivering drugs to the poor: will the TRIPS amendment help? Am J Law Med 34:107–124
Engelberg AB (1999) Special patent provisions for pharmaceuticals: have they outlived their usefulness? A political, legislative and legal history of U.S. law and observations for the future. J Law Technol 39:389–426
FDA (2003) Guidance for industry: bioavailability and bioequivalence studies for orally administered drug products — general considerations
Ghinea N, Lipworth W, Kerridge I (2016) Propaganda or the cost of innovation? Challenging the high price of new drugs. BMJ 352:i1284
Grabowski H (2002) Patents and new product development in the pharmaceutical and biotechnology industries. In: Duca JV, Yücel KM (eds) Science and cents: exploring the economics of biotechnology. Federal Reserve Bank of Dallas, Dallas, pp 87–104
IFPMA (2011) Encouraging Development of New Medicines
Malpani R (2009) All costs, no benefits: how the US-Jordan free trade agreement affects access to medicines. J Generic Med 6(3):206–217
Meitinger I (2005) Implementation of test data protection according to Article 39.3 TRIPS: the search for a fair interpretation of the term unfair commercial use. J World Intellect Prop 8:123
Olson M (1965) The logic of collective action. Harvard University Press, Cambridge
Palmedo M (2012) Do pharmaceutical firms invest more heavily in countries with data exclusivity? Curr Int Trade Law J 21:38
Reichman JH (2009) Rethinking the role of clinical trial data in international intellectual property law: the case for a public goods approach. Marquette Intellect Prop Law Rev 13:1
Sell SK (2003) Private power, public law: the globalization of intellectual property rights. Cambridge University Press, Cambridge
Shaffer ER, Brenner FE (2009) A Trade agreement's impact on access to generic drugs. Health Aff 28:957–968
Shaikh OH (2016) Access to medicine versus test data exclusivity: safeguarding flexibilities under international law. Springer, Berlin
Skillington GL, Solovy EM (2003) The protection of test and other data required by article 39.3 of the TRIPS agreement. Northwest J Int Law Bus 24:1
Song CH, Han JW (2016) Patent cliff and strategic switch: exploring strategic design possibilities in the pharmaceutical industry. SpringerPlus 5:1–14
Spina Alì G (2018) The 13th round: Article 39 (3) TRIPS and the struggle over "Unfair Commercial Use.". J World Intellect Prop 21(3-4):201–242
Wadlow C (2008) Regulatory data protection under TRIPs Article 39 (3) and Article 10bis of the Paris Convention: Is there a doctor in the house? Intellect Prop Q 4:355–415
Weiswasser ES, Danzis SD (2003) The hatch-waxman act: history, structure, and legacy. Antitrust Law J 71:585
Yu P (2020) China's innovative turn and the changing pharmaceutical landscape. U Pac L Rev 51:593–620

Chapter 2
An Overview of the Protection of Submitted Test Data

Abstract This chapter provides background information relevant to the discussion of the protection of submitted pharmaceutical test data throughout the rest of this book. Firstly, the role of pharmaceutical test data in the process of drug development is described. Secondly, this chapter provides an overview of the issues surrounding the protection of submitted pharmaceutical test data, and in particular the issues surrounding test data exclusivity. Both justifications for and criticisms of the protection of submitted test data are considered. A number of proposed alternative means of protecting submitted test data are detailed. Finally, a review is provided of the existing literature on the impact of test data exclusivity on access to medicines.

2.1 Introduction

Since the introduction of intellectual property rights in submitted pharmaceutical test data in the US in the early 1980s, there has been a vigorous debate amongst academics, policymakers, activists and members of the pharmaceutical industry regarding the justifications for and impact of such intellectual property rights. This chapter provides an overview of the issues surrounding the protection of submitted test data in order to inform the discussion and analysis in the remainder of this book.

2.2 Pharmaceutical Test Data and the Drug Development Process

As has been discussed in Chap. 1, the process of drug development is long and expensive. This is partially as a result of the complex scientific process of drug discovery and the fact that only a fraction of molecules identified as potentially therapeutic ever make it to market as pharmaceutical products; however, it is also the result of the fact that virtually all jurisdictions require that the safety and efficacy of a

A. Buick, *Intellectual Property Rights in Pharmaceutical Test Data*,
https://doi.org/10.1007/978-3-031-29436-5_2

drug must be demonstrated before it can be marketed.[1] The test data demonstrating the safety and efficacy of a drug must be generated through clinical trials carried out on human subjects.[2]

Clinical trials are traditionally divided into four phases, although in practice individual trials may encompass elements of different stages.[3] Following pre-clinical investigations, a prospective new drug enters phase I studies, which are aimed at determining the safety of the drug, as well as the dosage; trials typically involve a small number of healthy adults.[4] Phase II studies focus on the effectiveness of the drug in question and involve a small number of patients with a particular disease or condition.[5] Drugs which pass these 'early stage' trials continue to phase III studies. These are much larger in scale, potentially involving thousands of patients, and are aimed at determining both the safety of the drug in question and its efficacy in treating the relevant disease or condition. They are also the most expensive aspect of the clinical trial process.[6] Phase IV studies are post-marketing studies conducted after a product has entered public use to monitor its effects.[7]

Completing this process takes years, and only a minority of drugs which enter phase I testing will receive market authorisation; the exact numbers are unclear, but studies have suggested in the region of 9–14% of compounds make it through the process.[8] Estimates of the cost of this process are contested; the latest in a series of controversial studies on the cost of drug development by the Tufts Center for the Study of Drug Development estimated the cost of bringing a new compound to market at $2.87 billion USD, accounting for failed and abandoned compounds.[9] It should be noted that the Tufts Center receives a significant proportion of its funding from the research-based pharmaceutical industry,[10] and some commentators have accused the Tufts studies of inflating the overall cost of drug development in order to justify high pharmaceutical prices. Critics charge that there is insufficient transparency regarding the data used by the study (for example, the number of patients involved in the trials in the samples has not been disclosed in recent Tufts Center research; earlier Tufts Center research which did disclose these numbers produced significantly lower figures),[11] and that the methodology ignores tax deductions and

[1] Braithwaite and Drahos (2000), p. 393.

[2] Friedman et al. (2010), p. 4.

[3] Ibid.

[4] Ibid.

[5] Ibid p. 6.

[6] Grabowski (2002), p. 95.

[7] Friedman et al. (2010), pp. 7–10.

[8] Hay et al. (2014); Wong et al. (2019).

[9] DiMasi et al. (2016), pp. 20–33.

[10] Tufts Center for the Study of Drug Development, 'Financial Disclosure' https://csdd.tufts.edu/financial-disclosure (accessed 26 January 2023).

[11] See DiMasi et al. (2003).

government funding.[12] A substantial proportion (almost half) of the cost of drug development given by the study is also accounted for by the cost of capital, i.e. the opportunity cost a firm incurs by not using the research funding for another purpose—not an unreasonable assumption, but one which it may not be obvious has been factored into the headline price.[13] Other studies have suggested the price of bringing a novel drug to market is in the hundreds of millions—high, to be sure, but significantly below the Tufts Center figure.[14]

While the exact figure is unclear, it is certain that the cost of bringing a new drug to market is extremely expensive; if it was not, generic firms would not need to rely on originator data to gain marketing approval. As has previously been mentioned, research-based pharmaceutical firms are prepared to engage in this process because by patenting the products in question they may exclude direct competition for a time-limited period and thus charge prices significantly above the cost of manufacture.[15] Patents are typically justified on two grounds; firstly, that they act as an incentive for technological progress and secondly, that by having inventors disclose how to work their inventions to the public, competitors will quickly enter the market with their own version of the product upon patent expiration—thus balancing the need to reward innovation and encourage the dissemination of knowledge.[16] However, in the case of pharmaceutical products the requirement that the safety and efficacy of a product must be demonstrated imposes a significant additional barrier to market entry. Requiring generic competitors to conduct their own phase III trials to generate data on safety and efficacy would rarely be economically viable—with no hope of obtaining a patent over a product which is by definition non-novel, generic companies would have no way to recoup the costs of generating the data. As such, from the 1960s onwards most countries have introduced ‘abbreviated’ or ‘abridged’ approval pathways for generic pharmaceutical products. Because generic pharmaceuticals are chemically identical to the originator products of which they are copies, most jurisdictions only require that a generic product demonstrate that it is ‘bioequivalent’ (identical for all intents and purposes) to the originator; the product can then be approved on the basis that the test data previously submitted by the originator firm has already demonstrated that the drug in question is both safe and effective. Because bioequivalence studies can be conducted with only a few dozen healthy volunteers, the cost of gaining market entry for generic products is thus orders of magnitude lower than for originator products.[17]

---

[12] Ghinea et al. (2016) p. 1284.

[13] Avorn (2015), p. 1877.

[14] See, for example, Prasad and Mailankody (2017).

[15] Dutfield (2009), p. 297.

[16] Landes and Posner (2009), p. 295. Of course, in many cases this ‘disclosure’ is intentionally vague and difficult to understand in order to limit its usefulness to competitors.

[17] Ibid.

2.3 Test Data Exclusivity

Since the creation of abbreviated drug approval pathways, the research-based pharmaceutical industry has resented that their generic competitors are able to enter the market through reference to the test data which they generate at such expense. As a result, in the 1980s research-based pharmaceutical firms successfully lobbied first the US and later the EC to enact legislation restricting the ability of subsequent applicants to make reference to previously submitted test data for a time-limited period (see further Chap. 3). Such restrictions are now generally considered to be a form of intellectual property right in submitted test data, often referred to as test data exclusivity.[18]

Unlike other intellectual property rights such as patents or copyright, test data exclusivity does not provide an independent, actionable right to exclude third parties from the protected subject matter. Rather, test data exclusivity operates by automatically restricting access to a jurisdiction's abbreviated approval pathway; as such, its own existence is entirely dependent on the existence of such a pathway.[19] Test data exclusivity protection can restrict the ability of generic applicants to gain approval through reference to originator data in one of two ways—it can either prohibit a regulatory body from using submitted test data to process an abbreviated approval application in any way for the duration of the exclusivity period (data exclusivity *per se*), or it may permit regulators to use the previously submitted test data to process an abbreviated approval application provided that the application is not formally approved until the end of the exclusivity period (market exclusivity).[20] Some jurisdictions protect some forms of submitted data through data exclusivity *per se* while protecting other forms of submitted test data through market exclusivity[21]; others provide a period of data exclusivity *per se* concurrent with a longer period of market exclusivity with the intention that generic applications will be submitted and processed during the final stages of the exclusivity period and receive approval soon after its expiration.[22]

Test data exclusivity is not unique to the pharmaceutical industry. In theory, test data exclusivity rights could be granted with regards to any product which must submit data in order to receive regulatory approval,[23] although in practice the only other major products to which test data exclusivity laws apply are agrichemicals and

[18] Shaikh (2016), p. 3.

[19] Heled (2015), p. 305.

[20] Shaikh (2016), p. 6.

[21] See, for example, the five-year term of data exclusivity *per se* the US provides for new chemical entities versus the three-year period of market exclusivity it provides for new chemical indications.

[22] See, for example, the EU's system of test data exclusivity, in which an eight-year period of data exclusivity *per se* runs concurrently with a 10-year period of market exclusivity; as a result, abbreviated applications can be submitted and processed from 8 years after the approval of the originator product, although they cannot be approved for another 2 years.

[23] Thomas (2014), p. 370.

pesticides.[24] As is discussed in Chap. 3, test data exclusivity rights for pesticides actually predate test data exclusivity rights for pharmaceuticals by several years, and several international agreements, including TRIPS, deal with the protection of test data submitted to obtain marketing approval for pharmaceuticals and agrichemicals in similar terms.[25] While pharmaceutical test data is the focus of this book, on a number of occasions it will be relevant to discuss the protection of test data submitted regarding agrichemicals for comparative purposes.

2.3.1 *Test Data Exclusivity and Other Intellectual Property Rights*

Test data exclusivity for pharmaceutical products exists alongside a range of other intellectual property rights. The most common of these are patents, although the law of trade secrecy and other non-patent exclusivities also interact with test data exclusivity.[26] Understanding the relationship between these overlapping forms of exclusivity is key to understanding test data exclusivity.

2.3.1.1 The Relationship Between Test Data Exclusivity and the Patent System

In 2011, the International Federation of Pharmaceutical Manufacturers and Associations (IFPMA, an association of research-based pharmaceutical companies) observed that while patents and test data exclusivity rights both serve to protect pharmaceutical products from competition, they are quite distinct in that they protect different subject matter, have different terms of protection, and have different legal consequences.[27] Patents prevent third parties from, *inter alia*, making, using and selling the patented subject matter without the permission of the right holder, whereas test data exclusivity rights enable the right holder to prevent subsequent applicants from gaining marketing approval on the basis of the protected test data. While test data exclusivity rights in theory permit a subsequent applicant to gain approval by generating their own test data, this option is illusory in practice as the

[24] See, for example, the regulation of pesticides in the US under the Federal Insecticide, Fungicide, and Rodenticide Act (FIFRA).

[25] TRIPS Article 39.3; see also Free Trade Agreement between the EFTA States and Lebanon (EFTA-Lebanon FTA) (2004) Annex V; Trans-Pacific Partnership Agreement (TPP) (2016) Article 18.47.

[26] Pharmaceutical firms also use trade marks to protect their products—the vast majority of research-based pharmaceutical firms market their products under a propriety brand name rather than its 'generic' chemical name; however, trade marks have little bearing on test data exclusivity.

[27] IFPMA (2011), p. 5.

costs of clinical trials will present an insurmountable barrier in virtually all cases.[28] As such, both intellectual property rights produce the same result in practice—the prevention of generic pharmaceuticals entering the market during the term of protection. There is therefore a question of when test data exclusivity rights will have an impact beyond the protection typically provided by a patent or patents. Understanding the differences between the two intellectual property rights elucidates the circumstances under which test data exclusivity is likely to delay the market entry of a generic competitor.

Firstly, patents and test data exclusivity rights differ in the manner of their acquisition. Acquiring a patent involves the submission of an application in which the applicant must demonstrate to a patent examiner that the invention in question meets various standards, including novelty, inventive step and industrial application.[29] In contrast, test data exclusivity generally arises automatically upon the approval of a pharmaceutical product[30]; the criteria that must be met to receive protection vary by jurisdiction, but typically these include only that the submitted data be undisclosed, associated with a previously unapproved pharmaceutical product and be the product of considerable effort.[31] Test data exclusivity may thus be available in situations in which patent protection is not and *vice versa*; however, because the requirements for gaining test data exclusivity are, generally speaking, easier to meet than the requirements for patentability, and because patents must be actively applied for while test data exclusivity rights typically arise automatically upon the approval of a pharmaceutical product, the former scenario is by far the likelier one. The differing standards of novelty required by most patent and test data exclusivity laws further exacerbates this situation; because patent novelty is typically assessed globally (i.e. if the invention has been disclosed to the public anywhere in the world, it will not be considered novel),[32] patents for a particular invention must generally be filed at a similar time in all jurisdictions the prospective patent holder wishes to gain protection.[33] However, because test data exclusivity rights are typically available to pharmaceutical products provided they have not previously been approved in the relevant jurisdiction, they are often available for drugs even years after their global debut.[34]

---

[28] Gervais (2019), p. 367.

[29] See TRIPS Article 27.

[30] But see, for example, Malaysia, Directive on Data Exclusivity (2011).

[31] These are the criteria for submitted test data which must be protected per Article 39.3 of TRIPS.

[32] See, for example, Article 54(2) of the European Patent Convention (2000).

[33] Although 'convention priority' under the Paris Convention for the Protection of Industrial Property (1883) provides some flexibility here amongst members of the Paris Union; see Paris Convention for the Protection of Industrial Property (1883) Article 4.

[34] But note that there are exceptions to this; China would appear to only provide test data exclusivity to products first submitted in China, while Malaysia requires that products be submitted for approval in Malaysia soon after their global debut. Russia, on the other hand, does not seem to require that pharmaceutical products be new at all. See further Chap. 6.

Secondly, patents and test data exclusivity rights differ in their terms of protection. Under the TRIPS Agreement, the term of a patent is 20 years from the date of filing, with the possibility of an extension in some jurisdictions[35]; in contrast, most test data exclusivity terms last for around five years from the date of a pharmaceutical product's approval, with even the longest periods of exclusivity lasting for no more than 11 years.[36] This disparity has prompted Meir Pugatch to observe that it seems logical that the patent term will outlast the test data exclusivity term for the majority of drugs.[37] This observation, however, must be weighed against the fact that a significant proportion of the term of a pharmaceutical patent is likely to be consumed by the lengthy process of drug development and the time spent under regulatory review; studies have concluded that primary pharmaceutical patents in the US typically have only 12 years of the patent term remaining post-marketing approval, even accounting for patent term extensions.[38] Test data exclusivity, on the other hand, typically starts from the date of marketing approval; as a result, test data exclusivity may outlast patent protection when there has been a particularly long delay between the filing of the relevant patents and the grant of market authorisation. Test data exclusivity may also cause a delay in generic market entry even in cases in which the exclusivity period ends before the patent term if this prevents second applicants from seeking authorisation during the patent term under early-working provisions (sometimes known as 'Bolar' exceptions) with the intention of entering the market as soon as patent protection ends.[39]

Thirdly, patents and test data exclusivity rights differ in how they can be challenged. Patent protection can be compromised in a number of ways. Patents may be challenged on the grounds that the claimed invention did not, in fact, meet the requirements for patentability. Additionally, most jurisdictions have provisions to permit the compulsory licensing of patents. Compulsory licensing refers to a range of legal powers that allow a government to force a patent holder to permit either the government itself or a third party to make use of subject matter covered by a patent—this might be motivated by a public health crisis which necessitates the acquisition of large quantities of a patented pharmaceutical; for example, the COVID-19 pandemic prompted many national governments to take steps to facilitate compulsory licensing, although, as discussed in Chap. 8, few such licenses were ultimately issued during the pandemic.[40] Compulsory licenses have also been used to end anticompetitive behaviour enabled by a patent.[41] Test data exclusivity, however, is typically

[35] TRIPS Article 33.

[36] See e.g. Council Directive 2001/83/EC on the Community code relating to medicinal products for human use [2001] Article 10.

[37] Pugatch (2006), p.118.

[38] Grabowski and Vernon (2000) p. 116; Hemphill and Sampat (2012), p. 330.

[39] Obviously, this will have more impact when the test data exclusivity term expires close to the end of the patent term.

[40] Perehudoff et al. (2021).

[41] Dutfield (2008), pp. 109–110.

harder to challenge; few jurisdictions have specific mechanisms to invalidate test data exclusivity rights or suspend exclusivity in the event that a compulsory license is issued for patents covering the pharmaceutical product in question.

As such, if patent protection over a pharmaceutical product is compromised in some way, test data exclusivity can continue to maintain the monopoly position of the right holder by effectively blocking the launch of a generic version of the product in question—knowledge of this fact may deter would-be challengers from acting until the test data exclusivity period has ended. Even in jurisdictions where it is possible to challenge or suspend test data exclusivity, the additional costs this imposes may produce a similar chilling effect.

Fourthly, patents and test data exclusivity rights differ in terms of how they block competitors from the market. While patents provide extremely broad protection for the relevant invention, they must be actively enforced against infringers. Such enforcement can be expensive, as well as risky; counterclaiming that a patent should be revoked on the grounds that it is invalid is a common response by parties sued for patent infringement. Test data exclusivity, by contrast, is self-enforcing. Generic applicants are simply unable to gain approval based on the submitted test data during the period of protection—there is no need to identify potential infringers and file a suit against them, as is the case with patent infringement. As such, even in cases in which the originator of a drug holds a perfectly valid patent over it, test data exclusivity may have an impact by reducing the costs of enforcing exclusivity such as cease and desist letters or formal litigation.

Based on the above, there are at least four scenarios in which test data exclusivity rights may have an impact on the market entry of generic products. Firstly, scenarios in which a patent has never been acquired, either through choice, negligence or because the invention does not meet the criteria for patentability. Secondly, scenarios in which a patent is acquired but the patent term expires before the end of the test data exclusivity period or in which test data exclusivity rights prevent generic applicants from submitting abridged applications in the final stages of the patent term. Thirdly, test data exclusivity rights may continue to block market access for generic pharmaceuticals in scenarios in which patent protection is acquired but compromised before its normal expiration date, either because the patent is successfully challenged and revoked or because a compulsory license or similar measure designed to protect public health has been issued. Fourthly, even in situations in which the marketer of an originator pharmaceutical possesses an unexpired and uncompromised patent over the drug, test data exclusivity may provide a benefit by reducing enforcement costs.

It must be emphasised that each of these scenarios will be more common in some jurisdictions than others. There are many other factors affecting the relationship between patents and test data exclusivity; these include the differing economic, political, social and epidemiological conditions prevalent in a given jurisdiction. As a result, even textually similar test data exclusivity laws may produce significantly different results between jurisdictions. However, generally speaking, there is reason to suppose that test data exclusivity is more likely to have an impact in smaller pharmaceutical markets, especially those of developing countries. It is more likely, for example, that a pharmaceutical firm will not apply for patents in smaller pharmaceutical markets for reasons of cost effectiveness.[42] Test data exclusivity will also be more likely to outlast the patent term in smaller markets because pharmaceutical firms are less likely to prioritise launching a pharmaceutical product early in the patent term in these jurisdictions.[43] Developing countries have made greater use of compulsory licenses than developed countries in recent decades,[44] although their use remains uncommon amongst all countries, even in the aftermath of the COVID-19 pandemic. Reduced enforcement costs from test data exclusivity are likely to be most beneficial to right holders in jurisdictions in which the costs of suing infringers would be out of proportion with the value of the market and in jurisdictions in which it is difficult to enforce patent rights for reasons of ideology, corruption or incompetence; in addition, the reduction in enforcement costs provided by test data exclusivity rights will be greater in jurisdictions which lack so-called 'patent linkage' mechanisms that restrict the ability of national drug authorities to approve generics while the originator product is still under patent protection.[45] On the other hand, it seems probable that challenges over a patent's validity will be more common in developed countries and other countries with a large demand for pharmaceuticals as these provide the incentive of gaining access to a lucrative market and typically possess the lawyers with the skill to mount such challenges (and litigants with the funds to pay them).[46]

2.3.1.2 The Relationship Between Test Data Exclusivity and Trade Secrets

Test data exclusivity is closely related to the law of trade secrecy. Both concern the protection of undisclosed and commercially valuable information. Article 39 of TRIPS falls within the section of the Agreement on the 'protection of undisclosed information', and Articles 39.1 and 39.2 both deal with trade secrets (see further Sect. 2.3.2, below).[47] Pugatch has commented that the underlying logic of test data exclusivity 'suggests that it is an expression of trade secrets.'[48]

In spite of their similar subject matter, however, there is typically little interaction between the two intellectual property rights. Trade secrets typically prevent the disclosure of protected information, but test data is rarely, if ever, disclosed to the sponsor of a generic drug in an abbreviated drug application—the approval process is carried out by the government agency to which the data has already been

[42] Attaran (2004), p. 159.

[43] Goldberg (2010), p. 350.

[44] 't Hoen (2016), p. 64.

[45] Bouchard et al. (2011), p. 392.

[46] Drahos (2008), p.168.

[47] TRIPS Article 39.

[48] Pugatch (2006), p. 98.

submitted.[49] Indeed, in many cases the government agency may not directly access the previously submitted test data at all in an abbreviated drug application, and instead simply approves the generic applicant once it has been established that it is bioequivalent to the originator product. As such, while test data exclusivity has historical and theoretical ties with the law of trade secrets and protects a related subject matter, it performs a quite separate role in practice.

2.3.1.3 The Relationship Between Test Data Exclusivity and Other Forms of Non-Patent Exclusivity

In addition to test data exclusivity, a number of jurisdictions (mostly developed countries) also provide other non-patent exclusivities to pharmaceutical products under certain circumstances. These are especially common in the US, which in addition to test data exclusivity also provides a seven-year period of exclusivity for so-called ‘orphan drugs’ which treat rare conditions,[50] a six-month period of exclusivity for the first generic applicant to successfully challenge a patent over a pharmaceutical product under certain circumstances and a six-month extension to existing exclusivities (including patent protection and test data exclusivity) for drugs which submit clinical studies of the drug in paediatric populations.[51] The availability of such other non-patent exclusivities for pharmaceuticals will also inform the impact of test data exclusivity in a jurisdiction.

Yaniv Heled sees these non-patent exclusivities, including test data exclusivity, as part of a new class of administrative intellectual property he terms ‘regulatory competitive shelters’ which have developed to plug ‘gaps’ in the intellectual property system, mostly relating to the pharmaceutical industry.[52] It is certainly true that test data exclusivity shares many features with these other non-patent exclusivities, such as operating by barring regulatory approval; however, test data exclusivity can also be distinguished from other non-patent exclusivities by its unique subject matter. Test data exclusivity is also differentiated by the fact that of all the non-patent exclusivities which have developed in various national regulatory systems, test data exclusivity has been by far the most successful in terms of globalisation.

[49] Correa (2002), p. 80.

[50] USA, 21 USC § 360cc(a)(2).

[51] Heled (2015), p. 314.

[52] Ibid, p. 300.

2.3.2 Test Data Exclusivity at the International Level

The first law providing test data exclusivity for pharmaceutical test data was enacted in the US in 1984.[53] By the late 1980s, the EC had also adopted a test data exclusivity law.[54] Today, test data exclusivity rights are a feature of the national laws of more than 50 countries.[55] This globalisation of test data exclusivity has been the result of a push for increased requirements regarding the protection of submitted test data at the international level by developed countries—in particular, the US, EU and EFTA states.

As has already been discussed, attempts by the US and other developed countries to include a requirement to provide test data exclusivity in the TRIPS Agreement failed; however, as a compromise, an obligation for WTO members to provide protection to test data submitted to governments in order to gain approval for pharmaceutical and agricultural chemical products against 'unfair commercial use' was included in Article 39.3 of the TRIPS Agreement. In full, Article 39.3 reads:

> Members, when requiring, as a condition of approving the marketing of pharmaceutical or of agricultural chemical products which utilize new chemical entities, the submission of undisclosed test or other data, the origination of which involves a considerable effort, shall protect such data against unfair commercial use. In addition, Members shall protect such data against disclosure, except where necessary to protect the public, or unless steps are taken to ensure that the data are protected against unfair commercial use.[56]

Even on a casual reading, Article 39.3 is extremely ambiguous. The provision does not make clear what constitutes 'unfair commercial use' or what members must do to protect against it. The precise scope of Article 39.3 has never been definitively clarified and continues to generate considerable debate amongst academics and other commentators even to this day, as is discussed in more detail in Chap. 4. However, test data exclusivity provisions are a common feature of trade agreements negotiated by developed countries from the early 1990s onwards. Along with commitments made by developing countries during their accession to the WTO, these are the main means by which test data exclusivity has spread to new jurisdictions.

---

[53] USA, Drug Price Competition and Patent Term Restoration Act (1984).

[54] European Council directive 87/21/EEC amending Directive 65/65/EEC on the approximation of provisions laid down by law, regulation or administrative action relating to proprietary medicinal products [1986].

[55] See further Chap. 6.

[56] TRIPS Article 39.3.

2.4 The Test Data Exclusivity Debate

As with other intellectual property rights, the arguments around test data exclusivity centre on the extent to which it is necessary to prevent free-riding for a limited period in order to incentivise innovation. Proponents of test data exclusivity argue that it is necessary to protect the investments research-based companies put into generating the data submitted to regulators to gain marketing approval. As previously noted, it has been suggested that producing data for a pharmaceutical registration file accounts for 60% of the costs of developing a new drug.[57] In addition, it is argued that as the originator firms which bring pharmaceuticals to market assume the entire risk of the generation of the data in question, there would be no incentive to develop new pharmaceutical products if rival firms were immediately able to use this data to bring their own competitor products to market.[58] While competitors are most typically excluded from the market for a time-limited period through patent protection, patents are not always available for new pharmaceutical products. The IFPMA claims that more compounds are being developed which, for a variety of reasons, are not patent protected, with the result that data exclusivity is the only available intellectual property protection; as such, it is contended, the availability of test data exclusivity protection can be a significant factor in the decision to introduce a new drug to a particular market.[59] While critics charge that it would be wrong to grant monopolistic rights 'through the back door' to products which cannot demonstrate novelty or inventive step,[60] other commentators have noted that not every new pharmaceutical product or new indication that fails to qualify for patent protection can be said to be entirely lacking in social value—as such, a *sui generis* right such as test data exclusivity provides a way to work around the 'one size fits all' approach of the patent system in which the same protections, standards of patentability and term length apply equally to 'all fields of technology' regardless of the differing commercial realities faced by different industries.[61]

The argument that test data exclusivity is necessary to incentivise pharmaceutical research has many critics. Firstly, as with many intellectual property rights, it has never been demonstrated that test data exclusivity actually provides targeted incentives for socially productive research.[62] Others have also questioned the basic assumptions upon which the pro-test data exclusivity argument rests. Reichman points to the fact that the pharmaceutical industry derives significant benefits from public funding of 'upstream' medical research, in particular by the US Government; the US National Institutes of Health (NIH) spend some $30 billion on 'upstream'

---

[57] Grabowski (2002).

[58] IFPMA (2000), p. 2.

[59] Ibid.

[60] European Generic Medicines Association (2000), p. 6.

[61] Eisenberg (2006), p. 366.

[62] 't Hoen (2022), p. 186.

medical research every year.[63] Indeed, Reichman argues, given that so much of upstream pharmaceutical research is government funded or subsidised it is presumably largely *downstream* costs that justify strong patent rights over pharmaceutical products in the first place, raising the question of why an additional set of intellectual property rights are needed to further cover these costs.[64]

Other academics have challenged the notion that the need to conduct clinical trials to prove the safety and efficacy of pharmaceutical products is purely a cost for research-based pharmaceutical companies for which they should be compensated through additional protections. Ariel Katz suggests that while the argument that the costs of complying with regulatory requirements to demonstrate the safety and efficacy of pharmaceutical products negatively affects the incentives for new drug innovation is intuitively appealing, the requirement to conduct testing to demonstrate that new pharmaceuticals are safe and effective actually benefits research-based pharmaceutical companies, at least to some extent.[65] Katz notes that pharmaceuticals are what economists refer to as 'credence goods'—that is, consumers (for the most part) cannot easily ascertain the quality of pharmaceutical products, or indeed whether they need a particular pharmaceutical product at all, before purchase or even after consumption.[66] Even the physicians on whose advice prescription pharmaceuticals are purchased and consumed cannot determine the safety and efficacy of a pharmaceutical product by themselves beyond a very basic level. Katz observes that markets in which there are significant information asymmetries between sellers and consumers tend to result in untrustworthy sellers purveying low-quality products as high-quality ones because consumers cannot easily distinguish between them; this punishes trustworthy sellers of high-quality products, incentivising them to leave the market and thus further lowering the overall quality of the goods therein. This vicious circle may continue until the market stabilises at a significantly lower level of overall quality or even collapses—the so-called 'market for lemons' scenario first described by George Akerlof in 1970.[67] Clinical trials, Katz argues, are thus necessary for pharmaceutical companies to convince consumers to purchase their products at all. Furthermore, the fact that the submission of the results of such trials to an independent government body is mandatory provides additional advantages for research-based pharmaceutical firms; the credulity of the evidence is boosted by this process of independent review and the risk of low-cost and low-quality innovation undercutting high-quality innovation is reduced as costs are increased for all new drugs.[68]

---

[63] Reichman (2009), p. 41.

[64] Ibid.

[65] Katz (2007), p. 7.

[66] In contrast, many of the qualities of 'search goods' can easily be ascertained prior to purchase (table salt, for example) while many of the qualities of an 'experience good' can be easily ascertained after consumption (a meal in a restaurant, for example). Ibid, p. 11.

[67] Ibid, p. 11; Akerlof (1970).

[68] Katz (2007), p. 12.

Joseph Dumit has also recognised the role that clinical trials play in enabling the research-based pharmaceutical industry to operate. Dumit notes that the underlying function of clinical trials from the perspective of the research-based pharmaceutical industry is to extend the market in a prospective product to the maximum extent possible; clinical trials thus not only create the consumer trust that permits a market for high-quality pharmaceutical products to exist, it creates opportunities for pharmaceutical firms to 'grow medicine' by matching pharmaceutical products to medical conditions.[69] One result of this is that even with the credibility added by independent government assessment of clinical trial results, data produced by research-based pharmaceutical companies are still notoriously unreliable; there are numerous cases in which the positive effects of new drugs have been overstated or data on dangerous side effects downplayed.[70] The incentives to cheat here are obvious; as previously noted, drug development takes years and costs millions of dollars, and a failed trial may doom a promising product in which a huge amount has been invested. Clinical trials are thus a resource to be exploited by research-based pharmaceutical firms, occasionally at the expense of general health; the flip-side of evidence-based medicine is that markets are made through evidence—and that evidence is obtained through clinical trials conducted by companies with a financial interest in their success.[71]

The requirement to provide evidence of the safety and efficacy of a drug thus provides an assurance of quality which persuades consumers to purchase the product, and enables pharmaceutical companies to operate in the first instance.[72] Indeed, this requirement provides an opportunity for pharmaceutical firms to grow the markets for their products.[73] As such, they provide significant value to pharmaceutical firms. This weakens the argument that the completion of clinical trials represents an onerous burden on pharmaceutical companies which must be compensated with further exclusivities in the form of patent term extensions and test data exclusivity.

Concerns have also been raised over the ethical consequences of incentivising competitor firms to conduct duplicative clinical trials with human subjects in order to generate their own data to submit to regulatory authorities. The World Medical Association's Declaration of Helsinki on Ethical Principles for Medical Research Involving Human Subjects (Declaration of Helsinki) states that medical research involving humans must be based on a robust understanding of current scientific literature, be preceded by an assessment of the risks to individuals and communities involved in the research weighed against potential benefits to them and others, and that studies should be stopped immediately when risks are found to outweigh

[69] Dumit (2012), p. 12.

[70] Reichman (2009), p. 5.

[71] Dumit (2012), p. 95.

[72] Katz (2007), p. 12.

[73] Dumit (2012), p. 95.

benefits or if there is conclusive proof of a positive and beneficial outcome.[74] As Olasupo Owoeye observes, the implication of these provisions is that the repetition of clinical trials on human subjects cannot be justified when previous trials have already produced sufficient information on the question under investigation – e.g., that the pharmaceutical compound in question is safe and effective.[75] The Declaration is widely regarded as the cornerstone of medical research ethics.[76] It is unclear to what extent test data exclusivity incentivises duplicative clinical trials in practice (much as it is unclear to what extent test data activity incentivises any kind of research activity), but it is nonetheless troubling that an intellectual property theoretically designed to promote medical innovation and therefore human health creates incentives for such a violation of a fundamental tenet of medical research ethics.

2.4.1 *Conflicts Between Test Data Exclusivity and the Logic of Patent Law*

Even on the assumption that it is appropriate to protect submitted test data through exclusivity rights, there are fears that aspects of test data exclusivity conflict with features of patent law intended to serve the public interest. These issues include the incentivisation of delaying drug launches, the fear that test data exclusivity might undermine measures designed to protect public health such as compulsory licensing, the lack of disclosure of information associated with test data exclusivity and the lack of accountability or appeal mechanisms associated with test data exclusivity. While there are a number of measures that alleviate or outright prevents some of these issues, they are not found in the text data exclusivity laws of many jurisdictions as discussed in Chap. 6.

2.4.1.1 Incentivising Delayed Drug Launches

As noted at Sect. 2.3.1.1, the basic logic of the patent system is both that the time-limited exclusivity period granted by the patent will encourage the originator to exploit their invention, and that the disclosure of the invention in the patent specification will permit others to exploit it once this period has expired.[77] However, aspects of test data exclusivity can undermine these functions by incentivising delayed drug launches and providing opportunities for the 'evergreening' of pharmaceutical products.

---

[74] World Medical Association (2013), paras 12, 18 and 20.

[75] Owoeye (2014), p. 109.

[76] Bošnjak (2001), p. 179.

[77] Landes and Posner (2009), p. 295.

It is a well-known issue that pharmaceutical products often only enter developing markets a significant period of time after they are launched in the developed world.[78] This delay is deeply undesirable from an access to medicines perspective; patients cannot benefit from medicines which are simply not available in their jurisdiction. This drug delay occurs partly because research-based pharmaceutical companies prioritise the developed world markets in which the overwhelming majority of their profits are made; as markets for pharmaceuticals in the developing world have grown, the delay between the launch of pharmaceutical products in developed and developing jurisdictions has shrunk, but it can still amount to years.[79] It has also been suggested that drug launches are delayed in developing jurisdictions because the availability of drugs in these markets can undermine the profitability of developed drug markets. This can occur as a result of 'reference pricing', whereby the price a government is willing to pay for a drug is set by reference to its price in other jurisdictions, and 'parallel importation', the reimportation of branded pharmaceuticals from markets in which they were sold at a much lower price.[80]

Patent law theoretically incentivises introducing a new pharmaceutical product to a market as soon as possible in order to maximise the period of market monopoly because of the global standard of novelty typically applied by patent law.[81] Because the standard of novelty used for determining whether a product receives test data exclusivity is typically one of *local* novelty (that is, a drug will be considered novel if not previously approved in the jurisdiction, regardless of how long it has been used in other jurisdictions), originator firms receive no penalty in terms of reduced test data exclusivity protection if they choose to delay the launch of a drug. In certain circumstances, test data exclusivity may therefore further incentivise delaying the launch of a pharmaceutical product in a developing country in order to manage the issues of reference pricing and parallel importation as the originator firm will still be able to obtain a period of exclusivity when it eventually launches the product in that jurisdiction. Test data exclusivity may also incentivise the delaying of drug registration in order to prolong a company's monopoly on the best form of treatment for a condition—a firm may deliberately choose to release 'line extensions' of their products more slowly in order to minimise the overlap in their test data exclusivity terms. This issue is likely to be more acute in jurisdictions in which 'new indications' of an existing drug are entitled to a fresh period of exclusivity, such as the US.[82]

Incentivising companies to *delay* bringing drugs to market in this way contradicts the justification often given for intellectual property rights; that they promote

[78] Wileman and Mishra (2010), p. 54.

[79] Ibid 56.

[80] Spina Alì (2017), pp. 184–190.

[81] Although it should be noted that under article 4 of the Paris Convention for the Protection of Industrial Property, inventors are entitled to a period of one year from the filing of a patent in a member of the Paris Union during which the inventor or their successor in title may use the first filling date as the effective filing date in other states which are party to the agreement (the so-called 'convention priority right').

[82] Junod (2004), p. 511.

innovation. It has been suggested that part of the reason that companies are so slow to launch products in developing countries is that because smaller pharmaceutical markets mean acquiring a patent is not cost-effective, originator companies will therefore struggle to make a profit in these jurisdictions. As a result, the argument goes, test data exclusivity could provide a cost-effective mechanism to enable research-based pharmaceutical companies to earn profit in these jurisdictions and therefore incentivise earlier drug launches in smaller pharmaceutical markets.[83] While this may be the case for those jurisdictions in which acquiring a patent is legitimately not cost effective, such an approach is unlikely to be effective at reducing delays in drug launches incentivised by the management of reference pricing, restricting parallel importation or evergreening treatments. In these cases, a mechanism is required to prevent pharmaceutical companies delaying launches for as long as benefits them. As discussed in Chaps. 5 and 6, a number of jurisdictions provide such a mechanism either by only granting test data exclusivity when a product is submitted for approval in that jurisdiction within a certain period of its international debut, or by timing the exclusivity period from approval in a foreign jurisdiction in which it is likely to be launched promptly, such as the US or EU.

2.4.1.2 Undermining Measures Designed to Promote Public Health

Another widely discussed concern regarding test data exclusivity is that exclusivity rights undermine the ability of governments to make use of measures designed to promote public health. Attention has recently been focused on this issue by the COVID-19 pandemic, with commentators voicing alarm over the possibility that test data exclusivity provisions might frustrate either compulsory licenses issued by national governments or actions taken under the limited exceptions to TRIPS set out in the 2022 Ministerial Decision on the TRIPS Agreement.[84]

Compulsory licensing is provided for in the TRIPS Agreement at Article 31 (on use of patented inventions 'without authorization of the right holder'), which permits the practice as long as certain provisions are respected (these include requirements to engage in prior negotiations for a voluntary license on reasonable terms, to limit the license in terms of scope and duration, and to remunerate the right holder to some extent).[85] Compulsory licensing is a critical counterweight to the powerful monopolies conferred through the grant of patent rights—even working from the assumption that patents are in general a net positive, it is still necessary to provide some kind of measure to limit patent monopolies in those circumstances where they will cause obvious and avoidable harm. Such situations include threats to the public that require the use of the patented invention on a scale that the patent holder is unwilling or unable to meet, use of patent rights to facilitate an

[83] Spina Alì (2017), p. 204.

[84] See, for example, Chandler (2020).

[85] TRIPS Article 31.

anticompetitive abuse of a dominant market position or the emergence of a 'patent thicket' that impedes technological and scientific progress.[86]

The presence of test data exclusivity does nothing to prevent the actual grant of a compulsory license. However, as discussed at Sect. 2.3.1.1, test data exclusivity rights can render compulsory licenses ineffective in the context of pharmaceuticals by preventing the generic medicine produced under the license from using an abridged drug application to gain marketing approval. If the licensee has to produce their own test data, the market entry of the generics will be at the very least delayed (undesirable to say the least in an emergency), and potentially rendered completely economically unfeasible. The possibility of such a scenario has been highlighted by several commentators.[87] Graham Dutfield has suggested that the ability of test data exclusivity provisions to render a compulsory license worthless may explain why such provisions appear so frequently in FTAs.[88] Frederick Abbott goes further, and claims that test data exclusivity provisions seemed to be designed to restrict the effective use of compulsory licensing by preventing the approval of third party medicines.[89]

The threat of test data exclusivity rights undermining a compulsory license was highlighted in 2006 when Greg Perry, then the head of the European Generic Medicines Association (EGA), wrote to the European Commission's Directorate-General for Enterprise and Industry to enquire as to the possibility of EU countries using compulsory licenses to meet national demand for oseltamivir, a treatment for influenza then being stockpiled by governments at great cost amid fears that an Avian influenza pandemic with the potential to kill tens of millions was imminent.[90] In particular, Perry wanted to know if, in the event that such a license was issued by a national government, that government would be able to approve a generic version of oseltamivir produced under licence on the basis of previously submitted test data. Martin Terberger, the Head of Unit for Pharmaceuticals, replied that while issuing a compulsory license was a matter of national law for EU member states, because EU rules did not provide for any exceptions to this protection during the test data exclusivity period, and because oseltamivir was still under protection, applicants seeking marketing authorisation for a generic version in the EU would need to either provide their own clinical data demonstrating the safety or efficacy of the product, or confirm that the holder of the marketing authorisation had consented to the use of their own documentation by the applicant.[91] As such, drugs produced under a compulsory license could not be legally distributed in the EU without conducting

[86] Dutfield (2008), p. 111.

[87] Correa (2014), p. 46.

[88] Dutfield (2008), p. 111.

[89] Abbott (2004), p. 12.

[90] Lokuge et al. (2006), p. 16.

[91] European Commission (2006) Letter from the European Commission to Mr. Greg Perry, EGA-European Generic Medicines Association on the subject of Tamiflu application and data exclusivity in an emergency compulsory license situation.

fresh clinical trials or obtaining the permission of the right holder (which would obviously obviate any need for a compulsory license in the first instance). This gap in European legislation has never been addressed and, as will be discussed in Chap. 6, the test data exclusivity laws of many other jurisdictions fall into a similar position.

2.4.1.3 Lack of Disclosure of Information

Some commentators have also noted that while patent law incentivises the dissemination of information by disclosing the details of an invention to the public, test data exclusivity may restrict the disclosure of the information which it purports to incentivise the creation of.[92] A prohibition on the disclosure of submitted test data is not, technically speaking, test data exclusivity, but such prohibitions are often linked to test data exclusivity rights—Article 39.3 of TRIPS states that in addition to protection against unfair commercial use, submitted test data should be protected against disclosure except 'where necessary to protect the public, or unless steps are taken to ensure that the data are protected against unfair commercial use.'[93] Many of the FTAs which include test data exclusivity provisions have repeated this language.[94]

There are compelling reasons to disclose submitted test data. As noted above, many clinical trials results are fudged due to the immense investments they represent for pharmaceutical companies. Oseltamivir, the same drug that prompted the Terberger letter, is an infamous example. Between 1999 and 2014, national governments spent over $9 billion USD stockpiling oseltamivir.[95] However, as early as 2006 Cochrane, a British charity which advocates evidence-based medicine, had raised questions as to the actual effectiveness of oseltamivir as a treatment for influenza.[96] Cochrane made several requests to Hoffman-La Roche, the pharmaceutical firm which held the rights to oseltamivir, to access clinical study reports to further investigate these claims, which were refused.[97] In 2011, Cochrane managed to successfully obtain reports on several oseltamivir trials from the EU's pharmaceutical regulator, the European Medicines Agency (EMA).[98] Under mounting pressure, Roche released a larger number of reports in 2013.[99] In 2014, Cochrane

[92] Junod (2004), p. 516.

[93] TRIPS 39.3.

[94] For example, US-Chile FTA (2003), Article 17.10; EFTA-Turkey FTA (2018), Annex XX Article 6; EU-Korea FTA (2010), Article 10.36.

[95] Abbasi (2014), p. 348.

[96] Jefferson et al. (2009).

[97] Abbasi (2014), p. 348.

[98] British Medical Journal, 'Tamiflu campaign' https://www.bmj.com/tamiflu (Accessed 26 January 2023).

[99] Ibid.

released a review of oseltamivir based on this data which concluded that the drug shortened flu-like symptoms by only around half a day, did not reduce the number of hospitalisations, showed little evidence of reducing complications associated with influenza and had a number of significant adverse effects such as nausea, vomiting, headaches and renal and psychiatric events which had not been fully reported in the original publications.[100] Earlier disclosure of the test data submitted by Roche might therefore have saved national governments billions. Even when test data has been produced honestly, mistakes may be made; disclosing data permits third parties to verify it. Furthermore, the disclosure of scientific research adds to general scientific knowledge and thereby contributes to scientific progress.[101]

2.4.1.4 Absence of Appeal Mechanisms

Some commentators have expressed fears regarding the difficulty of contesting test data exclusivity rights in many jurisdictions. Patents, while powerful, will only be granted if an applicant can convince patent examiners that their invention meets the criteria for patentability.[102] Even if a patent application does meet these criteria, patents can be challenged by competitors who believe that the invention in question was improperly awarded a patent. Test data exclusivity, on the other hand, is typically granted automatically and cannot easily be challenged in many jurisdictions, even in cases where test data exclusivity is supposedly contingent on meeting specific requirements, such as being the product of considerable effort.[103] Test data exclusivity rights may thus provide exclusivity protection to pharmaceutical products which a patent office deems unworthy of protection, as well as reducing the incentive to challenge weak patents by preventing the marketing of a generic version of the patented drug even in the event that the patent in revoked.

2.5 Test Data Exclusivity and Biologic Drugs

Biological drugs, normally referred to as 'biologics', are medications comprised of or derived from living organisms[104]; examples of biologics include monoclonal antibodies, growth hormones and gene therapies.[105] All vaccines, including those used against COVID-19, are biologics, and biologic drugs represent an increasingly important area of medicine, providing many of the most promising treatments for

[100] Jefferson (2014).

[101] Spina Alì (2017), p. 232.

[102] TRIPS Article 27.

[103] Junod (2004), p. 516.

[104] Matthews (2017), p. 104.

[105] World Health Organization (2017).

various cancers, neurological disorders and autoimmune diseases amongst many others. Biologics differ from traditional 'small molecule' drugs in a number of important aspects; whereas small molecule drugs might be comprised of around 20–100 atoms, biologics are typically made up of 200 to 50,000 atoms,[106] and involve significantly more complicated methods of manufacture.[107] The result of these differences is that it is effectively impossible to create an exact copy of a biologic; small molecule drugs, in contrast, can be replicated cheaply and easily.[108] A biologic intended to imitate an originator product will be only 'highly similar' to it at best. Such follow-on biologics are known as 'similar biological medicinal products,'[109] 'similar biotherapeutic products,'[110] 'subsequent entry biologics,'[111] or simply 'biosimilars.'

These chemical differences between biologics and small molecule drugs have led to differences in how they are regulated, particularly regarding aspects of the abbreviated approval process. In addition, there is a debate over how the test data submitted in association with biologic drugs should be protected, if at all. Some point to the allegedly more expensive development process for biologics, as well as the fact that patents may be less effective in protecting biologics given that biosimilars are not exact copies of originator products, as evidence that biologic test data requires more protection than small molecule drug test data.[112] Others believe that biologic test data should simply be protected through existing test data exclusivity laws.[113] Understanding this debate requires some knowledge of the history of biologics and biosimilars.

2.5.1 The Origins and Development of Abbreviated Approval Pathways for Biosimilars

While abbreviated approval pathways for small molecule drugs first developed in the late 1970s and early 1980s (see further Chap. 3), abbreviated approval pathways for biosimilars have only developed more recently. This is partly because modern biologics are themselves relatively recent—the first new drug approvals for biologics in the US were made only in the early 1980s—but also due to the fundamental chemical differences between small molecule drugs and biologics.[114] Determining

[106] Matthews (2017), p. 105.

[107] Ibid.

[108] Ibid, p. 107.

[109] European Medicines Agency (2014).

[110] WHO (2009).

[111] Health Canada (2016), p. 6.

[112] Grabowski (2008), p.480.

[113] See, for example, Federal Trade Commission (2009).

[114] Grabowski (2008), p. 480.

whether two small molecule products are chemically identical is reasonable easy, especially as small molecule drugs generally have straightforward chemical structures. Determining whether two biological entities are similar enough that they will not produce clinically significant differences in patients is considerably more complicated.[115]

Despite these difficulties, many jurisdictions have now developed abbreviated approval pathways for biosimilars. The EU was the first jurisdiction to implement such a pathway; following a wave of biologic products coming off-patent in the mid-2000s, the EU amended its existing abbreviated approval pathway to permit the approval of biologic drugs on the basis of previously submitted test data if additional supplemental data was also submitted.[116] The standards set out by the EMA are extremely strict, requiring extensive testing to establish a high degree of similarity, which in turn raises the cost of entry for would-be biosimilar manufacturers: a 2010 paper placed the cost of getting a biosimilar to market in Europe as between $20–30 million USD, largely due to the stringent regulatory requirements of the EMA.[117]

The EU's guidelines have been extremely influential in how other jurisdictions have dealt with the issue of biosimilars. Australia, Canada, Japan, South Korea, Singapore, Malaysia and South Africa have all modelled the EU's standards in developing their own approval pathways.[118] In 2009, the WHO released further guidelines, largely based on the principles of the EU guidelines, which have also influenced the policies of national drug regulatory authorities.[119] The US created its own pathway for biosimilar approval in 2009 with the Biologics Price Competition and Innovation Act (BPCIA). While not directly modelled on the EU guidelines, the US approach is conceptually similar; sponsors may submit applications for approval of their product by showing that it is 'biosimilar' to a reference biologic, based on analytical studies showing that it is highly similar to the reference product, animal studies, and a clinical study or studies demonstrating that the safety, purity and potency of the product are in line with the originator.[120] The issue of test data exclusivity for test data submitted with respect to biologics is thus now a highly relevant one.

---

115 Macdonald et al. (2015), p. 665.

116 Council Directive 2001/83/EC, Article 10.

117 Mody et al. (2010), p. 28.

118 Krishnan et al. (2015), p. 21.

119 Macdonald et al. (2015), p.655.

120 USA, 42 USC § 262(i)(2).

2.5.2 Approaches to Test Data Exclusivity for Data Submitted in Association with Biologics

For a jurisdiction which has pre-existing test data exclusivity laws,[121] the issue of an abbreviated approval pathway for biosimilars suggests one of three approaches: to extend existing test data exclusivity rules to biologics, to create a separate (and potentially stronger) system of test data exclusivity for biologic products or to simply exclude test data submitted with respect to biologics from the scope of test data exclusivity altogether. The first approach treats small molecule drugs and biologics in the same way, while the second and third options suggest that there is some reason to differentiate between small molecule drugs and biologics when it comes to the protection of submitted test data.

The case for non-discrimination between test data exclusivity protection for small molecule drugs and biologics rests on the idea that they are not sufficiently dissimilar to warrant differential treatment. In the absence of evidence that the differences between biologics and small molecule drugs mean that they need to be treated differently, it is argued that existing test data exclusivity rights should therefore simply be extended to biologics.

The chief argument from proponents of a different set of test data exclusivity rules for biologics is that because biosimilars are never identical to innovator biologics, and because they may use different methods of formulation and manufacture, it is easier to avoid infringing the patents over an originator product while still availing of an abbreviated approval pathway.[122] Furthermore, biologics are supposedly more expensive to develop than small molecule drugs on average,[123] although the general absence of transparency around pharmaceutical development costs makes this claim difficult to assess. In 2008 (prior to the introduction of an abbreviated approval pathway for biologics in the US), Grabowski published a paper in which he concluded the breakeven lifetime for biologics was between 12.9 and 16.2 years.[124] Grabowski suggested that a 12 year period of test data exclusivity for biologics would act as an appropriate 'floor' on the minimum amount of exclusivity a biologic could expect to receive in cases in which patent protection was in some way compromised.[125]

Opponents of longer test data exclusivity for biologics observe that because of their molecular complexity and difficulties associated with the manufacturing process, biologics rarely face generic competition even post-patent expiration, and point to the high cost of gaining approval for a biosimilar in the EU, even using the

[121] It is theoretically possible that a jurisdiction which provides no test data exclusivity for small molecule drugs, such as Argentina, might decide that it wants to create a system of test data exclusivity for biologics alone, but this seems extremely unlikely to say the least.

[122] Grabowski (2008), p. 479.

[123] Tzeng (2010), p. 136.

[124] Grabowski (2008), p. 487.

[125] Grabowski et al. (2011), p. 16.

abbreviated approval pathway, as well as the smaller price reductions associated with biosimilar competition compared to competition with generic small molecule drugs.[126] A 2009 report by the US Federal Trade Commission (FTC) into follow-on biologic competition noted that there is no evidence that patents over biologics provide less protection than those over small molecule drugs, or that many biologic medicines are unpatentable.[127] It has also been observed that even assuming Grabowski's break-even periods are correct, the entire break-even period would be an unduly long term of exclusivity as innovators generally retain a sizeable market share and ability to generate profit even after the entry of follow-on competitors.[128]

These counterarguments to the case for stronger test data exclusivity rights for biologics also inform the argument that biologics are less deserving of test data exclusivity rights than small molecule drugs. The 2009 FTC report concluded that these barriers mean that biosimilar competition with originator biologics is 'much more likely to resemble brand-to-brand competition than the dynamics of brand-generic competition,'[129] and that as such patent protection and market-based pricing were likely to be sufficient to support biosimilar competition and biologic innovation even without 'special legislative incentives that restrict competition' (i.e. test data exclusivity), which might harm consumers.[130]

It is worth noting that since the passage of the BPCIA, there has not been a flood of biosimilars competing with innovator biologics still under patent, and biosimilars remain rare even in jurisdictions with test data exclusivity provisions much shorter than 12 years. In 2019, a study found that the mean total development time for both small molecule drugs and biologics approved by the FDA between 2007 and 2016 was about 12 years, suggesting that a significantly longer period of exclusivity for biologics was possibly unwarranted.[131] Still, many of the world's most expensive drugs are biologics, and most face no competition, even after the end of patent protection. It seems difficult to conclude from the state of the market today that the biologics industry is especially vulnerable to competition and therefore deserving of further protection, even on the assumption that the general public policy justifications for test data exclusivity for small molecule drugs are correct.

[126] See Engelberg et al. (2009).

[127] Federal Trade Commission (2009), p. viii.

[128] Tzeng (2010), p. 156.

[129] Federal Trade Commission (2009), p. iii.

[130] Ibid, p. vi.

[131] Beall et al. (2019), p. 708.

2.6 Alternatives to Test Data Exclusivity

While test data exclusivity has been the subject of much criticism, many commentators have acknowledged that the problem it purportedly solves—the need to incentivise the creation of a public good in the form of information regarding the safety and efficacy of pharmaceutical drugs—is a real one. Reichman acknowledges the soaring costs of clinical trials, and the need to find some kind of solution to ensure the sustainability of new medicine launches.[132] However, Reichman further argues that if the data produced by clinical trials are such an essential public good that as a society we must 'scrape the bottom of the intellectual property barrel' to incentivise their creation, we should address the risks of diminished investment directly by sharing the costs of the generation of the data.[133] A number of commentators have suggested a range of alternative measures to encourage the production of submitted test data.

One of the simplest solutions to the free-rider problems surrounding the creation of a public good is to create that good through the public sector. In the case of data on the safety and efficacy of pharmaceutical drugs, this would involve direct government funding and possibly supervision of clinical trials, obviating the issue of needing to reimburse the private companies for the generation of such data.[134] This approach would also have the benefit of reducing both the incentives and opportunities of pharmaceutical firms to manipulate or falsify clinical trial data.[135] In addition, whereas privately funded research is likely to be closely guarded by the firms involved in order to maintain their advantage over competitors, publicly funded research could be more widely shared between scientists. While such an approach would obviously be expensive, many governments effectively already fund the cost of clinical trials by purchasing pharmaceutical products at prices justified by the high costs of bringing those products to market. Indeed, the economies of scale that governments would bring to the process might even further reduce expenditure, while the increased transparency of such an approach would help to ensure that the price of drugs would more accurately reflect their development costs.[136]

Such a fundamental shift in the funding of the drug development process is not without its difficulties—Benjamin Roin argues that governments would not be able to correctly identify the most beneficial drugs to develop, and that governments have historically grossly underfunded clinical research.[137] Certainly, it cannot be assumed that an adequate amount of funding could be provided or that this funding would be efficiently allocated. There would also be a need for governments, especially in

[132] Reichman (2009), p. 45.

[133] Ibid, p. 45.

[134] Ibid, p. 58; Baker (2008), p. 731.

[135] Ibid, p. 732.

[136] Reichman (2009), p. 64.

[137] Roin (2008), p. 560.

developed countries, to coordinate regarding funding or the free-rider problem would merely shift from the private sector to the public.[138] Still, much pharmaceutical research is already funded or subsidised by governments,[139] avenues for cooperation exist through organisations such as the WHO,[140] and the issue of international cooperation to increase publicly funded medical research has received renewed attention in recent years, particularly in the aftermath of the COVID-19 pandemic.

Other commentators have suggested an approach in which competitors share the costs of generating data through some kind of compulsory liability regime.[141] In such a scheme, originators would have no power to exclude competitors from use of data which they had generated but competitors would be required to reimburse originators to some extent if they wished to rely on their data within a certain period. Compulsory liability regimes are already used to share the costs involved in the generation of test data submitted to gain approval for agrichemical products in some jurisdictions; for example, the US Federal Insecticide, Fungicide and Rodenticide Act (FIFRA) provides a 15-year period measured from the date of submission for certain data during which second applicants are free to reference the data provided they provide the originator with 'adequate payment' (certain types of originator data submitted under FIFRA may also qualify for a ten year period of test data exclusivity measured from the date of approval; as long as this period also applies to submitted data, it will not be possible to reference it).[142] A number of FTAs negotiated by EFTA in the mid-2000s explicitly permitted the signatories to provide a compulsory liability regime to protect pharmaceutical test data as an alternative to test data exclusivity, although it is not clear if any of the parties to these deals actually implemented such a scheme.[143] A price-sharing scheme would undoubtedly have many complicated details to work out, but existing compulsory liability models could provide a model. Aaron Fellmeth and Razvan Dinca have both made sophisticated suggestions for the calculation of costs in such a model.[144]

Spina Alì has also suggested taxation as a possible alternative means to share the cost of clinical trials.[145] An additional tax on generic products in proportion to the expenditure of the originator firm in generating the data in question for a fixed period would raise the prices of generic products and thus permit the originator to earn a premium during this time.[146] This approach can be distinguished from a compulsory

---

[138] Reichman (2009), p. 63.

[139] Ibid.

[140] Ibid.

[141] See, for example, Reichman (2009); Dinca (2005); Sanjuan et al. (2006); Fellmeth (2004).

[142] USA, 7 USC § 136a.

[143] EFTA-Lebanon FTA (2004), Annex V Article 4; EFTA-Tunisia FTA (2004), Annex V Article 4; EFTA-Korea FTA (2005), Annex XIII Article 3.

[144] Fellmeth (2004), p. 448; Dinca (2005), p. 520.

[145] Spina Alì (2018), p. 228.

[146] Ibid, p. 228.

liability system in that the proceeds of the tax would be collected by the government, rather than the originator—this could potentially be used to further fund or subsidise additional clinical research.[147]

Such non-monopolistic approaches would avoid the deadweight losses (that is, the losses which accrue to society when resources are not efficiently allocated) associated with grants of monopolies—although it should be noted that subsidies, levies and taxation are also associated with deadweight losses to an extent.[148] These schemes would also avoid many of the issues discussed above, such as incentivising duplicative trials, incentivising delays in drug launches, undermining compulsory licensing and preventing disclosure of data. These schemes are also likely compatible with Article 39.3 of the TRIPS Agreement, as discussed at Sect. 4.4.3.

2.7 The Impact of Test Data Exclusivity on Access to Medicine

The impact of test data exclusivity is uncertain. Like much of the intellectual property system its benefits have never been conclusively demonstrated. Still, a number of studies have been conducted which have aimed to assess some of the impact of test data exclusivity in certain contexts.

In 2007, Oxfam conducted a study on the impact of test data exclusivity in Jordan.[149] Jordan adopted a five-year term of test data exclusivity for new chemical entities in 2001 following its accession to the WTO and the conclusion of the negotiations which led to the US-Jordan FTA.[150] The Oxfam study found that of 108 medicines which faced no generic competitor at the time of the study, only five had patent protection—furthermore, analysis of the 103 drugs which did not have patents associated with them found that at least 79% faced no competition because of test data exclusivity.[151] Interviews with local industry and government revealed that most multinational companies had not filed patent applications in Jordan because Jordan was not a member of the Patent Cooperation Treaty meaning that many of the medicines would not have qualified for patent protection in Jordan due to the filing date, and because pharmaceutical companies were satisfied with the 5 years of effective market monopoly that test data exclusivity provides. The study did note that firms were beginning to file patents towards the end of the period studied, meaning that patent protection would presumably have a higher impact in future.[152]

[147] Ibid, p. 229.

[148] Ibid.

[149] Malpani (2009).

[150] US-Jordan FTA (2000), Article 4; Malpani (2009), p. 207.

[151] Malpani (2009), p. 209.

[152] Ibid 8.

The Oxfam study also found that pharmaceutical prices in Jordan had increased by 20% in Jordan between 2001 and 2006[153] and that new product launches in Jordan remained a fraction of those in the US (an analysis of the complete portfolios of a number of research-based pharmaceutical companies showed that only 33 out of 82 products were registered on Jordan's market).[154] Furthermore, there did not seem to have been any significant foreign direct investment by pharmaceutical companies seeking to synthesise or manufacture medicines in partnership with Jordanian firms.[155] This seems to be the case outside of Jordan as well—an analysis of 45 countries by Palmedo in 2013 revealed that there was no relationship between investment by the pharmaceutical industry and whether or not a country has passed test data exclusivity protection provisions.[156]

The impact of test data exclusivity in Jordan was also examined in a 2012 study by Ryan Abbott et al.[157] It found that enforcement of test data exclusivity resulted in additional expenditures of $18 million USD in 2004, a higher estimate than the Oxfam report, which had estimated a cost of between $6.3 and $22.04 million USD 2002 to 2006.[158] Overall, the Abbott study concluded that test data exclusivity had the most significant impact on the price of medicines of any form of intellectual property present in Jordan,[159] although it noted that this was at least partially due to the limited impact of Jordanian patents on the price of medicines, itself due to the fact the Jordan was not a signatory to the PCT and that patents filed post-2001 would likely only begin to significantly affect the Jordanian market after the 1999 to 2004 period studied.[160]

In 2009, Schaffer and Brenner conducted a study on the effects of test data exclusivity in Guatemala following the entry into force of the CAFTA-DR trade agreement between the US, several Central American countries and the Dominican Republic. They found that several drugs protected by test data exclusivity would remain protected against generic competition in Guatemala after they had become open for generic competition in the US, although they did not go into detail as to how much later exclusivity would end in Guatemala.[161] Schaffer and Brenner also observed that the prices for all drugs protected by test data exclusivity were higher than those of non-protected drugs in the same therapeutic class.[162]

A study assessing the impact of 10 years of test data exclusivity protection in Colombia by LAC-Global Alliance for Access to Medicines, *Misión Salud* and

[153] Ibid, p. 206.

[154] Ibid, p. 215.

[155] Ibid, p. 207.

[156] Palmedo (2012).

[157] Abbott et al. (2012).

[158] Ibid, p. 81.

[159] Ibid, p. 82.

[160] Ibid.

[161] Shaffer and Brenner (2009), p. 958.

[162] Ibid, p. 962.

IFARMA in 2011 found that of the 122 new chemical entities registered in Colombia between 2001 and 2011, 100% had requested data exclusivity protection, that it was denied in only 4.1% of cases, and that in all cases the products for which test data exclusivity was requested were owned by foreign companies.[163] The average date of registration for a generic competitor was 11.5 months after the expiration of the data exclusivity period, suggesting that test data exclusivity had delayed the market entry of generics in a significant number of cases.[164] The study also found that new chemical entities were more likely to be registered in Argentina or Venezuela, jurisdictions which lack test data exclusivity rules, before they were registered in Colombia.[165] The study also concluded that test data exclusivity had cost Colombians an extra $412 million USD over the 10 year period.[166]

These studies suggest that the introduction of test data exclusivity rights in developing countries are associated with decreased access to medicines. This does not in and of itself confirm that such intellectual property rights are a net negative; test data exclusivity may provide benefits that outweigh these costs, such as an increase in research and development from the research-based industry. However, clear evidence for these benefits remains lacking, while evidence that test data exclusivity imposes at least some costs seems clear.

2.8 Conclusion

As the discussion in this chapter has shown, the protection of submitted pharmaceutical test data is a highly contentious area. While the costs of generating the test data submitted to regulators as part of the process of approving a new pharmaceutical product are unquestionably high, there significant unanswered questions as to how and to what extent it is desirable to protect such data. The benefits of test data exclusivity remain unclear, while critics point to a wide range of concerns as to the potential negative impact of this intellectual property right, including the incentivisation of the duplication of experiments with human subjects, the risk of undermining various safeguards within the patent system, and the raising of the prices of medicines. Importantly, the impact of test data exclusivity is likely to vary significantly between jurisdictions.

---

[163] Cortés Gamba et al. (2012), pp. 33–36.

[164] Ibid, p. 39.

[165] Ibid, p. 42.

[166] Ibid, p. 9.

References

Abbasi K (2014) The missing data that cost $20 bn. BMJ 348:g2695

Abbott FM (2004) The Doha Declaration on the TRIPS Agreement and Public Health and the contradictory trend in bilateral and regional free trade agreements. Quaker United Nations Office (QUNO), Occasional Paper 14

Abbott RB, Bader R, Bajjali L, ElSamen TA, Obeidat T, Sboul H, Shwayat M, Alabbadi I (2012) The price of medicines in Jordan: the cost of trade-based intellectual property. J Generic Med 9(2):75–85

Akerlof GA (1970) The market for "Lemons": quality uncertainty and the market mechanism. Q J Econ 84(3):488–500

Attaran A (2004) How do patents and economic policies affect access to essential medicines in developing countries? Health Aff 23(3):155–166

Avorn J (2015) The $2.6 billion pill—methodologic and policy considerations. N Engl J Med 372(20):1877–1879

Baker D (2008) The benefits and savings from publicly funded clinical trials of prescription drugs. Int J Health Serv 38(4):731–750

Beall RF, Hwang TJ, Kesselheim AS (2019) Pre-market development times for biologic versus small-molecule drugs. Nat Biotechnol 37(7):708–711

Bošnjak S (2001) The declaration of Helsinki: the cornerstone of research ethics. Arch Oncol 9(3): 179–184

Bouchard RA, Cahoy D, Domeij B, Dutfield G (2011) Structure-function analysis of global pharmaceutical linkage regulations. Minnesota J Law Sci Technol 12:391

Braithwaite J, Drahos P (2000) Global business regulation. Cambridge University Press, Cambridge

Chandler DC (2020) Uh-oh we are in trouble! Compulsory Licences v data exclusivity in the EU: one more challenge to overcome in the race to find a COVID-19 vaccine? Eur Intellect Prop Rev 42(9):539–547

Correa C (2002) Protection of data submitted for the registration of pharmaceuticals: implementing the standards of the TRIPS agreement. South Centre, Geneva

Correa C (2014) The use of compulsory licensing in Latin America. In: Hilty R, Liu KC (eds) Compulsory licensing. Springer, Berlin, pp 43–60

Cortés Gamba ME, Francisco FR, Mayra Damaris VS (2012) Impacto de 10 años de protección de datos en medicamentos en Colombia. IFARMA

DiMasi JA, Hansen RW, Grabowski H (2003) The price of innovation: new estimates of drug development costs. J Health Econ 22(2):151–185

DiMasi JA, Grabowski HG, Hansen RW (2016) Innovation in the pharmaceutical industry: new estimates of R&D costs. J Health Econ 47:20–33

Dinca R (2005) The Bermuda triangle of pharmaceutical law: is data protection a lost ship? J World Intellect Prop 8:517

Drahos P (2008) "Trust me": patent offices in developing countries. Am J Law Med 34(2–3): 151–174

Dumit J (2012) Drugs for life: how pharmaceutical companies define our health. Duke University Press, Durham

Dutfield G (2008) Delivering drugs to the poor: will the TRIPS amendment help? Am J Law Med 34:107–124

Dutfield G (2009) Intellectual property rights and the life science industries: past, present and future. World Scientific, Singapore

Eisenberg RS (2006) The role of the FDA in innovation policy. Mich Telecommun Technol Law Rev 13:345

Engelberg AB, Kesselheim AS, Avorn J (2009) Balancing innovation, access, and profits—market exclusivity for biologics. N Engl J Med 361(20):1917–1919

European Commission (2006) Letter from the European Commission to Mr. Greg Perry, EGA-European Generic Medicines Association on the subject of Tamiflu application and data exclusivity in an emergency compulsory license situation

European Generic Medicines Association (2000) EGA Position Paper: Data Exclusivity: A major obstacle to innovation and competition in the EU pharmaceutical sector

European Medicines Agency (2014) Guideline on similar biological medicinal products

Federal Trade Commission (2009) Emerging health care issues: follow-on biologic drug competition

Fellmeth AX (2004) Secrecy, monopoly, and access to pharmaceuticals in international trade law: protection of marketing approval data under the TRIPs agreement. Harv Int Law J 45:443

Friedman LM, Furberg CD, DeMets DL (2010) Fundamentals of clinical trials. Springer, New York

Gervais D (2019) The patent option. North Carolina J Law Technol 20:357

Ghinea N, Lipworth W, Kerridge I (2016) Propaganda or the cost of innovation? Challenging the high price of new drugs. BMJ 352:i1284

Goldberg PK (2010) Intellectual property rights protection in developing countries: the case of pharmaceuticals. J Eur Econ Assoc 8(2–3):326–353

Grabowski H (2002) Patents and new product development in the pharmaceutical and biotechnology industries. In: Duca JV, Yücel KM (eds) Science and cents: exploring the economics of biotechnology. Federal Reserve Bank of Dallas, Dallas, pp 87–104

Grabowski H (2008) Follow-on biologics: data exclusivity and the balance between innovation and competition. Nat Rev Drug Discov 7(6):479–488

Grabowski H, Vernon JM (2000) Effective patent life in pharmaceuticals. Int J Technol Manag 19(1–2):98–120

Grabowski H, Long G, Mortimer R (2011) Data exclusivity for biologics. Nat Rev Drug Discov 10(1):15

Hay M, Thomas DW, Craighead JL, Economides C, Rosenthal J (2014) Clinical development success rates for investigational drugs. Nat Biotechnol 32(1):40–51

Health Canada (2016) Guidance document: information and submission requirements for biosimilar biologic drugs

Heled Y (2015) Regulatory competitive shelters. Ohio State Law J 76:299

Hemphill CS, Sampat BN (2012) Evergreening, patent challenges, and effective market life in pharmaceuticals. J Health Econ 31(2):327–339

IFPMA (2000) Encouragement of new clinical drug development: the role of data exclusivity

IFPMA (2011) Encouraging Development of New Medicines

Jefferson T, Jones M, Doshi P, Del Mar C (2009) Neuraminidase inhibitors for preventing and treating influenza in healthy adults: systematic review and meta-analysis. BMJ 339:b5106

Jefferson T, Jones M, Doshi P, Spencer EA, Onakpoya I, Henegah C (2014) Oseltamivir for influenza in adults and children: systematic review of clinical study reports and summary of regulatory comments. BMJ 348

Junod V (2004) Drug marketing exclusivity under United States and European Union law. Food Drug Law J 59(4):479–518

Katz A (2007) Pharmaceutical lemons: innovation and regulation in the drug industry. Mich Telecommun Technol Law Rev 14:1

Krishnan A, Mody R, Malhotra H (2015) Global regulatory landscape of biosimilars: emerging and established market perspectives. Biosimilars 5:19–32

Landes WM, Posner RA (2009) The economic structure of intellectual property law. Harvard University Press, Cambridge

Lokuge B, Drahos P, Neville W (2006) Pandemics, antiviral stockpiles and biosecurity in Australia: what about the generic option? Med J Aust 184(1):16–20

Macdonald JC, Hartman H, Jacobs IA (2015) Regulatory considerations in oncologic biosimilar drug development. MAbs 7(4):653–661

Malpani R (2009) All costs, no benefits: how the US-Jordan free trade agreement affects access to medicines. J Gen Med 6(3):206–217

Matthews D (2017) Exclusivity for biologics. In: Matthews D, Zech H (eds) Research handbook on intellectual property and the life sciences. Edward Elgar Publishing, Cheltenham, pp 104–121
Mody R, Varshney B, Patankar D (2010) Understanding variations in biosimilars: correlation with risk and regulatory implications. Int J Risk Safety Med 22(1):27–40
Owoeye OA (2014) Data exclusivity and public health under the TRIPS agreement. J Law Inf Sci 23(2):106–133
Palmedo M (2012) Do pharmaceutical firms invest more heavily in countries with data exclusivity? Curr Int Trade Law J 21:38
Perehudoff K, 't Hoen E, Boulet P (2021) Overriding drug and medical technology patents for pandemic recovery: a legitimate move for high-income countries, too. BMJ Glob Health 6(4): e005518
Prasad V, Mailankody S (2017) Research and development spending to bring a single cancer drug to market and revenues after approval. JAMA Intern Med 177:1569–1575
Pugatch M (2006) Intellectual property, data exlcusivity, innovation and market access. In: Roffe P, Tansey G, Vivas-Eugui D (eds) Negotiating health: intellectual property and access to medicine. Earthscan, London, pp 97–132
Reichman JH (2009) Rethinking the role of clinical trial data in international intellectual property law: the case for a public goods approach. Marq Intellect Prop Law Rev 13(1):1
Roin BN (2008) Unpatentable drugs and the standards of patentability. Texas Law Rev 87:503
Sanjuan JR, Love J, Weissman R (2006) Protection of pharmaceutical test data: a policy proposal. KEI Research Paper: 1
Shaffer ER, Brenner FE (2009) A trade agreement's impact on access to generic drugs. Health Aff 28:957–968
Shaikh OH (2016) Access to medicine versus test data exclusivity: safeguarding flexibilities under international law. Springer, Berlin
Spina Ali G (2017) Article 39 (3) TRIPS: understanding the obligations, exploiting the flexibilities. The University of Hong Kong
Spina Alì G (2018) The 13th round: Article 39 (3) TRIPS and the struggle over "Unfair Commercial Use.". J World Intellect Prop 21(3–4):201–242
't Hoen E (2016) Private patents and public health: changing intellectual property rules for access to medicines. Health Action International, Amsterdam
't Hoen E (2022) Protection of clinical test data and public health: a proposal to end the stronghold of data exclusivity. In: Correa C, Hilty RM (eds) Access to medicines and vaccines. Springer, Cham, pp 183–200
Thomas JR (2014) Toward a theory of regulatory exclusivities. In: Okediji RL, Bagley MA (eds) Patent law in global perspective. Oxford University Press, Oxford, pp 345–376
Tzeng L (2010) Follow-on biologics, data exclusivity, and the FDA. Berkeley Technol Law J 25: 135
Wileman H, Mishra A (2010) Drug lag and key regulatory barriers in the emerging markets. Perspect Clin Res 1(2):51
Wong CH, Siah KW, Lo AW (2019) Estimation of clinical trial success rates and related parameters. Biostatistics 20(2):273–286
World Health Organization (2009) Expert committee on biological standardization: guidelines on evaluation of similar biotherapeutic products (SBPs)
World Health Organization (2017) Report on the expert consultation on improving access to and use of similar biotherapeutic products
World Medical Association (2013) World medical association declaration of Helsinki: ethical principles for medical research involving human subjects. JAMA 310(20):2191–2195

Chapter 3
The Origins of Test Data Exclusivity

Abstract This chapter sets out the history of how intellectual property rights in pharmaceutical test data first developed in the 1980s. The analysis of the origins of test data exclusivity presented shows that these intellectual property rights emerged in the US as a result of political expediency rather than a reasoned argument or other evidence as to their public benefit. This approach was then quickly adopted by the European Communities with little consideration of its implications. Along with the parallel development of a similar system in Japan, this meant that almost all centres of the research-based pharmaceutical industry entered the negotiations that would lead to the establishing of the World Trade Organisation, and therefore the TRIPS Agreement, with similar perspectives on the protection of submitted pharmaceutical test data.

3.1 Introduction

Like other major reforms to pharmaceutical regulation over the course of the twentieth century, the origins of test data exclusivity lie in the response of the US government to a perceived crisis and the subsequent globalisation of that response. As is discussed below, what is now known as 'data exclusivity' or 'test data exclusivity' for pharmaceuticals first came into existence as a product of a politically expedient solution to the peculiarities of this particular crisis, rather than because of any evidence that it was a sound policy that would benefit the public interest. Furthermore, the first transmission of test data exclusivity to a new jurisdiction—its adoption by the EC in 1986—was not the result of careful deliberation by lawmakers or new evidence of the benefits of the policy, but rather the result of the EC modelling the US abbreviated approval pathway system with little reflection or adaptation to the European context. Both of these facts cast doubts upon the benefits of test data exclusivity, as well as claims as to its universal applicability.

By coincidence, Japan had concurrently developed a system whereby second applicants were prevented from entering the market for a number of years after the approval of an originator product in response to the thalidomide disaster. While the Japanese system was motivated by public safety concerns rather than any desire to

A. Buick, *Intellectual Property Rights in Pharmaceutical Test Data*,
https://doi.org/10.1007/978-3-031-29436-5_3

protect submitted test data, it created a similar effect to test data exclusivity. As a result, most of the major centres of the research-based pharmaceutical industry, with the notable exception of Switzerland,[1] had domestic non-patent exclusivity periods restricting the market entry of generics as they entered the Uruguay Round of GATT negotiations in 1986. These circumstances would prove to have a significant effect on the negotiations that would eventually lead to the TRIPS Agreement, as is discussed in the next chapter.

3.2 The History of Pharmaceutical Regulation in the US and the Origins of Test Data Exclusivity

Before examining the precise circumstances leading to the creation of test data exclusivity rights for pharmaceuticals in the US, this section summarises the general development of the modern system of pharmaceutical regulation. This development is intrinsically bound up with the origin of test data exclusivity, both because test data exclusivity operates as part of this system and because this history helps explain how test data exclusivity itself originated.

The modern system of pharmaceutical regulation developed in the US over the course of the twentieth century and has been subsequently modelled, to a greater or lesser extent, by virtually all other jurisdictions.[2] This development and subsequent globalisation has been highly influenced by three crises; firstly, a mass poisoning in the US in the 1930s which led to the enactment of the first requirements for pre-market safety checks. Secondly, the thalidomide tragedy in the late 1950s and early 1960s that led most other countries to adopt US-style regulations requiring pre-marketing approval and prompted authorities within the US itself to raise the standards required for marketing approval. Finally, a crisis in both the research-based and generic pharmaceutical industries in the US in the 1970s and early 1980s which resulted in a reform which both expanded abbreviated approval pathways for generic drugs and created test data exclusivity for originator drugs. The role of crises in prompting regulatory action is well documented—Braithwaite and Drahos observe that crises 'trigger media frenzies and mass demand for a response' which

---

[1] Switzerland did not in fact adopt test data exclusivity at the federal level until 2002. Prior to this, the Swiss cantons entered into the Intercantonal Convention on the Control of Therapeutic Products to implement Article 39(3) TRIPs in 1998. See further Holzer (2012).

[2] This is probably the result of the domination of the pharmaceutical industry by the US over the course of the twentieth century, and in particular after the Second World War. With this industrial capacity came regulatory expertise which became world-leading, especially following the thalidomide tragedy as discussed below; an FDA official interviewed by Braithwaite and Drahos in the 1990s commented that it was only recently that the FDA had stopped with the expectation that they would write the regulations and the rest of the world would follow; Braithwaite and Drahos (2000), p. 72.

creates opportunities for actors to present regulatory solutions.[3] This is not necessarily undesirable, of course—many crises have systemic causes that must be addressed and, regrettably, it often takes a tragedy to focus the attentions of political elites on such issues. However, crises are by definition exceptions to the normal operating conditions of society. The details of a regulation may be overly informed by factors that are not generalisable outside of the crisis to which it is a response, and the pressure to act created by a crisis can lead to hurried law making in which potential consequences are insufficiently considered. Countries who rush to model regulation without sufficient local adaptation risk importing regulation unsuitable for their context.[4] Both these trends are evident, to some extent at least, regarding the origins of test data exclusivity.

3.2.1 *Elixir Sulfanilamide, Thalidomide and Pre-marketing Approval*

The beginning of the modern system of pharmaceutical regulation began in 1937. In that year, over 100 people died across the US after taking a toxic 'medicine' known as elixir sulfanilamide.[5] This crisis prompted the passage of the Food, Drug and Cosmetic Act (FDCA) of 1938, the first piece of American legislation to require pre-market regulatory checks based on scientific evidence to establish the safety of drugs.[6] While there had been older laws on the regulation of drugs such as the Pure Food and Drug Act 1906, these had all focused on false advertising or standards of cleanliness during production; the new regime required manufacturers of new drugs to submit a new drug application (NDA) to the Food and Drug Administration (FDA), containing 'full reports of investigations which had been made to show whether or not the drug was safe for use' before they could bring it to market—in other words, the submission of test data.[7] The need to conduct 'investigations' in order to prove the safety of a drug obviously imposed costs on manufacturers, but these were relatively modest. Companies protected this data through trade secrecy and contract law, a practice enabled by the FDA's policy of considering all unpublished data submitted in an NDA to be confidential.[8]

The FDCA represented the beginning of the modern system of pharmaceutical regulation which required pre-market authorisation in order to market a pharmaceutical product. However, at this stage the system required only evidence of safety rather than safety *and* efficacy and was chiefly confined to the US. The impetus for

[3] Ibid, p. 257.

[4] Ibid, p. 591.

[5] Ballentine (1981), p. 15.

[6] Carpenter and Sin (2007); Cavers (1939), p. 22.

[7] USA, 21 USC § 355(b)(1).

[8] Flannery and Hutt (1985), p. 275.

the mass globalisation of the US system of pre-market safety checks was the thalidomide disaster of the late 1950s and early 1960s, in which an under-tested 'wonderdrug' called thalidomide caused birth defects amongst thousands of children whose mothers had taken it to alleviate morning sickness while pregnant, mostly in Europe.[9] This event prompted the beginning of the mass globalisation of the US system of pharmaceutical regulation. Few countries other than the US had a system of rigorous pre-market safety checks at the time of the disaster, and the fact that the US was largely unaffected by the crisis helped drive this widespread modelling of the US system. Today, virtually all countries have a system of pre-market authorisation for pharmaceutical products, with almost all of these having been adopted post-thalidomide.[10]

Within the US itself, the thalidomide tragedy prompted calls for higher standards of evidence for marketing approval. Even though the disaster had occurred primarily in Europe and had been an issue of safety rather than efficacy, Senator Estes Kefauver and Representative Oren Harris proposed reforms to the FDCA to require pharmaceutical manufacturers to prove the efficacy of new drugs for their stated purpose.[11] Kefauver had been attempting to reform US pharmaceutical regulation since 1959 but had faced vigorous opposition from Congress;[12] however, the media hype and mass public demand for a regulatory response engendered by the thalidomide tragedy caused this opposition to collapse and the Kefauver-Harris bill easily passed Congress in 1962, despite the concerns over the effect it would have on the pharmaceutical industry.[13]

The requirement for pre-market evidence of a drug's efficacy is an important measure in protecting the general public from the predations of quacks and charlatans, and the 1962 Amendment deserves recognition as the first piece of legislation to write such requirements into law. However, the provisions of the Amendment were unintentionally flawed. While proving the safety of a drug could be done relatively quickly and cheaply, proof of efficacy required years of testing. The costs of the tests reduced the originators' profits, and the years the clinical trials took to complete ate into the patent term in which they stood the best chance of recovering the costs of drug development.[14] There were negative consequences for America's young generics industry, too—under the new regime, generics firms were compelled to submit the same level of evidence of safety and efficacy as a new chemical entity, even if their drug was chemically identical to one already on the market. Without the possibility of even a diminished patent term in which to recoup this expense, most generics firms could not afford to conduct the significant testing

---

[9] Braithwaite and Drahos (2000), p. 393.

[10] Ibid, p. 393.

[11] USA, 76 Stat 780 (1962).

[12] Robert and Bodenheimer (1982), p. 584.

[13] Ibid.

[14] Weiswasser and Danzis (2003), p. 588.

required to generate data of their own, and the FDA's policy of treating unpublished studies as non-disclosable trade secrets meant they could not rely on originator data.

While the Kefauver-Harris Amendments contained no specific pathway for generic products, two provisions facilitated generic market entry under certain circumstances. Manufacturers of generic pharmaceuticals could avail of so-called 'paper NDAs', wherein the applicant relied on published scientific data to establish their drugs' safety and efficacy, although such data were not available for most products.[15] In addition, drugs approved prior to 1962 benefitted from a 'grandfather clause' which meant they did not have to demonstrate safety and efficacy; as a result, generic versions of these drugs did not qualify as 'new drugs' and therefore did not need to submit a full NDA.[16] In addition, antibiotic generics did not need to submit an NDA regardless of whether the reference product had been submitted pre- or post-1962.[17]

3.2.2 The Crisis of the Late 1970s and the Drug Price Competition and Patent Term Restoration Act

The full implications of the 1962 Amendment were not immediately apparent. However, by the late 1970s there was little doubt that the Kefauver-Harris Amendment had created significant problems for both the research-based and generics industries in the US. The delays caused by the FDA's review process had become longer and longer—despite the global dominance of US research-based firms (around half of all new major drugs launched in this period were developed in the US),[18] a 1977 study found two thirds of US-originated drugs were available in the UK before they were available in the US itself.[19] On top of this, the costs of bringing a new drug to market, including clinical trials, had increased dramatically. By 1973, the cost of developing a new drug was 13 times greater than it was in 1962.[20] Some pointed to an 81% decrease in new chemical entities approved between the early 1950s and late 1970s as evidence that the Kefauver-Harris Amendment had caused a 'crisis in innovation,' although others countered that this was largely due to an elimination of drugs with little therapeutic value and the picking of the 'low hanging fruit' of drug discovery.[21] The generics industry was also suffering. The effects of the Kefauver-Harris Amendment on generics manufacturers had been somewhat delayed because for many years after the amendment entered into force the drugs

[15]Engelberg (1999) [n 12] 396.

[16]Levine (1973), p. 770.

[17]Sanjuan et al. (2006), p. 3.

[18]Dutfield (2009), p. 153.

[19]Grabowski and Vernon (1977), p. 359.

[20]Wheaton (1985), p. 450.

[21]Ibid.

coming off-patent had almost all been approved prior to 1962, meaning generic versions of these could thus be approved without the need to submit a full NDA. But by the late 1970s, most drugs coming off patent had been approved post-1962, meaning that a prospective generic competitor would be required to submit a full NDA. As a result, many important drugs were essentially free from any generic competition despite the expiration of their associated patents, with obvious consequences for their prices.[22]

This crisis took much longer to resolve than the crises prompted by the elixir sulfanilamide and thalidomide incidents. One reason for this were the differences between this crisis and those that had gone before—the FDCA and Kefauver-Harris Amendment had both been precipitated by highly published, shocking tragedies, and both had been enacted quickly, while their respective disasters still dominated the headlines; a classic 'reactive sequence' of regulation in which a disaster creates media hype and mass public demand for a regulatory response, enabling regulatory entrepreneurs to pull pre-existing regulatory innovations such as the FDCA and Kefauver-Harris Amendments 'from the desk' to meet this public demand.[23] The crisis facing the pharmaceutical industry in the late 1970s was much less visible, even though the potential death and suffering from a lack of pharmaceutical innovation and affordable medicine far exceeded that of either the elixir sulphanilamide or thalidomide tragedies; this required a proactive regulatory approach in which would-be regulators would need to seek to enrol organisational power.[24] Working against this was the fractious nature of the US legislative process and the internal division of the pharmaceutical industry between its research-based and generics arms. Resolving the crisis meant reconciling two seemingly contradictory aims—increasing the profit margins of the research-based industry, while making it easier for generic medicines to enter the market.

Multiple unsuccessful bills were proposed from the mid-1970s onwards to resolve the crisis. It would appear that this period was when suggestions for what we would now recognise as test data exclusivity first arose. A bill introduced in 1975 would have reformed the marketing approval process by permitting abbreviated approvals for generics after a time-based data exclusivity period, but this failed to pass the House of Representatives. In 1978 two other bills with test data exclusivity provisions were advanced—another which proposed abbreviated approvals in exchange for a test data exclusivity period for pharmaceuticals, as well as an amendment to the Federal Insecticide, Fungicide and Rodenticide Act (FIFRA). The FIFRA amendment authorised the Environmental Protection Agency (EPA) to use data submitted by an applicant in order to register a pesticide to evaluate a generic application after a 10-year period of exclusivity and/or a 15-year period of compulsory liability. The pharmaceutical bill once again failed to pass the House,

[22] Engelberg (1999), p. 397.

[23] Braithwaite and Drahos (2000), p. 33.

[24] Ibid.

but the FIFRA amendment became law.[25] As discussed in Chap. 5, this connection between the protection of data submitted for the approval of agricultural chemical products and pharmaceutical products has persisted into the trade agreements of the following decades.

With the failure of the compromise bills in the 1970s, both the research-based industry and the generics industry made unsuccessful unilateral efforts to resolve the problems that the 1968 Amendment had created for their respective industries. In 1982, a bill that would have allowed for patent-term extensions of up to seven years to compensate for the time supposedly lost during the approval process failed to pass the House of Representatives by only five votes.[26] Attempts were made in 1983 to reintroduce the patent term extension proposals in the new Congress. However, they faced strong opposition—the mood in Congress had begun to swing in favour of ensuring access to affordable medicine.[27] Even so, the deadlock continued; a third bill to extend the abbreviated drug application process was introduced by Representative Henry Waxman in 1983, but could not gain the support necessary to pass the House on its own.[28]

It was now apparent that some kind of compromise would have to be reached between the pro-research and pro-generics elements in Congress. Waxman began negotiations between the Pharmaceutical Manufacturers' Association (PMA, now known as PhRMA, the main trade group of the research-based industry) and the Generic Pharmaceutical Industry Association (GPIA) in 1983 to attempt to achieve this compromise. By January of 1984, an agreement in principle between the two groups had been reached which would give the research-based industry patent term extensions and allow the generics industry to seek approval via abbreviated approval pathways for a wider range of drugs, subject to certain conditions.[29]

Initially, the planned compromise had featured test data exclusivity provisions similar to the bills proposed in 1975 and 1978. The original House draft contained provisions that would have prevented the FDA from approving an abbreviated application on the basis of originator data for four years after its submission, provided the drug was a new chemical entity and could not be patented. However, this provision was stricken from the bill by a patent sub-committee of the House Judiciary Committee on the grounds that the creation of 'second class patents' could not be justified without a strong showing of need.[30] The Committee also noted that the granting of what were in effect exclusive rights was a power that should be kept within the United States Patent and Trademark Office (USPTO), not delegated to the FDA. This seemed to be relatively uncontroversial, and negotiations continued over

[25] Gannon (1979), p. 599.

[26] Engelberg (1999), p. 398.

[27] Ibid.

[28] Wheaton (1985), p. 457.

[29] Engelberg (1999), p. 400.

[30] Kastenmeier (1984), p. 7.

more pressing issues, such as abbreviated applications submitted regarding drugs whose patent terms had not yet elapsed.[31]

Test data exclusivity might have remained stricken from the bill had it not been for a surprise decision of the Court of Appeals for the Federal Circuit. In 1983, a district court had ruled that the 'early working' of patent protected pharmaceuticals in order to obtain scientific evidence to submit to the FDA was not a patent infringement in *Roche v Bolar*. [32] The case had been appealed, but it was generally assumed the first-instance decision would be upheld. As such, the draft bill had included a codified version of the *Bolar* exception. However, on the 23rd of April, mere weeks after the House Judiciary Committee had struck the test data exclusivity provisions from the draft Bill, the Federal Circuit released a judgment which unexpectedly reversed and remanded the decision of the district court, finding that 'early working' did indeed constitute patent infringement. [33] The Federal Circuit's reversal meant that rather than merely codifying the *status quo*, the early working exception in the draft bill now handed a significant concession to the generics industry. The proposed compromise had suddenly become a much worse deal for PMA and its members. The consensus reached by Waxman broke down, and a faction of powerful pharmaceutical firms within the PMA—including such heavy-weights as Merck, Johnson & Johnson and Hoffman-La Roche—reneged on the agreement in principle. The negotiations ground to a standstill once again. Various carrots and sticks deployed throughout the summer by Senator Orin Hatch, the Republican co-sponsor of the Bill and long-time ally of the research-based industry, failed to compel them to endorse the proposed legislation. The situation deteriorated to the point that by August of 1984 it seemed unlikely that the legislation could be passed before the end of the 98th Congress.

It was here that test data exclusivity re-entered the negotiations. A new compromise was suggested by Hatch on August 10th; the legislation would permit the approval of generic drugs that could prove bioequivalence with a previously approved version of the drug through an Abbreviated New Drug Application (ANDA), but such an application could not be submitted for five years from the approval of the originator product (with the caveat that if a patent over the reference product was successfully challenged by the applicant, the exclusivity period would be reduced to 4 years).[34] In addition, the bill would also grant three years of exclusivity for new clinical investigations (other than bioavailability studies) for

[31] Ibid.

[32] *Roche Products v Bolar Pharmaceutical* 572 F Supp 255 (District Court 1983).

[33] *Roche Products v Bolar Pharmaceutical* 733 F2d 858 (Federal Circuit 1984).

[34] Under the HWA, a generic applicant must list the patents associated with the product in question and must make one of four certifications regarding why its drug will not infringe these. A paragraph I certification states that no such patents have been filed with the FDA, a paragraph II certification states that the listed patents have expired, a paragraph III certification states the date of expiration of the listed patents and explains that the generic product will not go on the market before then, and a paragraph IV certification states that the listed patents are invalid, unenforceable or will not be infringed by the manufacture, use or sale of the drug product for which the ANDA is submitted. It is

pharmaceutical products which had already been approved. The compromise held, and the Drug Price Competition and Patent Term Restoration Act, more commonly known as the Hatch-Waxman Act (HWA), received the presidential signature on 24 September 1984.

As with the earlier reforms to pharmaceutical regulation, the provisions of the HWA were informed by the particulars of the crisis to which it was a response. Test data exclusivity was not a vital part of the expansion of the abbreviated approval system (indeed, it was almost not a part of the system at all) and was certainly not based on any evidence that such exclusivity would promote higher levels of innovation. Rather, it was a concession offered to the research-based industry in order to make a reform that would have reduced their market dominance more palatable.

3.3 The Origins of Test Data Exclusivity in Europe and Japan

Test data exclusivity rights might have remained confined to the US, like many other quirks of its system of pharmaceutical regulation, if not for the fact that the combination of abbreviated drug approvals and test data exclusivity for originator products was quickly adopted by the EC. Coupled with the fact that Japan had developed a system which operated in a similar manner to test data exclusivity (although based on a quite different justification) this meant that as the Uruguay Round of GATT negotiations began, most of the major centres of the research-based pharmaceutical industry had similar domestic policies on the issue, something that would make achieving consensus between them much easier.

The European Commission proposed what would eventually become Directive 87/21/EEC on 25 September 1984—one day after the HWA was signed into law in the US by President Ronald Reagan.[35] The speed with which this modelling had taken place suggests that there could not have been much reflection on the system that the HWA had established in the US. The Commission's own justification in the explanatory memorandum accompanying the proposal consisted of a single paragraph, and simply stated that it appeared 'advisable' to introduce an exclusivity period for 10 years to allow for the partial recovery of investment in research when other forms of protection, such as a patent, were not available.[36] The preamble (which is identical in both the proposal and final Directive) further stated that while 'it is advisable to stipulate more precisely the cases in which the results.... of clinical trials do not have to be provided' during the drug approval process, there

a successful Paragraph IV certification that reduces the test data exclusivity term to 4 years. 21 USC § 314.94(a)(12)(i)(A)(1)-(4).

[35]European Commission (1984).

[36]Ibid.

was also a need to ensure 'that innovative firms are not placed at a disadvantage.'[37] It has been suggested that the inclusion of the exclusivity period was motivated by a desire to introduce some kind of protection for new pharmaceuticals in EC members, such as Italy, Spain and Portugal, which did not provide patent protection for pharmaceuticals at the time.[38] A bureaucrat involved in the drafting of the 2001 Directive that would eventually replace 87/21/EEC subsequently stated that the 10 year period was not based on any mathematical equation, and was a purely political decision.[39]

At less than two pages long, the European proposal was much shorter than the HWA, focusing only on establishing an abbreviated approval pathway and test data exclusivity. The proposal, identical to the final Directive in all substantive parts aside from the duration of the exclusivity term itself,[40] would have amended the existing regime of pharmaceutical approval in the EC by permitting the approval of drugs through 'detailed references to published scientific literature'—a provision largely equivalent to the 'paper NDA' found in the HWA—or if applicants could demonstrate that the medicinal product in question was 'essentially similar' to a product already authorised in the country concerned in the application, provided that the originator of that medical product had consented to the use of this data during the examining of the application or if that product had been marketed in the relevant Member State for more than 10 years. This approximated the US ANDA process and test data exclusivity.[41]

The proposal was subject to little further scrutiny as it moved through the EC's legislative process over the next 2 years. The Economic and Social Committee offered no more comment than to suggest that the 10-year period of test data exclusivity should be capable of being shortened in the public interest.[42] The European Parliament did suggest that member states be allowed to replace the test data exclusivity requirement with 'a compulsory licensing system' (presumably a form of liability based cost-sharing scheme of the type discussed at Sect. 2.6), but this seems to have been ignored.[43] The Directive was passed into law on 22 December 1986, with the only changes from the initial proposal being that member states could choose between a six or a 10-year exclusivity period and

[37] Council directive 87/21/EEC amending Directive 65/65/EEC on the approximation of provisions laid down by law, regulation or administrative action relating to proprietary medicinal products [1986].

[38] Junod (2004), p. 502.

[39] Adamini et al. (2009), p. 993.

[40] The original proposal provided for a uniform 10-year exclusivity period; the final Directive allowed Member States to choose either a six of 10-year period, with the further option of limiting data exclusivity to the period of the patent term.

[41] Council directive 87/21/EEC.

[42] OJ No C160, 01/07/1985, 18.

[43] OJ No C36 17/02/1986, 156.

choose to limit the test data exclusivity period to the duration of the term of a patent associated with the pharmaceutical product.[44]

The Japanese policy now generally recognised as a form of *de facto* test data exclusivity actually developed quite separately from the US and European system, preceding the HWA by several years. The Japanese system provides for a re-examination period for pharmaceutical products; essentially, a period of post-marketing surveillance. This system took effect from April of 1980, and currently lasts for between four and 10 years.[45] During this period, other versions of the drug (i.e. generics) are barred from approval—as such, the system provides a period of exclusivity to pharmaceutical products after their launch, but one that is justified on the grounds of protecting public health rather than compensating the efforts of originators who created the data. The connection between the post-market surveillance period and the protection of an originator firm's investment in the generation of submitted test data does not seem to have been clear in the mid- to late-1980s, but would become more fully articulated post-TRIPS. The Japanese policy is now universally regarded as meeting Japan's international commitments regarding the protection of submitted test data.[46]

Interestingly, these policies that are now viewed as test data exclusivity rights do not seem to have been widely considered to be intellectual property rights at this time. This is particularly clear in the case of Japan, where the restrictions on access to the abbreviated approval system for generics was explicitly justified on the grounds of public safety rather than any consideration for the rights of the originators of submitted test data. In the EC, too, the issue appears to have been viewed as a regulatory one rather than a matter of intellectual property; indeed, many commentators do not consider the EC to have become involved with intellectual property at the legislative level until the Software Directive of 1991.[47] In both the US and EC legislation, an exclusivity period was the *implication* of the fact that the abbreviated approval pathway can only be used by generics after a certain period of time from the approval of the originator product than being formulated as an explicit right in the submitted test data itself. The principle that referencing previously submitted test data in a generic drug application was an intellectual property issue, as opposed to a general question of health policy, was still not fully articulated even amongst the jurisdictions which would come to promote test data exclusivity so aggressively.

[44] Council directive 87/21/EEC.

[45] Japan Pharmaceutical Manufacturers Association (2019), p. 131.

[46] Intellectual Property Policy Headquarters (2005), p. 51.

[47] See, for example, Huet and Ginsburg (1992).

3.4 Conclusion

The history of the origin of test data exclusivity in the US and its spread to Europe should make us wary of claims as to its role in incentivising socially useful innovation and to claims as to its universal applicability. The purpose of test data exclusivity within the HWA was resolving a uniquely American political stalemate rather than performing an essential regulatory function. At the time, there was no evidence that test data exclusivity would serve the wider public interest. However, test data exclusivity was then quickly modelled by the EC in spite of this lack of evidence and without any significant further consideration or local adaptation. As a result of this modelling and the parallel developments in Japan, the countries in which the research-based pharmaceutical industry was concentrated would enter the Uruguay Round of GATT negotiations with similar approaches to abbreviated approval processes for generic pharmaceuticals; as is discussed in the next chapter, this would have significant implications for the protection of submitted test data in the TRIPS Agreement.

References

Adamini S, Maarse H, Versluis E, Light DW (2009) Policy making on data exclusivity in the European Union: from industrial interests to legal realities. J Health Polit Policy Law 34(6):979–1010

Ballentine C (1981) Taste of raspberries, taste of death: the 1937 elixir sulfanilamide incident. FDA Consumer Magazine

Braithwaite J, Drahos P (2000) Global business regulation. Cambridge University Press, Cambridge

Carpenter D, Sin G (2007) Policy tragedy and the emergence of regulation: the food, drug, and cosmetic act of 1938. Stud Am Polit Dev 21(2):149–180

Cavers DF (1939) The food, drug, and cosmetic act of 1938: its legislative history and its substantive provisions. Law Contemp Probs 6:2

Dutfield G (2009) Intellectual property rights and the life science industries: past, present and future. World Scientific, Singapore

Engelberg AB (1999) Special patent provisions for pharmaceuticals: have they outlived their usefulness? A political, legislative and legal history of U.S. law and observations for the future. J Law Technol 39:389–426

European Commission (1984) Proposal for a Council Directive on the approximation of national measures relating to the placing on the market of high-technology medicinal products, particularly those derived from biotechnology. COM 1984:437

Flannery EJ, Hutt PB (1985) Balancing competition and patent protection in the drug industry: the drug price competition and patent term restoration act of 1984. Food Drug Cosmetic Law J 40: 269

Gannon JF (1979) FIFRA and the taking of trade secrets. Boston Coll Environ Aff Law Rev 8:593

Grabowski HG, Vernon JM (1977) Consumer protection regulation in ethical drugs. Am Econ Rev 67(1):359–364

Holzer S (2012) Regulatory data protection of medicinal products from a Swiss perspective. Bio-Sci Law Rev 12(5):184–191

Huet J, Ginsburg JC (1992) Computer programs in Europe: a comparative analysis of the 1991 EC software directive. Columbia J Transnatl Law 30:327

Intellectual Property Policy Headquarters (2005) Intellectual Property Strategic Program

Japan Pharmaceutical Manufacturers Association (2019) Pharmaceutical Administration and Regulations in Japan

Junod V (2004) Drug marketing exclusivity under United States and European Union law. Food Drug Law J 59(4):479–518

Kastenmeier R (1984) Report together with additional news. US House of Representatives

Levine SM (1973) Recent "New Drug" litigation involving the "Grandfather Clause" and hearing rights. Bus Lawyer, pp 769–784

Robert BS, Bodenheimer DZ (1982) The Drug Amendments of 1962: the anatomy of a regulatory failure. Ariz State Law J: 581

Sanjuan JR, Love J, Weissman R (2006) Protection of pharmaceutical test data: a policy proposal. KEI Research Paper: 1

Weiswasser ES, Danzis SD (2003) The Hatch-Waxman act: history, structure, and legacy. Antitrust Law J 71:585

Wheaton JJ (1985) Generic competition and pharmaceutical innovation: the drug price competition and patent term restoration act of 1984. Catholic Univ Law Rev 35:433

Chapter 4
The Protection of Submitted Test Data and the TRIPS Agreement

Abstract This chapter considers Article 39.3 of TRIPS and its relationship with test data exclusivity. It begins with an examination of the negotiating history of what would become Article 39.3 during the Uruguay Round of GATT negotiations, before moving to analyse the terms of the provision itself. On the basis of this analysis, it is argued that Article 39.3 does not require members of the WTO to implement test data exclusivity laws. WTO members have a wide degree of discretion as to how to implement the protection of submitted test data, and indeed the degree of protection which should be given.

This chapter also considers how the difficulties in interpreting Article 39.3 may have influenced the globalisation of test data exclusivity. It is contended that despite not requiring test data exclusivity rights, Article 39.3 has nevertheless played a critical role in the globalisation of these rights because the lack of a definitive interpretation of the article has made developing alternative TRIPS-compliant means for the protection of submitted test data difficult. As a consequence, states are incentivised to model the predominant means of meeting the obligations of Article 39.3, which is test data exclusivity.

4.1 Introduction

In 1986, the eighth round of international trade talks under the GATT was launched in Punta del Este, Uruguay. Originally intended to focus on reforming trade in sensitive areas such as agriculture and to expand the trading system into new areas such as services, the Uruguay Round ultimately led to the creation of the WTO and its associated agreements, including the Agreement on Trade-Related Aspects of Intellectual Property Rights (TRIPS), which remains the most comprehensive multilateral agreement on intellectual property. While the Agreement contains no explicit requirement for test data exclusivity, the third paragraph of Article 39 of the Agreement requires members to protect test data submitted in order to receive marketing approval for pharmaceutical and agricultural chemical products.

Almost three decades on from the signing of the TRIPS Agreement, exactly how members must protect submitted test data under Article 39.3 is still the subject of

A. Buick, *Intellectual Property Rights in Pharmaceutical Test Data*,
https://doi.org/10.1007/978-3-031-29436-5_4

debate amongst commentators. This chapter concludes that Article 39.3 gives members of the WTO a wide degree of discretion regarding the protection of submitted test data, and does not require members to implement test data exclusivity rights. This interpretation, however, is but one of many. Given the lack of consensus over the interpretation of Article 39.3, there is a question as to what role the article has played in the globalisation of test data exclusivity. This chapter argues that despite its disputed meaning, Article 39.3 has nevertheless played a critical role in the globalisation of test data exclusivity. Precisely because the lack of a definitive interpretation of Article 39.3 has made developing alternative TRIPS-compliant approaches to the protection of submitted test data difficult, states have been incentivised to model existing means of implementing Article 39.3 in the form of test data exclusivity laws; the ambiguity of the article thus paradoxically causes national laws on the protection of submitted test data to become more, rather than less, similar.

4.2 Article 39.3

The full text of Article 39 of TRIPS is as follows—

Article 39

1. In the course of ensuring effective protection against unfair competition as provided in Article 10*bis* of the Paris Convention (1967), Members shall protect undisclosed information in accordance with paragraph 2 and data submitted to governments or governmental agencies in accordance with paragraph 3.
2. Natural and legal persons shall have the possibility of preventing information lawfully within their control from being disclosed to, acquired by, or used by others without their consent in a manner contrary to honest commercial practices so long as such information:

    (a) is secret in the sense that it is not, as a body or in the precise configuration and assembly of its components, generally known among or readily accessible to persons within the circles that normally deal with the kind of information in question;
    (b) has commercial value because it is secret; and
    (c) has been subject to reasonable steps under the circumstances, by the person lawfully in control of the information, to keep it secret.

3. Members, when requiring, as a condition of approving the marketing of pharmaceutical or of agricultural chemical products which utilize new chemical entities, the submission of undisclosed test or other data, the origination of which involves a considerable effort, shall protect such data against unfair commercial use. In addition, Members shall protect such data against disclosure, except where necessary to protect the public, or unless steps are taken to ensure that the data are protected against unfair commercial use.[1]

Article 39.3 requires members to protect some forms of clinical data submitted to governments in order to demonstrate the safety and efficacy of a pharmaceutical or agrichemical product from 'unfair commercial use.' However, unlike the reference

[1]TRIPS Article 39.

to 'honest commercial practices' in Article 39.2, which is defined by an extensive footnote, unfair commercial use is not defined. There has been considerable debate over what is meant by this term and how members are obliged to protect against it.

WTO members have offered wildly different interpretations of the meaning of the provision. In 1995, a few months after TRIPS had entered into force, the Office of the United States Trade Representative (USTR) released a press statement regarding Article 39.3 claiming that compliance with the article required a time-limited period in which test data could not be used to approve other applications; in other words, test data exclusivity. The USTR statement reads:

> ...[The] TRIPS Agreement negotiators understood [unfair commercial use] to mean that the **data will not be used to support, clear or otherwise review other applications for marketing approval for a set amount of time** unless authorized by the original submitter of the data. Any other definition of this term would be **inconsistent with logic and the negotiating history of the provision.**[2] [emphasis added]

This position lacks credibility; as we shall see, the negotiating history of TRIPS shows that requirements for test data exclusivity were explicitly rejected. However, more sophisticated arguments linking test data exclusivity to Article 39.3 have been advanced. In 2001, the European Commission published its own statement on Article 39.3, asserting that negotiators of TRIPS had intended for test data exclusivity to be the 'envisaged way' to protect against unfair commercial use, although the Commission conceded that it was possible, in theory at least, that other means could provide protection from submitted test data:

> **Both the logic and the negotiating history** of Article 39.3 of TRIPS leave no doubt that providing **data exclusivity for a certain period of time was the envisaged way to protect data against unfair commercial use as prescribed by Article 39.3** ... Whether any system other than data exclusivity over a reasonable period of time would meet the requirements of Article 39.3 of the TRIPS Agreement is to be assessed on a case-by-case basis, but examples of actual application by WTO Members of alternative – and TRIPS compliant – systems to non-reliance over a certain period of time do not appear to exist[3] [emphasis added]

Other countries, chiefly in the developing world, have interpreted Article 39.3 at the other extreme. In 2001, several developing countries released a statement arguing that Article 39.3 required no more than that WTO members prevent submitted test data from misappropriation:

> The protection is to be granted against 'unfair commercial use' of confidential data. This means that a third party could be prevented from using the results of tests undertaken by another company as background for an independent submission for marketing approval, if the data had been acquired through dishonest commercial practices. However, **Article 39.3 does permit a national competent authority to rely on data in its possession to assess a second and further applications, relating to the same drug, since this would not imply unfair commercial use**[4] [emphasis added]

---

[2]USTR (1995).

[3]European Commission (2001).

[4]Council for Trade-Related Aspects of Intellectual Property Rights (2001).

Disputes regarding the meaning of international treaties by signatories are not uncommon. For precisely this reason, the WTO has a system for the settlement of disputes regarding WTO rules, and this system is explicitly intended to clarify the provisions of WTO agreements in accordance with customary rules of interpretation of public international law.[5] In May 1999, the US began dispute settlement proceedings against Argentina regarding, *inter alia*, failure to provide sufficient protection to submitted test data per Article 39.3 (Argentina protects submitted test data only against disclosure and 'dishonest' commercial use such as misappropriation; see further Sect. 6.2.2 below). [6] Had the matter continued through the WTO's dispute settlement system, an authoritative interpretation of the requirements of Article 39.3 might have been forthcoming; however, the proceedings ended in 2002 when the US and Argentina came to a mutual understanding regarding the issue. [7] In the document notifying the WTO of their solution, the two countries explained that they had settled most of their disputes—regarding restrictions of parallel importations of patented goods, for example, both countries agreed Argentina's law was in fact in compliance with TRIPS, while the Argentine government agreed to introduce legislation amending its laws on the burden of proof in patent cases.[8] However, on the matter of the protection of submitted test data, the US and Argentina simply agreed to disagree—Argentina would continue with its policy towards submitted test data, and the US would drop the issue until such time as the DSB should clarify the rights related to undisclosed test data submitted for marketing approval under Article 39.3. If and when this happened, both countries would accept the ruling.[9] This clarification never came; to date, no WTO dispute settlement panel has attempted to clarify the meaning of Article 39.3. In the absence of such clarity, lawyers and academics have argued over the interpretation of Article 39.3 for almost three decades.

4.3 The History of the Protection of Submitted Test Data in TRIPS

4.3.1 Intellectual Property and the Uruguay Round

Prior to the Uruguay Round, intellectual property had not received much attention in the GATT negotiations. The US had pushed for the inclusion of some intellectual

[5] Understanding on rules and procedures governing the settlement of disputes (1994) Article 3.2.

[6] *Argentina – certain measures on the protection of patents and test data,* WT/DS196/1 (6 June 2000).

[7] *Argentina – certain measures on the protection of patents and test data,* WT/DS196/4 (31 May 2002).

[8] Ibid, para 3 and 5.

[9] Ibid, para 9.

property measures towards the end of the previous Tokyo Round of GATT talks in 1979, but these had been limited to anti-counterfeiting measures and in any case failed to produce a substantive agreement.[10] However, by the 1980s intellectual property had grown in importance for the US economy. A quarter of American exports by value were now intellectual property-reliant goods like chemicals, scientific equipment and entertainment—double the proportion at the end of the Second World War.[11] Due partly to the economic turmoil of the 1970s and anxiety over the long-term sustainability of America's economic dominance, increased attention was being paid to intellectual property.[12] Unfavourable comparisons between the economic performance of the US and countries such as Japan were partly blamed on foreign nations 'cheating' by free-riding on American research and development.[13] Voices within intellectual property reliant industries, in particular the entertainment, software, and pharmaceutical industries, insisted that higher intellectual property standards were key to economic growth and creating American jobs.[14] Increasingly, the narrative from these groups emphasised intellectual property as a 'right' and its unauthorised use by others as 'theft' or 'piracy,' characterisations that glossed over the contingent nature of intellectual property laws and instead framed them as inviolable and absolute rights whose trespass constituted a moral wrong rather than a mere act of competition.[15]

The US government was receptive to these overtures. In 1982, the Reagan administration set up the US Court of Appeals for the Federal Circuit, an appellate court that was given, *inter alia*, exclusive jurisdiction over final district court decisions that dealt with patents and which some commentators have argued has been overly sympathetic to right holders.[16] In 1984, Gerald Mossinghoff, the then Assistant Secretary of Commerce and Commissioner of Patents and Trademarks, gave an official statement emphasising the US government's commitment to increasing worldwide intellectual property protection.[17] That same year, Congress passed the Trade Act 1984; this act empowered the US to take unilateral action against countries whose intellectual property standards were deemed inadequate.[18] Section 301 of the Trade Act 1974 had permitted the US President to suspend benefits to or impose duties upon countries which had adopted policies that placed 'unjustifiable, unreasonable, or discriminatory burdens' on US trade.[19] The 1984 Act incorporated intellectual property into this structure by defining a failure to give

[10] Bradley (1987), p. 65.

[11] Sell (1995), p. 163.

[12] Drahos and Braithwaite (2002), p. 85.

[13] Sell (2003), p. 80.

[14] Drahos and Braithwaite (2002), p. 85.

[15] Weissman (1996), p. 1088.

[16] Palombi (2015), p. 58.

[17] Mossinghoff (1984).

[18] Matthews (2003), p. 15.

[19] USA, 19 USC § 2101.

adequate intellectual property protection as an unreasonable act and making certain tariff elimination privileges dependent on adequate intellectual property protection.[20] The 1984 Act also gave private industry a large role in the new regime, enabling them to petition the USTR to investigate countries for such 'unreasonable acts.'[21] The USTR was already an organisation receptive to industry concerns—the changes to trade policy of the 1980s made it tantamount to an official cabinet-level lobbyist for American business interests.[22]

The new Section 301 was soon put to use. Acting on a complaint from the Motion Picture Association of America (MPAA), the Republic of Korea was threatened with sanctions under Section 301 for inadequate copyright protection—Korea quickly acquiesced to the US demands for higher copyright protection standards.[23] The threats of sanctions were not empty—in 1988, the US used Section 301 to impose 100% tariffs on a range of Brazilian imports as a result of that country's failure to provide patent protection for pharmaceuticals (Brazil, only recently emerging from military rule and deep in the middle of a hyperinflation crisis, quickly folded).[24] Such successes only increased the view of the intellectual property-based industries (and their sympathisers within the US government) that unilateral trade pressure from the US could bring about the global intellectual property order that they desired. In 1988, the Omnibus Trade and Tariff Act enhanced the USTR's powers under Section 301, introducing so-called 'Special 301.' Special 301 transferred many of the Section 301 powers previously held by the President to the USTR and required the USTR to conduct an annual review of global intellectual property rights (in practice, this report is compiled largely from industry submissions).[25] The USTR report classifies the most grievous 'offender' nations as 'priority foreign countries,' (a designation that has been described as 'death row' for countries facing sanctions), and designates lesser offenders as 'priority watch list' and 'watch list' countries.[26]

By the late 1980s, the US had thus identified intellectual property as a central pillar of its trade policy—one that remains to this day. It had also implemented a formal legal mechanism enabling businesses and business organisations to enrol the power of the US state to economically coerce other states into raising standards of intellectual property protection, and deployed this to successful effect. It was against this background that the US entered the Uruguay Round of GATT negotiations.

In 1985, the Preparatory Committee of the GATT met to identify issues to be addressed by the Uruguay Round. The US proposed that all intellectual property rights be discussed while developing countries (led by Brazil and India) insisted that

[20] Ibid.

[21] Sell (2003), p. 86.

[22] Ibid, p. 36.

[23] Drahos and Braithwaite (2002), p. 71.

[24] Matthews (2003), p. 16.

[25] Ibid, p. 26.

[26] Drahos and Braithwaite (2002), p. 90.

the GATT was not the appropriate forum for intellectual property rights.[27] The US, backed by other developed countries, remained firm; its position was 'no IP, no round.'[28] In September 1986, the Uruguay Round was formally launched with the Punta del Este Ministerial Declaration, which set out the list of issues up for debate—including 'trade-related aspects of intellectual property, including counterfeit goods.' The statement was vague, and what exactly this would entail was unclear. However, it did not explicitly limit the negotiations to specific fields of intellectual property, and implied that the Round would discuss more than just counterfeit goods.[29]

Substantive negotiations got underway in 1987. A General Negotiation Plan was released in February 1987, which included the 'Trade-Related Aspects of Intellectual Property Rights, Including Counterfeit Goods Negotiation Plan.'[30] However, the intellectual property Negotiation Plan was as vague as the Punta del Este Declaration on exactly which intellectual property rights would be discussed and the level of harmonisation any agreement would lead to—the Plan's objectives were given as clarifying existing GATT rules and elaborating new ones 'as appropriate' in order to reduce distortions and impediments to international trade, as well as the promotion of adequate and effective protection for intellectual property while ensuring that the measures to enforce intellectual property rights did not themselves become a barrier to trade.[31] Developed countries (in particular, the 'Quad' of the US, EC, Japan and Canada) and developing nations (particularly the 'Group of Ten', led by India and Brazil) were divided over how strong the intellectual property rights to be included in the agreement should be.[32]

From 1987 onwards the 'Negotiating Group on Trade-Related Aspects of Intellectual Property, Including Counterfeit Goods,' or Negotiating Group 11 (NG11), consisting of representatives of the GATT countries and chaired by Lars Anell of Sweden, met regularly to negotiate an agreement on intellectual property.[33] The negotiations were carried out by representatives of the various governments of the states party to GATT; while there was no industry representation during these negotiations, national representatives (particularly those of developed countries) considered reflecting the interests of multinational business as an important aspect of the talks.[34]

---

[27] Matthews (2003), pp. 16–17.

[28] Braithwaite and Drahos (2000), p. 56.

[29] GATT, *Punta del Este Declaration* (20 September 1986), Part 1 D.

[30] GATT, *Information - The Uruguay Round - Decisions of 28 January 1987*, GATT/1405 (5 February 1987), p. 21.

[31] Ibid.

[32] Drahos and Braithwaite (2002) [n 302] 133, 138. The Quad also sometimes met with other developed countries (the 'Quad+'). The Group of Ten consisted in full of India, Brazil, Argentina, Cuba, Egypt, Nicaragua, Nigeria, Peru, Tanzania and Yugoslavia.

[33] Matthews (2003), p. 16.

[34] Bradley (1987), p. 29.

4.3.1.1 Parallel Negotiations

It should be noted that the NG11 negotiations were not the only means by which the US sought to export its standards of intellectual property in the late 1980s and 1990s. Parallel to the GATT talks, the US was also engaged in the negotiation of various trade deals which included intellectual property chapters. Many of these agreements contained provisions on the protection of submitted test data. The most well known of these is the North American Free Trade Agreement (NAFTA), signed in 1992, which required a reasonable period (normally 'not less than five years') of test data exclusivity for undisclosed data submitted as a condition for approving the marketing of pharmaceutical or agricultural products at Article 1711.[35] However, similar test data exclusivity provisions had also appeared in bilateral agreements between the US and Sri Lanka,[36] Bulgaria,[37] Albania,[38] Ecuador[39] and Jamaica[40] by the time of the signing of the TRIPS Agreement, with more concluded shortly afterwards. The provisions of these agreements, discussed in detail in Chap. 5, are very closely modelled on the 'bracketed' version of the July 1990 Brussels Draft discussed below; this demonstrates that the negotiations around the protection of submitted test data in the TRIPS Agreement were only one aspect of a broader and co-ordinated effort to globalise test data exclusivity rights.

4.3.2 *The Protection of Undisclosed Data*

The protection of submitted data is, of course, only a small part of the overall TRIPS Agreement. However, its inclusion was fiercely contested throughout the negotiations—a factor which contributed significantly to the vagueness and uncertainty of the final version of Article 39.3. To begin with, the debate focused on whether there should be any kind of protection for undisclosed data in TRIPS whatsoever. This debate was not purely a North-South issue; the Japanese representatives—which as we have seen had a system similar to test data exclusivity by the time of the Uruguay Round, albeit based on the logic of public health rather than the protection of commercially valuable information—made clear early on that they did not feel that trade secrets and ither undisclosed information were intellectual

[35] North American Free Trade Agreement (1992) Article 1711.

[36] United States-Sri Lanka Intellectual Property Rights Agreement (1991) Article 2.

[37] United States-Bulgaria Agreement on Trade Relations (1991) Article 2.

[38] United States-Albania Trade Relations Agreement (1992) Article IX.

[39] United States-Ecuador Intellectual Property Rights Agreement (1993) Article 8.

[40] United States-Jamaica Intellectual Property Rights Agreement (1994) Article 11.

property and as such were not appropriate for inclusion in TRIPS.[41] India and others supported this view.[42] This disagreement was hardly unexpected—the issue of whether trade secrets were intellectual property rights had only been settled in the US in 1984 with the case of *Ruckelshaus v Monsanto*. [43] However, as negotiations continued the developed countries became more united on the issue of trade secrets; by 1990, the Japanese representative told the Negotiating Group that his government now recognised the importance of protection for trade secrets and was 'seriously considering' the issue.[44] Resistance from developed countries had collapsed.

Protection for submitted test data does not appear in the official records of the Uruguay Round until 1988. Its first inclusion appears to have been precipitated by the publication of the influential 'Basic framework of GATT provisions on intellectual property: statement of views of the European, Japanese and United States business communities' (Statement of Views), a large document consisting of recommendations from various business communities in the developed world that has been described as forming a 'multilateral blueprint' for the developed country negotiators and which endorsed the inclusion of provisions on trade secrets in TRIPS.[45] Of particular interest for the purposes of this chapter, the Statement of Views contained the following proposal regarding information submitted to governments in connection with approval of a product:

1. Information required by a government to be disclosed by any Party shall not be used commercially or further disclosed without the consent of the owner.
2. Information disclosed to a government as a condition for registration of a product shall be **reserved for the exclusive use of the registrant for a reasonable period from the day when government approval based on the information was given.** The reasonable

[41] GATT, *Negotiating Group on Trade-Related Aspects of Intellectual Property Rights, Including Trade in Counterfeit Goods - Meeting of 23–24 November 1987 - Note by the Secretariat*, MTN.GNG/NG11/5, (14 December 1987), p. 22.

[42] GATT, *Negotiating Group on Trade-Related Aspects of Intellectual Property Rights, Including Trade in Counterfeit Goods - Meeting of 12–14 July 1989 - Note by the Secretariat*, MTN.GNG/NG11/14 (12 September 1989), p. 90; GATT, *Negotiating Group on Trade-Related Aspects of Intellectual Property Rights, Including Trade in Counterfeit Goods - Meeting of 30 October-2 November 1989 - Note by the Secretariat*, MTN.GNG/NG11/16 (4 December 1989), p. 63; GATT, *Negotiating Group on Trade-Related Aspects of Intellectual Property Rights, Including Trade in Counterfeit Goods - Meeting of 11, 12 and 14 December 1989 - Note by the Secretariat*, MTN.GNG/NG11/17 (23 January 1990), p. 49; GATT, *Negotiating Group on Trade-Related Aspects of Intellectual Property Rights Including Trade in Counterfeit Goods - Meeting of the Negotiating Group of 1 November 1990 - Note by the Secretariat.* MTN.GNG/NG11/27 (14 November 1990), p. 3. With the exception of India, exactly which countries are voicing opposition to the inclusion of trade secrecy is unclear—the statements are normally attributed to 'several representatives 'or 'a representative speaking of behalf of several developing countries.'

[43] *Ruckelshaus v Monsanto* 467 US 986 (1978). The Court found that trade secrets were indeed intellectual property rights.

[44] GATT, *Negotiating Group on Trade-Related Aspects of Intellectual Property Rights, Including Trade in Counterfeit Goods - Meeting of Negotiating Group of 14–16 May 1990 - Note by the Secretariat*, MTN.GNG/NG11/21 (22 June 1990).

[45] Drahos and Braithwaite (2002), p. 123.

period shall be adequate to protect the commercial interests of the registrant.[46] [emphasis added]

This proposal for a 'reasonable' period of exclusive use of submitted test data reserved for the originator of the data closely resembles the test data exclusivity provisions of the Hatch-Waxman Act discussed in the previous chapter. This consensus regarding submitted test data amongst the business communities of the US, Europe and Japan (or at least the individuals and entities within those business communities which had collaborated on the Statement of Views) was no doubt influenced by the similar approaches of the US, EC and Japan to abbreviated approvals for generics and the economic clout of their domestic research-based pharmaceutical industries. This consensus regarding the protection of submitted test data would influence the issue throughout the remainder of the Uruguay Round; while Japan never submitted a proposal for the protection of submitted test data specifically, several proposals by the US, Switzerland and the EC followed.

4.3.3 The Proposals on the Protection of Submitted Test Data

The first submission on submitted test data came from the US. In their revised submission of October 1988, the US representatives included a subsection on 'conditions on government use' of trade secrets.[47] This included the following provision:

> 6. Conditions on Government Use
>
> Trade secrets submitted to governments shall not be disclosed or used for the benefit of third parties except in compelling circumstances involving major national emergencies posing an imminent unreasonable risk to health or the environment, or to facilitate required health and safety registrations. Government use or disclosure on the basis of a national emergency may only be made where other reasonable means are not available to satisfy the need for which the government seeks to disclose or use the trade secret, and the government may use it only for the duration of that emergency. **Government use or disclosure to facilitate required health and safety registrations may only be made if the trade secret has not been submitted within the previous ten years and full compensation is made for the use or disclosure.** In any case, a government shall not use or disclose a trade secret to an extent greater than required to achieve one of the above needs without providing the submitter with a reasonable opportunity to oppose the proposed use or disclosure, including the opportunity to secure judicial review, or without providing for the payment of full compensation as in the case of personal property.[48] [Emphasis added]

This proposal would have gone even beyond the US's own domestic provisions on test data exclusivity. It would have applied to government 'use' as well as disclosure,

[46] UNCTAD-ICTSD (2005), p. 523.

[47] GATT, *Negotiating Group on Trade-Related Aspects of Intellectual Property Rights, including Trade in Counterfeit Goods - Suggestion by the United States for Achieving the Negotiating Objective – Revision*, MTN.GNG/NG11/W/14/Rev.1, (17 October 1988), p. 6.

[48] Ibid, p. 6.

and specifically referred to the facilitation of health and safety registration—in addition, reliance on previously submitted data would only have been possible after 10 years of exclusivity, and even then, only if 'full compensation' was made for the use of the data.

However, the October 1988 submission by the US was not the most restrictive proposal on the protection of submitted test data made during the Uruguay Round. In July of 1989, the Swiss submitted an addendum on 'proprietary information'[49] to a previous draft proposal.[50] The relevant section of the proposal reads:

> Protection of Proprietary Information
>
> [. . .]
>
> (iv) There shall be **no compulsory licensing** of proprietary information.
>
> (v) Proprietary information provided to a governmental agency in order to obtain permission to produce or market a product, such as results of clinical or safety tests, shall not be disclosed without the consent of the proprietor, except to other governmental agencies if necessary to protect human, plant or animal life, health or the environment.
>
> Governmental agencies **shall not be entitled to use the information for commercial purposes. They may disclose it only to the extent indispensable to inform the general public about the actual or potential danger of a product**.[51] [emphasis added]

This proposal would have prevented reliance on submitted test data seemingly in perpetuity, as well as preventing the compulsory licensing of proprietary information. Neither the US nor Swiss proposals on submitted test data receive much discussion in the official records of NG11.

Between 1987 and 1989 progress on the negotiations had been slow, partly because of the amount of technical information that had to be amassed but also due to the disagreements between developed and developing countries over what intellectual property rights should be included (including, as previously noted, trade secrecy).[52] By 1990, however, this opposition had largely been overcome. The US had both threatened and made use of unilateral economic action to divide the developing countries and force the most defiant into compliance—this included the 1988 sanctions against Brazil, which effectively broke the Brazil-India axis of

---

[49] GATT, *Negotiating Group on Trade-Related Aspects of Intellectual Property Rights, including Trade in Counterfeit Goods - Standards and Principles concerning the Availability, Scope and Use of Trade-Related Intellectual Property Rights - Communication from Switzerland - Addendum on Proprietary Information,* MTN.GNG/NG11/W/38/Add.1 (11 December 1989).

[50] GATT, *Negotiating Group on Trade-Related Aspects of Intellectual Property Rights, including Trade in Counterfeit Goods - Standards and Principles concerning the Availability, Scope and Use of Trade-Related Intellectual Property Rights - Communication from Switzerland - Addendum on Proprietary Information,* MTN.GNG/NG11/W/38 (11 July 1989), p. 8.

[51] GATT, Negotiating Group on Trade-Related Aspects of Intellectual Property Rights, including Trade in Counterfeit Goods - Standards and Principles concerning the Availability, *Scope and Use of Trade-Related Intellectual Property Rights - Communication from Switzerland - Addendum on Proprietary Information,* MTN.GNG/NG11/W/38/Add.1 (11 December 1989), p. 3.

[52] Gervais (1998), p. 15.

opposition (India, Thailand, China, South Korea, Argentina, Egypt and Yugoslavia also found themselves threatened with unilateral action under Special 301 during the negotiation process).[53]

With the substantive negotiations ramping up, and the issue of trade secrecy now more settled, the protection of submitted data re-entered the negotiations. The EC for the first time submitted a proposal on the protection of submitted test data, and the US submitted a revised version of its 1988 suggestion. The EC proposal contained the following provision under 'undisclosed information':

> Article 28
>
> (b) Contracting parties, when requiring the publication or submission of test or other data, the origination of which involves a considerable effort, shall protect such efforts against unfair exploitation by competitors. **The protection shall last for a reasonable time commensurate with such efforts, the nature of the data required, the expenditure involved in their preparation and shall take account of the availability of other forms of protection.**[54] [Emphasis added]

The US text, submitted a few months later, contained the following provisions as under 'trade secrets':

> Article 33
>
> (1) Contracting parties which require that trade secrets be submitted to carry out governmental functions, shall not use the trade secrets **for the commercial or competitive benefit of the government or of any person other than the right-holder except with the right-holder's consent, on payment of the reasonable value of the use, or if a reasonable period of exclusive use is given the right-holder.**
> (2) Contracting parties may disclose trade secrets to third parties, only with the right-holder's consent or to the degree required to carry out necessary government functions. Wherever practicable, right-holders shall be given an opportunity to enter into confidentiality agreements with any non-government entity to which the contracting party is disclosing trade secrets to carry out necessary government functions.
> (3) Contracting parties may require right-holders to **disclose their trade secrets to third parties to protect human health or safety or to protect the environment only when the right-holder is given an opportunity to enter into confidentiality agreements with any non-government entity receiving the trade secrets to prevent further disclosure or use of the trade secret.**[55] [emphasis added]

The EC proposal used language similar to that which would be found in the final version of Article 39.3, although it was less vague and specified measures that the term of protection might be set with respect to. As with Article 39.3, it was unclear whether the protection of submitted test data against 'unfair exploitation by

[53] Drahos and Braithwaite (2002), pp. 134–137.

[54] GATT, *Negotiating Group on Trade-Related Aspects of Intellectual Property Rights, Including Trade in Counterfeit Goods - Draft Agreement on Trade-Related Aspects of Intellectual Property Rights,* MTN.GNG/NG11/W/68 (29 March 1990), p. 12.

[55] GATT, *Negotiating Group on Trade-Related Aspects of Intellectual Property Rights, including Trade in Counterfeit Goods - Draft Agreement on the Trade-Related Aspects of Intellectual Property Rights - Communication from the United States,* MTN.GNG/NG11/W/70 (11 May 1990), p. 14.

competitors' would have precluded reliance on such data by generic drug applications, although official statements from the EU after the conclusion of the TRIPS Agreement claim that this was indeed the intention of the European negotiators.[56] The US proposal would have explicitly protected submitted test data from reference in subsequent applications but, in a clear moderation of the 1988 US proposal, would have permitted protection either through test data exclusivity or through a payment to the data originator (one of 'reasonable value' rather than 'full compensation').

Shortly after these EC and US proposals, the negotiations underwent a qualitative shift and moved to a focus on more informal meetings to choose between various 'bracketed' options. In July 1990, Lars Anell produced a consolidated draft text in which provisions over which there was still disagreement appeared in brackets. Officially entitled 'Status of work in the negotiating group – Chairman's Report to the GNG', this became known as 'the Anell Draft' or 'the Chairman's Draft.'[57] While a large number of issues remained unresolved (both between the members of the Quad as well as between the developed and developing countries) Daniel Gervais, who was working at the GATT Secretariat at the time, believes that the Chairman's draft put the negotiations on a 'single track until the end.'[58] The Chairman's Draft contained three different 'options' for the protection of 'undisclosed information.' These mirrored the most recent proposals of the EC, US and Switzerland discussed above (including the prohibition on the compulsory licensing of proprietary information proposed by the Swiss), along with the possibility of not including any requirement to protect submitted data at all.[59] The Swiss proposal would have provided the strongest protection for submitted test data and the vague EC suggestion the weakest, with the US suggestion falling in the middle. In full, the relevant provisions of the Chairman's Draft read:

> Section 7: acts contrary to honest commercial practices including protection of undisclosed information
>
> [...]
>
> 2Ab There shall be no compulsory licensing of proprietary information. **[From the December 1989 Swiss proposal]**
>
> 3. Government Use
>
> 3Aa PARTIES, when requiring the publication or submission of undisclosed information consisting of test [or other] data, the origination of which involves a considerable effort, shall protect such data against unfair exploitation by competitors. The protection shall last for a reasonable time commensurate with the efforts involved in the origination of the data, the

---

[56] European Commission (2001).

[57] GATT, *Negotiating Group on Trade-Related Aspects of Intellectual Property Rights, Including Trade in Counterfeit Goods - Status of Work in the Negotiating Group - Chairman's Report to the GNG,* MTN.GNG/NG11/W/76 (23 July 1990) 9.

[58] Gervais (1998), pp. 17–18.

[59] GATT, *Negotiating Group on Trade-Related Aspects of Intellectual Property Rights, Including Trade in Counterfeit Goods - Status of Work in the Negotiating Group - Chairman's Report to the GNG,* MTN.GNG/NG11/W/76 (23 July 1990), p. 9.

nature of the data, and the expenditure involved in their preparation, and shall take account of the availability of other forms of protection. **[From the March 1990 EC proposal]**

3Ab.1 PARTIES which require that trade secrets be submitted to carry out governmental functions, shall not use the trade secrets for the commercial or competitive benefit of the government or of any person other than the right holder except with the right holder's consent, on payment of the reasonable value of the use, or if a reasonable period of exclusive use is given the right holder.

3Ab.2 PARTIES may disclose trade secrets to third parties, only with the right holder's consent or to the degree required to carry out necessary government functions. Wherever practicable, right holders shall be given an opportunity to enter into confidentiality agreements with any non-government entity to which the PARTY is disclosing trade secrets to carry out necessary government functions.

3Ab.3 PARTIES may require right holders to disclose their trade secrets to third parties to protect human health or safety or to protect the environment only when the right holder is given an opportunity to enter into confidentiality agreements with any non-government entity receiving the trade secrets to prevent further disclosure or use of the trade secret. **[From the May 1990 US proposal]**

3Ac.1 Proprietary information submitted to a government agency for purposes of regulatory approval procedures such as clinical or safety tests, shall not be disclosed without the consent of the proprietor, except to other governmental agencies if necessary to protect human, plant or animal life, health or the environment. Governmental agencies may disclose it only with the consent of the proprietor or to the extent indispensable to inform the general public about the actual or potential danger of a product. They shall not be entitled to use the information for commercial purposes.[60] **[From the December 1989 Swiss proposal (note the slight rewording)]**

In December of 1990 a ministerial meeting was held in Brussels with the intention of finishing the Round per the original timetable agreed at Punta del Este. By this stage, negotiations had advanced to the point that what would become the TRIPS Agreement had a broad structure in which the various remaining options were clearly articulated.[61] This 'Brussels Draft' contained a general provision for the protection of submitted undisclosed data under which governments would be unable to disclose the information unless necessary to protect the public, and an additional bracketed subclause that would have added a requirement for a test data exclusivity period of 'generally no less than five years.' The Swiss-proposed prohibition on the compulsory licensing of proprietary information did not appear in the Brussels Draft. In full, the provision reads:

PARTIES, when requiring, as a condition of approving the marketing of new pharmaceutical products or of a new agricultural chemical product, the submission of undisclosed test or other data, the origination of which involves a considerable effort, shall [protect such data against unfair commercial use. Unless the person submitting the information agrees, the data may not be relied upon for the approval of competing products for a reasonable time, generally no less than five years, commensurate with the efforts involved in the origination of the data, their nature, and the expenditure involved in their preparation. In addition,

[60] Ibid.

[61] Gervais (1998), p. 22.

> PARTIES shall] protect such data against disclosure, except where necessary to protect the public.[62]

The Brussels ministerial meeting ultimately broke down due to a failure to reach consensus over agriculture, but the TRIPS negotiations had reached such a stage that a number of commentators believe that the agreement might well have been completed if not for this unrelated collapse.[63] Based on the text of the Brussels Draft, this could have resulted in two very different sets of obligations with respect to submitted test data. On the one hand, without the bracketed text quoted above, the provision would simply have prevented signatories from disclosing submitted test data. With the bracketed provision, however, TRIPS would have unambiguously required five years of test data exclusivity at minimum, with the possibility of raising the exclusivity term higher. It is clear that even with the end of the TRIPS negotiations in sight, the question of protection for undisclosed information was still far from settled. A representative quoted in the notes on an NG11 meeting held between 27 and 28 June 1991 stated that while much discussion had taken place, no progress had been made regarding the protection of submitted test data.'[64]

In 1991 Arthur Dunkel, the GATT's Director-General, moved to bring the Uruguay Round to a close by tabling the 'Draft Final Act Embodying the Results of the Uruguay Round,' a single unified document without any bracketed provisions.[65] The TRIPS section of this Draft had been prepared by Anell. The provision on the protection of undisclosed submitted information had moved away from either of the extremes presented in the Brussels Draft. The language was virtually identical to that of the eventual Article 39.3 of TRIPS:

> PARTIES, when requiring, as a condition of approving the marketing of pharmaceutical or of agricultural chemical products which utilise new chemical entities, the submission of undisclosed test or other data, the origination of which involves a considerable effort, shall protect such data against unfair commercial use. In addition, PARTIES shall protect such data against disclosure, except where necessary to protect the public, or unless steps are taken to ensure that the data are protected against unfair commercial use.[66]

What exactly this requires is unclear, as evidenced by the debates over Article 39.3 that continue to this day. It seems likely that this vagueness was a feature rather than a bug; Anell needed to present a document in which all participants could see their preferred interpretations. In any case, by December 1991 the explicit requirement for test data exclusivity was gone, but so to was the wording that unambiguously

[62] GATT, *Trade Negotiations Committee - Draft Final Act Embodying the Results of the Uruguay Round of Multilateral Trade Negotiations, MTN.TNC/W/35* (26 November 1990), p. 215.

[63] Drahos and Braithwaite (2002), p. 142; Gervais (1998), p. 26.

[64] GATT, *Negotiating Group on Trade-Related Aspects of Intellectual Property Rights, Including Trade in Counterfeit Goods - Meeting of Negotiating Group of 27 and 28 June 1991 - Note by the Secretariat,* MTN.GNG/TRIPS/l, (25 July 1991).

[65] GATT, *Draft Final Act Embodying the Results of the Uruguay Round of Multilateral Trade Negotiations,* MTN.TNC/W/FA (20 December 1991).

[66] Ibid.

required signatories to protect submitted test data only against disclosure. With the exception of some minor points, the Draft Final Act was essentially identical to the final TRIPS Agreement, which was signed in April 1994 as Annex 1C of the Marrakesh Agreement Establishing the World Trade Organization.[67]

The US, EC and Switzerland had failed to achieve their aim of an international obligation to provide test data exclusivity rights over submitted test data. Furthermore, what obligations they had secured were unclear. However, the principle that submitted test data should be protected had been established, and the direction of regulatory travel had been set.

4.4 Interpreting Article 39.3

As a WTO agreement, TRIPS should be interpreted according to 'the customary rules of interpretation of public international law,'[68] including Articles 31 and 32 of the VLCT.[69] As stated at Section 1.4, Article 31 of the VCLT states that treaties should 'be interpreted in good faith in accordance with the ordinary meaning to be given to the terms of thc trcaty in their context and in the light of its object and purpose',[70] while Article 32 states that recourse may be made to the *travaux préparatoires* of the treaty in order to confirm Article 31 or when applying Article 31 leaves the meaning ambiguous or obscure or leads to a conclusion that is manifestly absurd.[71]

In addition, Article 31(3)(a) of the VCLT states that 'a subsequent agreement between the parties regarding the interpretation of the treaty or the application of its provisions' shall be taken into account, together with its context, when interpreting a treaty. The Declaration on the TRIPS Agreement and Public Health of 14 November 2001 (popularly known as the Doha Declaration) is such a subsequent agreement to TRIPS,[72] as is the Ministerial Decision on the TRIPS Agreement adopted in response to the COVID-19 pandemic in June 2022.[73] While the Declaration does not deal directly with the protection of submitted test data, it does confirm that 'the TRIPS Agreement does not and should not prevent Members from taking measures to protect public health', and that 'the Agreement can and should be interpreted and implemented in a manner supportive of WTO Members' right to protect public

[67] Marrakesh Agreement Establishing the World Trade Organization (1994).

[68] Understanding on rules and procedures governing the settlement of disputes (1994) Article 3(2).

[69] WTO, *United States – Standards for Reformulated and Conventional Gasoline* [1996], WT/DS2/AB/R.

[70] Vienna Convention on the Law of Treaties (1969) Article 31(1).

[71] Ibid, Article 32.

[72] WTO, *Declaration on the TRIPS Agreement and Public Health of November 2001*, WT/MIN(01)/DEC/2 (20 November 2001) (Doha Declaration).

[73] WTO, *Ministerial Decision on the TRIPS Agreement*, WT/MIN(22)/30 (22 June 2022).

health and, in particular, to promote access to medicines for all.'[74] The Ministerial Decision does explicitly engage with Article 39.3 of the TRIPS Agreement at Paragraph 4—this is discussed as Sect. 4.4.3.1, below.

This section discusses the interpretation of Article 39.3, first considering the meaning of the term 'unfair commercial use' before moving to consider other terms in the provision.

4.4.1 Unfair Commercial Use

The crux of the debate over Article 39.3 is the meaning of 'unfair commercial use,' and in particular under what circumstances, if any, reference to previously submitted test data in an abbreviated drug approval application will constitute unfair commercial use. As we have already seen, some have advanced the argument that such reliance without the consent of the originator does constitute unfair commercial use and must therefore be prevented for at least some period of time through exclusive rights,[75] while others have taken the position that unfair commercial use means only misappropriation by competitors.[76] At least one of these views must be incorrect.

Only commercial uses of submitted data which are *unfair* must be protected against per Article 39.3; as such, this is perhaps the most important word in determining the necessary amount of protection for submitted test data required under TRIPS. It is also the most unclear; as multiple commentators have observed, the ordinary meaning of the word 'unfair' relates to an absence of justice or honesty, terms which are no more specific than 'unfair' itself.[77] Article 39.1 establishes that the protection granted by the article is being given 'in the course of ensuring effective protection against unfair competition as provided in Article 10*bis* of the Paris Convention,' which might be expected to provide some further illumination.[78] However, while Article 10*bis* clarifies that unfair competition is 'any act of competition contrary to honest practices in industrial or commercial matters' and that acts creating confusion, false allegations intended to discredit and acts intended to mislead the public in particular are unfair, this goes no further towards answering the question of what is contrary to honest business and commercial practices in the first place.[79]

Correa argues that because 'unfairness' has no internationally defined meaning and goes undefined in the TRIPS Agreement itself, what is 'contrary to honest practices in industrial or commercial matters' depends on the values of a given

---

[74] Ibid, para 4.

[75] Skillington and Solovy (2003), p. 2.

[76] Correa (2002), p. 80.

[77] Fellmeth (2004), p. 461; Shaikh (2016), p. 44; Spina Alì (2018), p. 210.

[78] TRIPS Article 39.1.

[79] TRIPS Article 39.1.

society; as these vary across different times and places, it is therefore for individual members of the WTO to decide on what is unfair.[80] Under this interpretation, national governments are consequently free to determine whether a given practice, including referencing originator data to gain marketing approval, is permissible under Article 39.3 provided that such a determination meets the minimum threshold of protection against those practices specifically highlighted by Article 10*bis* of the Paris Convention.[81] Correa further notes that Article 10*bis* of the Paris Convention at no point suggests the creation of intellectual property rights (protection against false allegations is not typically dealt with through the law of intellectual property, for example) and that unfair competition law does not generally create exclusive rights.[82] As such, Correa believes that the minimum requirements of Article 39.3 can be met through laws which protect against no more than the dishonest misappropriation of submitted test data.[83]

Correa's position has intuitive appeal, especially given the principle of *in dubio mitius* ('leniency in doubt'), which cautions against the interpretation of imprecise language to impose onerous obligations on signatories and which has been recognised by WTO panels.[84] However, Correa's position is also open to an obvious criticism; the principle of effective interpretation, which WTO bodies have consistently applied to the interpretation of WTO Agreements,[85] holds that interpreters may not reduce provisions to inutility or redundancy.[86] Giving members virtually complete discretion as to what practices to consider unfair would impose no international requirement on members and thus be useless.[87] Holding that Article 39.3 only requires protection against fraud or misappropriation would be redundant, as Article 39.2 of TRIPS already protects undisclosed information against dishonest commercial practices. The meaning of 'unfair' commercial uses in Article 39.3 must therefore somehow go beyond the mere protection against dishonest commercial practises set out in Article 39.2.[88]

Other commentators have suggested that the meaning of unfairness in the context of Article 39.3 of TRIPS is *economic* unfairness. Reading the phrase 'unfair' in light of the terms 'commercial' and 'considerable effort' used elsewhere in Article 39.3, Skillington and Solovy take the view that the article refers to 'unfair' acts such as competitors 'free riding' on the work of innovators (including through reliance on

80 Correa (2002), pp. 77–78.

81 Ibid, p. 77.

82 Correa (2010), p. 713.

83 Correa (2002), p. 83.

84 Fellmeth (2004), p. 459.

85 Ibid.

86 See, for example, WTO, *Korea – Definitive Safeguard Measure on Imports of Certain Dairy Products*, WT/DS98/AB/R, para 81; WTO, *United States – Section 211 Omnibus Appropriations Act of 1998* WT/DS176/AB/R, para 338.

87 Fellmeth (2004), p. 460.

88 Spina Alì (2018), p. 216.

previously submitted data, unless some kind of economic compensation is available).[89] Fellmeth develops this argument further, arguing that the definition of 'unfair' in Article 39.3 relates to the concept of getting 'that to which one is entitled'—in this case, the value of the submitted test data.[90] According to Fellmeth, in order for commercial use of submitted information to not be unfair, the originator must not be denied the economic value which the data has by virtue of not being known.[91] As Spina Alì notes, this is supported by Article 7 of TRIPS, which states that the objective of the Agreement is to promote technological innovation and technology transfer and dissemination (although Spina Alì also notes that the fact that this should be to the 'mutual advantage of producers and users of technological knowledge and in a manner conducive to social and economic welfare' suggests that the need to protect against unfair commercial use cannot be assumed to require strict exclusive rights or full compensation of the value of test data—this is discussed further at Sect. 4.4.3, below).[92] Finally, this interpretation of 'unfair' has the considerable advantage of not reducing Article 39.3 to redundancy.

The ordinary meanings of 'commercial' includes both engaged in commerce and relating to commerce. Correa observes that in most cases in which a generic drug application seeks to rely on previously submitted data, it is normally a governmental body rather than a commercial one which refers to the data in question—as such, he argues, use of submitted test data in an abbreviated drug application is not commercial.[93] However, this objection ignores the second meaning of 'commercial' set out above; reference to submitted originator data in order to grant commercial approval for competing products is clearly commercial in the sense that it relates to commerce.[94] In the context of Article 39.3, it seems clear that the second meaning is the intended one; the article expressly concerns situations in which test data has been submitted to a government for the purpose of gaining approval for marketing (i.e. *commercial*) approval.

This then brings us to the meaning of the word 'use' in Article 39.3. As Spina Alì observes, Article 39.3 employs the word 'use' in its sense as a noun rather than a verb.[95] The ordinary meanings of 'use' in this sense include using something or the state of being used for a purpose, as well as the act or practice of using something.[96] When a regulatory agency examines submitted data to achieve an end, such as approving a generic version of a drug, this is clearly a 'use' of that data within the

[89] Skillington and Solovy (2003), p. 30.

[90] Fellmeth (2004), p. 462.

[91] Ibid, p. 463.

[92] Spina Alì (2018), p. 212.

[93] Correa (2002), pp. 79–80. See also the case of *Bayer v The Attorney General of Canada* 84 CPR (3d) 129, where the Canadian Court of Appeal came to a similar conclusion regarding a provision of NAFTA.

[94] Skillington and Solovy (2003), p. 29.

[95] Spina Alì (2018), p. 209.

[96] Ibid.

ordinary meaning of the word. However, Correa points to two circumstances in which an abbreviated approval application for a generic may not constitute use of the submitted originator test data—scenarios in which the regulatory agency does not actually access to the submitted data but instead approves the generic purely based on its bioequivalence to a previously approved drug (indirect reliance), and scenarios in which a generic is approved based on its bioequivalence with a product approved in another jurisdiction, such as the US or EU (foreign reliance).[97]

Skillington and Solovy, Fellmeth and Meitinger argue that indirect reliance is indeed use of submitted test data because 'but for' that data, the information that the originator product has been approved for marketing could not exist—reliance on the regulatory status of a drug approved as a result of submitted test data therefore necessarily relies upon (and uses) the submitted data itself.[98] Dinca further argues that based on the maxim *ubi lex non distinguit, nec nos distinguere debemus* ('when the law does not distinguish [between several categories], neither must the interpreter distinguish'), the term 'use' must therefore be assumed to include both direct and indirect uses.[99] However, these rebuttals ignore the crux of Correa's argument; indirect reliance and reliance on foreign approvals do not actually rely on or use submitted data at all; rather, they use the positive regulatory decision that a particular drug is safe and efficacious. Indirect 'use' of submitted test data is 'use' of the submitted test data only in a colloquial sense—an entirely separate piece of information is being used, even if it is derived from the first. Use of this second, derived piece of information cannot be assumed to also entail use of the first; by way of analogy, consider a person who wishes to use the publicly available information on which individuals are authorised to provide a particular regulated service in order to compile a database of such individuals. The information that someone is authorised to provide such a service will generally be based on 'submitted data' of some sort (at the very least an application form and possibly some kind of examination), and the regulatory decision to approve an individual to, for example, practice law could not exist but for the submission of this data. However, using the information that an individual is authorised to provide such a service does not mean indirectly using the data upon which that information is based, and certainly does not violate the intellectual property rights that subsist in the application or the transcript of the examination (similarly, the reader may wish to reflect on whether in using this book by reading it, they are necessarily also 'using' the notes that were necessary for its creation but which do not appear in the final text). This line of reasoning was followed by the Canadian Federal Appeal Court in the 1999 case of *Bayer v Canada (Attorney General).* [100] While this case focused on Article 1711 of NAFTA rather than TRIPS, its logic easily applies to Article 39.3; Article 1711 of

[97] Correa (2002), pp. 72–79.

[98] Skillington and Solovy (2003), p. 6; Fellmeth (2004), p. 459; Meitinger (2005), p. 132.

[99] Dinca (2005), p. 527.

[100] *Bayer v The Attorney General of Canada* 84 CPR (3d) 129.

NAFTA requires a higher standard of protection for submitted test data than Article 39.3,[101] and in any case, Canada is also a signatory to TRIPS and was so equally bound by Article 39.3 at the time of the decision. The Canadian court found that 'indirect reliance' on submitted test data was not barred by Article 1711(5) of NAFTA on the grounds that such reliance is based on the fact of an originator drug's approval rather than the submitted data on which it is based. While this decision of a Canadian court is obviously not a binding interpretation of Article 39.3, it demonstrates the sound reasoning behind distinguishing between submitted data and information derived from submitted data.

Based on the analysis of this section, this book takes the view that the term 'unfair commercial use' imposes more than an obligation to protect submitted data against misappropriation, and that entirely unrestrained use of originator data in subsequent drug approvals is likely to fall foul of the provision. However, many forms of generic approval applications will not fall foul of the provision (in particular, those that approve generics purely on the basis of its bioequivalence with a drug that has been approved domestically or abroad). Furthermore, as we shall see, Article 39.3 gives members an extremely high level of discretion as to how to protect against unfair commercial use.

4.4.2 Other Terms

While the meaning of unfair commercial use is the most important aspect of the debate over the meaning of Article 39.3, a number of other terms are also unclear, and it is relevant to understand their meanings as this book moves forward.

Firstly, protection against unfair commercial use is only required for *undisclosed* data, the origination of which involves a *considerable effort*, *submitted* to members as a condition of approving the marketing of pharmaceutical or agricultural chemical products which *utilise new chemical entities*. This imposes a further set of qualifications on when submitted test data must be protected under Article 39.3; determining what exactly these qualifications entail is thus essential to understanding the requirements of the article. Secondly, members must 'protect such data against disclosure, except where necessary to protect the public, or unless steps are taken to ensure that the data are protected against unfair commercial use.' This also raises a number of questions as to the obligations of members of the WTO regarding the protection of submitted test data.

[101] NAFTA (1992) Article 1711 requires 'that 'no person other than the person that submitted [test data], without the latter's permission, [may] rely on such data in support of an application for product approval during a reasonable period of time after their submission.'

4.4.2.1 New Chemical Entity

Only data submitted as a condition of approving the marketing of pharmaceutical or agricultural chemical products which 'utilise new chemical entities' must be protected under Article 39.3. This raises two questions; what is meant by 'new' and what is meant by 'chemical entity'?

First, let us consider 'new.' It is clear that data submitted with respect to new indications, dosages and other variations of 'old' chemicals are not protected under Article 39.3 as it is the entity rather than the use which must be new.[102] A further question, however, is under which circumstances a chemical entity can be considered 'new.' The term 'new' can be understood in an absolute sense; something which has only recently come into existence, or in a relative sense—i.e., something which is novel to the person or persons presently considering it. Understanding in which sense the word is used in Article 39.3 is important because the former definition implies that only data submitted regarding recently developed chemical entities must be protected under Article 39.3, while the latter definition implies that data submitted in association with any chemical entity which is new to the jurisdiction must be protected, regardless of the time since the chemical entity's initial development.

The *travaux* provide little guidance on the meaning of newness—the word first appears in relation to submitted test data in the Brussels draft and receives no discussion.[103] Skillington and Solovy argue that as Article 39.3 deals with data in the context of its submission to regulators, the term should be understood as meaning a chemical entity with respect to which data has not been previously submitted to the national regulator.[104] However, this argument is tenuous; the mere fact that the data in question must be submitted to governments cannot be read as meaning that the newness of the chemical entity in question must be assessed from the perspective of whether the government has previously approved such an entity any more than the requirement that an invention must be 'new' in Article 27 of TRIPS should be assessed based on whether the relevant patent office has previously granted a patent over the invention in question on the grounds that TRIPS requires that the invention be sufficiently disclosed to that patent office.[105]

Spina Alì argues that subsequent state practice confirms that the term should be assessed from the perspective of national regulators, further noting that post-TRIPS WTO parties have endorsed this meaning in dozens of FTAs.[106] It is true that the vast majority of jurisdictions with test data exclusivity laws have opted for the 'local' definition of novelty, as is discussed in Chap. 6. However, a number of FTAs and jurisdictions also place significant limitations on novelty—for example, by tying the

---

[102] Spina Alì (2017), p. 222.

[103] GATT, *Draft Final Act Embodying the Results of the Uruguay Round of Multilateral Trade Negotiations,* MTN.TNC/W/FA (20 December 1991).

[104] Skillington and Solovy (2003), p. 25.

[105] TRIPS Articles 27 and 29.

[106] Spina Alì (2017), p. 222.

availability of test data exclusivity or the length of the exclusivity term to requirements to seek approval within the jurisdiction within a certain period after the pharmaceutical product has been approved in other jurisdictions. China, for example, appears to define 'new chemical entities' and 'new drugs' as those for which initial marketing authorisation is first sought in China, with the result that those first submitted for approval in other jurisdictions will not qualify for test data exclusivity.[107] Vietnam, Malaysia, Chile and Taiwan all require that a new chemical entity be submitted for approval in the national jurisdiction within a few years of its international debut to qualify for test data exclusivity.[108] Meanwhile, the trade agreements negotiated with Peru and Colombia by both the US and EU permit parties to measure the term of exclusivity from its approval in another party, provided that the originator application is approved by that party within six months of its submission; such a position obviously has the result of preventing a chemical entity from gaining test data exclusivity protection if the delay between its first approval in a party and its submission in the second party is greater than the exclusivity period.[109] This diversity of state practice demonstrates that the issue is less than settled.

Correa argues that as the term is undefined, members are free to define the term as either referring to 'new' in the sense of having recently come into existence, or 'new' in the sense of 'not previously approved', perhaps even going so far as to apply the extreme level of novelty used in patent law, i.e. a product will not be considered new if it has been previously disclosed to the public anywhere in the world.[110] Given the genuine absence of clarity on this issue, this seems to be the correct approach. The ambiguity of the term 'new' is such that it can neither be seen as imposing a requirement for absolute novelty nor an obligation to protect the data submitted regarding all chemical entities not previously approved by the national regulator. Members thus have the freedom to define the standard of 'new' in either absolute or relative terms.[111]

The term 'chemical entity' has also generated debate. It is obvious that the term covers the traditional 'small molecule' drugs which comprise the majority of pharmaceuticals. However, questions arise when considering whether Article 39.3 requires protection for only test data submitted with respect to these small molecule drugs, or also to drugs derived through biological processes, i.e., biologics. These questions have become more relevant due to the advent of abbreviated approval procedures for biologics in many jurisdictions, as discussed at Sect. 2.5. On the one hand, biologics are still composed of chemicals in a literal sense, and as such some

[107] USTR, 2017 *Special 301 Report* (2017), p. 33.

[108] Vietnam, Circular No. 17/2011/TT-BNNPTNT 2011; Malaysia, Directive on Data Exclusivity (2011); Chile, Law 19.039 on Industrial Property (as amended) and Taiwan, Pharmaceutical affairs act, article 40-2(4).

[109] US-Peru TPA (2006) Article 16.10; US-Colombia TPA (2006) Article 16.10; Trade Agreement between the EU and Peru, Colombia (2012) Article 231.

[110] Correa (2002), p. 74.

[111] Correa (2002), p. 74; Shaikh (2016), p. 84.

commentators believe that they should fall within Article 39.3's scope.[112] However, in the pharmaceutical context 'chemical drugs' are commonly understood to refer to small molecule entities, with biologically derived drugs being referred to as biologics.[113] Indeed, in the US the term 'new chemical entity' *explicitly* refers only to small molecule drugs;[114] given that at the time of the TRIPS negotiations the US represented an even larger share of the world pharmaceutical market than today, the stakeholders involved in the negotiation of TRIPS would have been familiar with this terminology. Shaikh notes that the drafters of TRIPS chose the phrase 'chemical entity' rather than 'active moiety' or 'substance,' the generic phrases normally used to refer to both chemical drugs and biologics.[115] Indeed, the Brussels draft used the term 'new pharmaceutical *product*', the ordinary meaning of which would seemingly cover any new pharmaceutical, including biologics; the fact that this term was changed to 'pharmaceutical or agricultural chemical products *which utilise new chemical entities*' [emphasis added] in the final draft of TRIPS suggests an intentional narrowing of the scope of the provision. It would appear, therefore, that test data submitted regarding biologics is not included within the scope of Article 39.3.

4.4.2.2 The Submission of Undisclosed Test or Other Data

The concept that only *undisclosed* test data must be protected per Article 39.3 seems relatively straight forward but has nonetheless managed to generate debate. While it is unambiguous that only submitted test data which is not publicly available must be protected under Article 39.3, a point of contention remains as to whether members must continue to protect data that is undisclosed at the time of submission but which subsequently becomes disclosed. Skillington and Solovy note that there is no express condition that the data must remain undisclosed after submission in the article, and that therefore the protection against unfair competition must remain for the period necessary to recover costs even if data becomes disclosed.[116] The obvious counterargument to this point is that just as Article 39.3 contains no express provision that data should remain undisclosed after submission, it contains no express requirement that submitted data which becomes disclosed must retain its protection. As discussed below, members must protect the test data against disclosure except where such a disclosure is necessary to protect the public or unless steps are taken to ensure that the disclosed data is protected against unfair commercial use;

[112] de Carvalho (2008), p. 287.

[113] Shaikh (2016), p. 82.

[114] See, for example, FDA, 'New Drugs at FDA: CDER's New Molecular Entities and New Therapeutic Biological Products' https://www.fda.gov/drugs/development-approval-process-drugs/new-drugs-fda-cders-new-molecular-entities-and-new-therapeutic-biological-products (Accessed 26 January 2023).

[115] Shaikh (2016), pp. 82–83.

[116] Skillington and Solovy (2003), p. 35.

this suggests that whatever protection a government provides to submitted test data should continue if that government discloses that data, unless that disclosure is for reasons of public health. However, Article 39.3 does not require that test data which is disclosed by the applicant or another party must remain protected.

It should also be noted that as Article 39.3 deals with test data that has been submitted as part of a requirement by a member state for the approval of a pharmaceutical (or agricultural) product, data which has been submitted in foreign countries but not the member state itself is not protected—this further strengthens the argument that approvals of generic pharmaceuticals on the basis of approval decisions in foreign jurisdictions is not prohibited by Article 39.3.[117]

4.4.2.3 Considerable Effort

Only test data 'the origination of which involves a considerable effort' is protected under Article 39.3. Again, this term is left undefined in the text. Correa notes that whatever is meant by 'considerable', Article 39.3 permits national governments to request evidence that the effort involved in the origination of test data was indeed 'considerable.'[118] Shaikh observes that as the considerable effort has to relate to the generation of the specific data in question, members are free to request evidence relating to the drug in question rather than total spending on research and development, and are free to exclude failed trials from the definition of considerable as these trials by definition do not generate any of the data that is actually submitted.[119] Focusing on the phrase 'the origination of which', Skillington and Solovy observe that data which required trivial efforts regarding translation and reformatting prior to submission will still be covered as long as the data required considerable effort at its creation.[120]

4.4.2.4 Prohibition on Disclosure

Article 39.3 ends with a requirement for members to protect submitted data of the kind described in the article from disclosure, except where the disclosure is necessary to protect the public or where steps are taken to ensure that the data will be protected against unfair commercial use.

The second exception is, on first impression, somewhat puzzling. The exception permits the disclosure of submitted test data if the data will be protected from unfair commercial use; however, given that Article 39.3 already requires protection from unfair commercial use, this seems to imply that mere compliance with the first part of

---

[117] Correa (2002), p. 75.

[118] Ibid.

[119] Shaikh (2016), p. 90.

[120] Skillington and Solovy (2003), p. 28.

Article 39.3 frees a member from any actual obligations under the second part, reducing it to redundancy. However, it must be recalled that Article 39.3 provides members with a wide degree of freedom regarding the means of protecting data against unfair commercial use. In some cases, it is likely that disclosure of the submitted test data might permit a competitor to effectively by-pass the mechanism by which unfair commercial use is normally achieved; for example, in the US a generic drug might reference disclosed data in a 'paper NDA' and thus gain marketing approval based on originator data during the test data exclusivity period. As such, the second exception should be properly understood as confirming that while members may disclose submitted test data, they must ensure that it continues to be protected against unfair commercial use after such disclosure. An example of this can be seen with the EMA's 'Policy on publication of clinical data for medicinal products for human use.'[121] The data is only made available under strict terms; commercial use is still forbidden, certain 'commercial confidential information' (any non-publicly available data the disclosure of which might undermine the legitimate commercial interests of the originator) may be redacted,[122] and the EU's test data exclusivity rules are unaffected (the EMA's policy is discussed further at Sect. 6.4.5).

Having established the meaning of the second exception, the meaning of the first exception is therefore straightforward; when a threat to the public necessitates the disclosure of submitted test data, it is not necessary to continue to protect the submitted test data from unfair commercial use. This could permit a country with test data exclusivity laws to disclose test data in order to enable it to be used in an abbreviated approval application for a generic version of a drug produced under compulsory license during a pandemic, for example. Of course, the fact that the disclosure must be 'necessary' to protect the public imposes a high threshold on when such an exception might actually be used; noting the practice of GATT and WTO dispute panels, Fellmeth observes that the 'necessity' provision likely prohibits disclosure unless the disclosure is the only reasonable possible means of protecting the public.[123]

4.4.3 What Must Members Do to Comply with Article 39.3?

The fundamental question for national governments is what they must actually do to conform with TRIPS. As the above discussion has demonstrated, it is quite obvious that Article 39.3 does not oblige members to adopt test data exclusivity. The removal of explicit test data exclusivity provisions after the Brussels Draft of the Agreement makes it clear that such an obligation was rejected by the negotiators. To insist that

[121] EMA, 'European Medicines Agency policy on publication of clinical data for medicinal products for human use' (2019) EMA/144064/2019.

[122] Ibid, p. 7.

[123] Fellmeth (2004), p. 451.

the Article requires test data exclusivity would be to ignore that a requirement to protect submitted test data through a particular means was deleted by the drafters, demonstrating an intention to provide members with freedom in the choice of means they adopt in order to comply with Article 39.3.[124] This is further confirmed through Article 1.1 of TRIPS, which states that members are free to 'determine the appropriate method of implementing the provisions of this Agreement within their own legal system and practice.'[125] Against this, Skillington and Solovy argue that protection against unfair commercial use requires strong exclusive rights, although not necessarily test data exclusivity of the sort found in the Hatch-Waxman Act. They note that previous WTO panels have chosen to interpret the phrases 'conflict with a normal exploitation of the work' (relating to copyright in Article 13 of TRIPS) and 'unreasonably conflict with the normal exploitation of the patent' (relating to patents in Article 30 of TRIPS) to refer to economic competition with the holder of the intellectual property right in question. From this, they conclude that the normal exploitation of the submitted test data will be best protected through a right granting near total control over it, as with a copyright or patent.[126] This comparison is unconvincing—the essence of a copyright or patent is an exclusive right, while the existence of such a right is exactly what is under debate regarding Article 39.3. The comparison between the unfair commercial use of submitted test data and the conflict with the normal exploitation of a patent or copyright only makes sense if we have already concluded that submitted test data is protected by an exclusive right equivalent to copyright or patent—such a circular argument cannot be given credence.

Article 39.3 mandates only that submitted test data be 'protected' against unfair commercial use. As Spina Alì observes, protection—whose ordinary meaning is 'to keep safe from harm'—does not entail a *prohibition* on unfair commercial use, only that the originators of such data be protected against its detrimental effects.[127] This fits with Fellmeth's observation, noted above, that any commercial use of submitted test data that is rendered 'fair' will be permissible.[128] This could, of course, be achieved through a test data exclusivity period, but it could also be achieved through alternative mechanisms such as those highlighted in Chap. 2. Direct funding of clinical trials obviously removes the issue of commercial use of the submitted data being unfair because the originator has either already been directly compensated by the government, or the government itself has generated the data. Compulsory liability regimes and taxation on generic products for a time-limited period after the submission of the data also provide the originator with compensation in exchange for the use of the data, either directly in the case of the liability regime, or indirectly by providing the originator firm with a tax discount compared to its

[124] Spina Alì (2018), p. 218.

[125] TRIPS Article 1.1.

[126] Skillington and Solovy (2003), p. 30.

[127] Spina Alì (2018), p. 211.

[128] Fellmeth (2004), p. 462.

competitors.[129] Indeed, members might even argue that their patent terms and other forms of supplementary protection for pharmaceuticals are enough to ensure an 'economically fair' monopoly period for originators in a majority of cases, only offering additional protection for submitted test data when patent protection is not available.

Of course, the question remains as to what extent submitted test data must be protected against commercial use by competitors until such use ceases to be 'unfair.' It has been argued that permitting reliance on submitted test data before the originator's investment in the production of that data is entirely recouped will violate Article 39.3.[130] This seems implausible for a number of reasons. Firstly, the negotiating history of TRIPS does not support such a view; the only proposal to mention 'full compensation' for the submitted data was the 1988 US proposal, and while other attempts to tie the cost of the production of the data to its protection (the requirement for payment of the 'reasonable value' of the data in the 1990 US proposal or the suggestion that the 'reasonable term of protection' be commensurate with the effort which went into the production of the data in the 1990 EC proposal and Brussels Draft), all these provisions were rejected from the final Article 39.3. In any case, *no* WTO members require 'full compensation' prior to permitting reliance on originator approval data—even the most generous test data exclusivity terms simply grant a uniform period of exclusivity after which generic reliance is possible, regardless of whether the originator has been 'fully compensated' or not.[131] Article 7 of TRIPS also suggests against such an extreme meaning; as Spina Alì observes, requiring the full compensation of the costs of the submitted test data would unbalance the market position of the generic firms as originators would be fully reimbursed for the costs of test data generation while the generic firms would have to cover the costs of bio-equivalence checks.[132]

For members who do choose to protect submitted test data through test data exclusivity, what features must this exclusivity have? Firstly, while an absurdly short term of protection such as a few days would clearly not be in compliance with TRIPS as it would render the concept of protection from unfair commercial use meaningless, members do have a wide degree of latitude regarding the term of protection. Furthermore, this protection can be either market exclusivity, data exclusivity *per se* or a combination of the two (see further Sect. 2.3). Indirect reliance on data through reference to the mere fact of approval is permissible, as is reference to foreign approvals. Members are also free to determine what standard of 'newness' is required to qualify for protection, whether this be objective or relative. In addition, members are not obliged to provide protection to data submitted in association with

[129] Spina Alì (2018), p. 228.

[130] Skillington and Solovy (2003), p. 5.

[131] As we shall see, a number of FTAs and national laws do mention a 'reasonable' term and/or otherwise suggest that the term of protection should somehow be linked to the effort expended in creating the data, but none appear to actually apply this in practice.

[132] Spina Alì (2018), p. 224.

new indications for old pharmaceuticals or biologics, for data which cannot be demonstrated to have been the result of considerable effort or for data which has been disclosed. Members are also free to disclose submitted data, provided that its protection from unfair competition continues or that this disclosure is necessary to protect the public.

4.4.3.1 Does Article 39.3 Prohibit the Use of Submitted Test Data in Relation to Compulsory Licensing or Other Measures Design to Promote Public Health?

As noted at Sect. 2.4.1.2, one of the criticisms of the protection of submitted test data in general, and test data exclusivity in particular, is that such protection undermines the ability of governments to issue compulsory licenses over pharmaceutical products by preventing generics produced under such a license from gaining approval through an abbreviated pathway. There are a number of obvious ways that such a conflict could be avoided. Members could disclose data in order for it to be used in a paper NDA or equivalent mechanism in cases where such disclosure would be necessary to protect the public as discussed at Sect. 4.4.2.4. In addition, members could provide for the waiver of whatever means by which submitted test data is protected or through the compulsory licensing of the submitted test data itself.

While neither the waiver of rights in submitted test data nor the compulsory licensing of such data is expressly accounted for in the text of Article 39.3, it seems likely that both are permissible under it. Firstly, as noted by Nuno Pires de Carvalho, restrictions on compulsory licensing elsewhere in the TRIPS Agreement—such as the prohibition on the compulsory licensing of trademarks at Article 21, or the restrictions on use of patents without the authorisation of the right holder at Article 31—are phrased in the negative; this suggests that absent an explicit restriction, compulsory licensing of subject matter protected by TRIPS is permissible.[133] This is further supported by the fact that the Swiss proposal expressly prohibiting the compulsory licensing of confidential information was rejected from the final version of TRIPS.

Furthermore, as Article 39.3 requires only protection against *unfair* commercial use, exceptions to the normal means of submitted test data protection will be permissible provided they are fair or at least shield the originator from the unfair consequences of the use. For example, while test data exclusivity might be suspended or the submitted test data it protects compulsorily licensed in the event of a public health crisis, so long as the right holder is remunerated to an adequate level this use would not be unfair. In addition, Spina Alì notes that it is a well-established principle of international law that an interpreter should read silences narrowly rather than using them to infer onerous obligations, as expressed in the Latin maxim '*ubi lex voluit dixit, ubi noluit tacuit*' ('when the law wills, it speaks;

[133] De Carvalho (2008), p. 309.

when it does not, it is silent').[134] Reading this in line with Article 8.1 of TRIPS and the Doha Declaration, this suggests members may implement exceptions to their general means of submitted test data protection provided these means are consistent with the general requirements of Article 39.3.

This interpretation of Article 39.3 has been lent further credence as a result of the Ministerial Decision on the TRIPS Agreement adopted by the WTO's 12th Ministerial Conference in June 2022. The Ministerial Decision, which is discussed in more detail at Sect. 8.2.2.1, mentions Article 39.3 only briefly, at Paragraph 4. This states:

> Recognizing the importance of the timely availability of and access to COVID-19 vaccines, it is understood that Article 39.3 of the Agreement does not prevent an eligible Member from enabling the rapid approval for use of a COVID-19 vaccine produced under this Decision.[135]

As indicated by the phrase 'it is understood', Paragraph 4 of the Ministerial Decision simply provides a clarification regarding the interpretation of Article 39.3, rather than altering the obligations under the article in any way.[136] The clarification is framed cautiously—it is only acknowledged that Article 39.3 does not prevent the rapid approval of vaccines in the specific context of the Ministerial Decision. However, this could only be the case if the general interpretation of Article 39.3 is consistent with permitting the rapid approval of pharmaceutical products in at least some circumstances. Indeed, several commentators have welcomed Paragraph 4 of the Ministerial Declaration as providing clarification that a general exception or safeguard of the sort outlined in this section exists within Article 39.3 to prevent it from frustrating compulsory licenses or other measures designed to promote public health in emergency situations.[137]

4.5 The Significance of Article 39.3

This chapter has discussed in considerable detail the meaning of Article 39.3, as many authors have before. However, the arcane debate over the meaning of Article 39.3 does not explain why virtually all significant pharmaceutical markets now protect submitted test data through test data exclusivity rights despite such a requirement being rejected from TRIPS, the uncertainty regarding virtually every aspect of the article and the absence of any formal attempts to enforce one particular interpretation of the article other that the inconclusive US-Argentina case discussed above.[138]

---

[134] Spina Alì (2016), p. 749.

[135] WTO, *Ministerial Decision of the TRIPS Agreement*, WT/MIN(22)/30 (22 June 2022).

[136] Solovy (2022), p. 10; Ranjan and Gour (2022), p. 8.

[137] Mercurio and Upreti (2022), p. 7; Ranjan and Gour (2022), p. 8; Mitchell et al. (2022), p. 126.

[138] WTO, *Argentina – certain measures on the protection of patents and test data*, WT/DS196/4 (31 May 2002).

It might be argued that Article 39.3 has simply been unimportant in the globalisation of test data exclusivity, or that it has even been a setback for the developed country proponents of test data exclusivity which those countries have managed to overcome in the post-TRIPS period. However, the next two chapters of this book advance the case that Article 39.3 has played an important role in the globalisation of test data exclusivity. Prior to the TRIPS Agreement, jurisdictions which did not have a domestic research-based pharmaceutical industry had little reason to enact special protections for submitted test data to safeguard the investments of foreign pharmaceutical companies, especially if this meant increasing the costs of medicines for their citizens. Article 39.3 established the principle that submitted test data should receive special protections and as such set the direction of regulatory change, with mechanisms such as non-reciprocal adjustment, coercion and systems of reward then employed by developed countries to promote detailed test data exclusivity rules in the post-TRIPS period.[139]

In addition to establishing this principle, the ambiguity of Article 39.3 has also played a significant role in globalising test data exclusivity rights post-TRIPS. As Braithwaite and Drahos observe, the development of new regulatory approaches imposes costs in the form of time, money, mental effort and conflict.[140] This is especially true when the 'new way' in question must implement an obligation which is fundamentally unclear; a government wishing to develop a new means of protecting submitted test data would have to bear the cost of coming up with this new approach, implementing it and withstanding the inevitable backlash from developed countries, who would also almost certainly be able to construct a semi-plausible argument that this new means of protecting submitted test data was not in conformity with Article 39.3 given the Article's considerable interpretive malleability. As a result, states are incentivised to model the existing response to Article 39.3—that is, test data exclusivity—despite the fact that this approach will typically be poorly adapted to their context.

As discussed in the next chapter, some states implemented test data exclusivity laws soon after TRIPS despite the absence of any obvious benefit to their own economies or any bilateral pressure.[141] However, in addition to this straightforward modelling of existing test data exclusivity laws, the ambiguity of Article 39.3 has also enhanced the ability of the US, EU and EFTA to negotiate test data exclusivity terms with states that are more resistant to adopting such laws. States which have not enacted measures to implement Article 39.3 are open to the accusation that they have not met their WTO obligations; this strengthens the position of the US, EU and EFTA when attempting to secure a commitment to provide test data exclusivity during negotiations. This can most clearly be seen with regard to the fact that a number of states, including China, have made commitments to provide test data

[139] Braithwaite and Drahos (2000), p. 19.

[140] Ibid, p. 585.

[141] For example, New Zealand and Mauritius; see Sect. 6.4 below.

exclusivity during the process of accession to the WTO despite the fact that test data exclusivity is not an obvious requirement of any WTO treaty.

Specific obligations obviously produce specific outcomes; however, extremely non-specific obligations such as Article 39.3 may also produce such outcomes under certain circumstances because they raise the cost of developing an original means of implementing the obligation to the point that the modelling of an existing response becomes the most viable option. This is not to suggest that Article 39.3 was *deliberately* designed to be ambiguous for this reason; the negotiating history of TRIPS clearly shows that the US, EC and Switzerland pushed hard for explicit restrictions on the ability of generic firms to gain approval based on previously submitted data during the Uruguay Round. However, this is the role that Article 39.3 has come to play in globalising test data exclusivity post-TRIPS.

4.6 Conclusion

It seems likely that Article 39.3 does require more than the mere protection of submitted test data against misappropriation, and entirely unrestricted use of submitted test data by subsequent drug applications is likely to fall foul of the article. However, the obligations imposed by Article 39.3 provide members with a wide discretion as to how to protect submitted test data. There are many ways in which Article 39.3 could be implemented, including through direct funding of clinical trials as suggested by Reichman, a compensation model as suggested by Fellmeth and Dinca, or through taxes on generic products as suggested by Spina Alì.[142] If members do provide test data exclusivity, they are free to include features such as higher standards of novelty or exceptions to the test data exclusivity period. In addition, many types of drug approvals that rely on originator data will not be caught by Article 39.3 at all, such as those which rely on the fact of an originator's approval rather than the submitted test data itself (whether domestically or in another jurisdiction) or those which rely on data submitted regarding a biologic product.

However, while test data exclusivity was rejected from TRIPS in the Uruguay Round, Article 39.3 of TRIPS has nonetheless played an important role in its globalisation. Article 39.3 established the principle that submitted test data should receive special protections. In addition, the difficulties of determining the meaning of Article 39.3 impose a high cost for developing an original means of protection for submitted test data. As discussed in the next two chapters, this has facilitated the promulgation of test data exclusivity in trade negotiations in the post-TRIPS period.

[142] Reichman (2009); Fellmeth (2004), p. 461; Dinca (2005), p. 528; Spina Alì (2017), p. 228.

References

Bradley AJ (1987) Intellectual property rights, investment, and trade in services in the Uruguay Round: laying the foundations. Stanford J Int Law 23:57

Braithwaite J, Drahos P (2000) Global business regulation. Cambridge University Press, Cambridge

Correa C (2002) Protection of data submitted for the registration of pharmaceuticals: implementing the standards of the TRIPS agreement. South Centre, Geneva

Correa C (2010) Data exclusivity for pharmaceuticals: TRIPS standards and industry's demands in free trade agreements. In: Correa C (ed) Research handbook on the protection of intellectual property under WTO rules: intellectual property in the WTO. Edward Elgar Publishing, Cheltenhem, pp 713–728

Council for Trade-Related Aspects of Intellectual Property Rights (2001) Submission to the TRIPS Council by the African Group, Barbados, Bolivia, Brazil, Cuba, Dominion Republic, Ecuador, Honduras, India, Indonesia, Jamaica, Pakistan, Paraguay, Philippines, Peru, Sri Lanka, Thailand and Venezuela

de Carvalho NP (2008) The TRIPS Agreement for antitrust and undisclosed information. Kluwer, The Hague

Dinca R (2005) The Bermuda Triangle of pharmaceutical law: is data protection a lost ship? J World Intellect Prop 8:517

Drahos P, Braithwaite J (2002) Information feudalism: who owns the knowledge economy. Routledge, London

EMA (2019) European Medicines Agency policy on publication of clinical data for medicinal products for human. EMA/144064/2019

European Commission (2001) Questions on TRIPs and Data Exclusivity: An EU Contribution

Fellmeth AX (2004) Secrecy, monopoly, and access to pharmaceuticals in international trade law: protection of marketing approval data under the TRIPs Agreement. Harv Int Law J 45:443

Gervais D (1998) The TRIPS Agreement: drafting, history and analysis. Sweet and Maxwell, London

Matthews D (2003) Globalising intellectual property rights: the TRIPS Agreement. Routledge, London

Meitinger I (2005) Implementation of test data protection according to Article 39.3 TRIPS: the search for a fair interpretation of the term unfair commercial use. J World Intellect Prop 8:123

Mercurio B, Upreti P (2022) From necessity to flexibility: a reflection on the negotiations for a TRIPS waiver for Covid-19 vaccines and treatments. World Trade Rev 21(5):633–649

Mitchell AD, Taubman A, Samlidis T (2022) The legal character and practical implementation of a TRIPS waiver for COVID-19 vaccines. Fordham Intellect Prop Media Entertain Law J 33:100

Mossinghoff GJ (1984) The importance of intellectual property protection in international trade. Boston Coll Int Comp Law Rev 7:235

Palombi L (2015) The patenting of biological materials in the United States: a state of policy confusion. Perspect Sci 23(1):35–65

Ranjan P, Gour P (2022) The TRIPS waiver decision at the World Trade Organization: too little too late! Asian J Int Law:1–12

Reichman JH (2009) Rethinking the role of clinical trial data in international intellectual property law: the case for a public goods approach. Marquette Intellect Prop Law Rev 13(1):1

Sell SK (1995) The origins of a trade-based approach to intellectual property protection: the role of industry associations. Sci Commun 17(2):163–185

Sell SK (2003) Private power, public law: the globalization of intellectual property rights. Cambridge University Press, Cambridge

Shaikh OH (2016) Access to medicine versus test data exclusivity: safeguarding flexibilities under international law. Springer, Berlin

Skillington GL, Solovy EM (2003) The protection of test and other data required by article 39.3 of the TRIPS agreement. Northwest J Int Law Bus 24:1

Solovy EM (2022) The TRIPS waiver for COVID-19 vaccines, and its potential expansion: assessing the impact on global IP. George Mason University Centre for Intellectual Property x Innovation Policy

Spina Alì G (2016) The sound of silence: international treaties and data exclusivity as a limit to compulsory licensing. Eur Intellect Prop Rev 38(12):744–754

Spina Alì G (2017) Article 39 (3) TRIPS: understanding the obligations, exploiting the flexibilities. The University of Hong Kong

Spina Alì G (2018) The 13th Round: Article 39 (3) TRIPS and the struggle over "Unfair Commercial Use". J World Intellect Prop 21(3–4):201–242

UNCTAD-ICTSD (2005) Resource book on TRIPS and development. Cambridge University Press, Cambridge

USTR (1995) The Protection of Undisclosed Test Data in Accordance with TRIPS Article 39.3

USTR (2017) 2017 Special 301 Report

Weissman R (1996) A long, strange TRIPS: the pharmaceutical industry drive to harmonize global intellectual property rules, and the remaining WTO legal alternatives available to Third World countries. Univ Pa J Int Law:1069

Chapter 5
The Globalisation of Test Data Exclusivity

Abstract This chapter analyses how test data exclusivity has become so thoroughly globalised in spite of its rejection from TRIPS, as well as how test data exclusivity requirements in trade agreements and other instruments have evolved over time and between parties. The chapter firstly examines the role that trade agreements negotiated by the US, EFTA/Switzerland and EU have played in the globalisation of test data exclusivity. Then, the chapter moves to examine how the process of accession to the WTO and more coercive measures have been used to pressure countries to adopt test data exclusivity laws. Finally, this chapter discusses why test data exclusivity has globalised so successfully post-TRIPS.

5.1 Introduction

In the previous chapter, it was observed that requirements to provide test data exclusivity were rejected from what would become the TRIPS Agreement during the Uruguay Round. In addition, it was concluded that while entirely unrestricted use of submitted test data in an abbreviated application likely constitutes unfair commercial use per Article 39.3, members of the WTO retain wide discretion as to the means by which submitted test data should be protected; alternative means of protecting submitted test data are entirely permissible under TRIPS, and even if a member does meet its Article 39.3 obligations through test data exclusivity, it may qualify this exclusivity in a number of ways. Nevertheless, test data exclusivity is now a feature of the regulatory systems of virtually all large pharmaceutical markets, far surpassing the globalisation of other TRIPS-plus measures such as patent linkage and patent term extensions. This chapter analyses how test data exclusivity has become so globalised.

A. Buick, *Intellectual Property Rights in Pharmaceutical Test Data*,
https://doi.org/10.1007/978-3-031-29436-5_5

5.2 The Protection of Submitted Test Data and Trade Post-TRIPS

Despite the rejection for an explicit requirement for test data exclusivity from TRIPS during the Uruguay Round, the claim that Article 39.3 did in fact require test data exclusivity began almost immediately after the signing of the TRIPS Agreement. The USTR released its statement that Article 39.3 required that submitted data not be used to 'support, clear or otherwise review' subsequent applications for marketing approval for a set amount of time in May of 1995,[1] and the US began its case against Argentina over, *inter alia*, its failure to provide test data exclusivity protection in 1999.[2] This push for a 'maximalist' interpretation of TRIPS was not limited to the protection of submitted test data; the US also became involved in a spat with South Africa regarding the South African government's attempt to make use of compulsory licensing to secure access to affordable HIV medication, as well as bringing a case against Brazil through the WTO's dispute settlement process regarding 'local working' provisions in Brazil's patent law.[3] However, by 2001 the US had backed down in all three cases, with the South African debacle in particular provoking an embarrassing backlash.[4] An additional blow had been dealt to the US's use of unilateral pressure to promote higher standards of intellectual property protection in 1999 when a challenge to the Special 301 system was brought through the WTO's dispute settlement process; the panel report, adopted by the Dispute Settlement Body (DSB), confirmed that the US could only impose sanctions against another WTO member after exhausting its options within the WTO.[5]

More circumspect approaches to increasing the level of protection for submitted test data proved more effective, however. As previously noted, towards the end of the TRIPS negotiations the US had begun negotiating provisions on test data exclusivity in a number of bilateral agreements. These provisions were clearly modelled on the bracketed version of the provisions on undisclosed data found in

[1] USTR (1995a).

[2] WTO, *Argentina: Patent Protection for Pharmaceuticals and Test Data Protection for Agricultural Chemicals – Notification of Mutually Agreed Solution*, WT/DS196/4 (20 June 2002).

[3] 't Hoen (2002), p. 29.

[4] The South African case was dropped unconditionally. In the Brazilian case the Mutually Agreed Solution permitted Brazil to maintain its local working provisions but committed Brazil to hold prior talks with the US if a compulsory license on a patent held by a US company was actually to be issued under the local working provisions. In the Argentine case, Argentina agreed to comply with most of the US demands, but the issue of test data exclusivity was left undecided, as discussed in the previous chapter. See further 't Hoen (2002), WTO, *Brazil: Measures Affecting Patent Protection – Notification of Mutually Agreed Solution* WT/DS199/4 (19 July 2001); and WTO, *Argentina: Patent Protection for Pharmaceuticals and Test Data Protection for Agricultural Chemicals – Notification of Mutually Agreed Solution,* WT/DS196/4 (20 June 2002).

[5] WTO, *Panel Report, United States—Sections 301–310 of the Trade Act of 1974*, WT/DS152/R (22 December 1999).

the Brussels Draft of TRIPS.[6] The US continued to negotiate such deals after TRIPS was signed, and from the mid- to late-2000s onwards, the EU, EFTA and Switzerland also began to negotiate commitments to provide test data exclusivity in trade agreements. In addition to this, from the early 2000s onwards a number of countries have either formally committed to providing test data exclusivity or indicated that they will provide such protection in order to conform with Article 39.3 during the negotiations around their accession to the WTO.

These commitments in trade and accession negotiations have been the major means by which test data exclusivity has spread to new jurisdictions post-TRIPS. However, test data exclusivity has also globalised through other means. Negotiations more explicitly backed by the threat of economic coercion have also led states to adopt test data exclusivity laws, as has outright military coercion on at least one occasion. In addition, a small number of countries simply modelled the test data exclusivity provisions of other countries, as the EC did in the 1980s. Switzerland adopted test data exclusivity laws modelled after those of the EC post-TRIPS, although this is hardly surprising, given Switzerland's large research-based pharmaceutical industry and its aggressive stance on the protection of submitted test data in the Uruguay Round.[7] Other jurisdictions without such obvious motivations to increase intellectual property protection for pharmaceuticals also passed test data exclusivity laws soon after TRIPS was signed; New Zealand adopted its current test data exclusivity law in 1994, for example.[8]

5.3 Test Data Exclusivity in Trade Agreements

At least 54 trade agreements have been signed with provisions which require either test data exclusivity protection or closely related measures. These agreements have been signed between the US (which has signed at least 26 such agreements), the EFTA states (at least 17 agreements signed by EFTA as a block with a further two signed only by Switzerland) or the EU (at least 9 agreements) and a third party or parties. The only notable jurisdiction with a large domestic research-based pharmaceutical industry which has not made us of FTAs to promote test data exclusivity is Japan, a state which has long been noted for its surprisingly weak influence on global regulation.[9]

Table 5.1 shows the trade agreements with test data exclusivity provisions which had been signed as of January 2023, although it should be noted that some of these agreements are yet to be ratified and, in the case of the Trans-Pacific Partnership

[6] GATT, *Draft Final Act Embodying the Results of the Uruguay Round of Multilateral Trade Negotiations,* MTN.TNC/W/35 (26 November 1990), p. 215.

[7] Holzer (2012), p. 184.

[8] New Zealand, Medicines Act Amendment 1994.

[9] Braithwaite and Drahos (2000), p. 478.

Table 5.1 Trade agreements with provisions on test data exclusivity by year

Year	Agreement	Year	Agreement
1991	USA & Sri Lanka	*2007*	USA & Panama
1991	USA & Bulgaria	*2007*	EFTA & Egypt[a]
1992	USA & Albania	*2008*	EFTA & Colombia
1992	USA, Canada & Mexico	*2009*	EFTA & Albania
1993	USA & Ecuador	*2009*	Switzerland & Japan
1994	USA & Jamaica	*2010*	EFTA & Serbia
1994	USA & Latvia	*2010*	EFTA & Peru
1994	USA & Trinidad and Tobago	*2010*	EFTA & Ukraine
1996	USA & Cambodia	*2010*	EU & Korea
1998	USA & Nicaragua	*2011*	EFTA & Hong Kong
2000	USA & Vietnam	*2011*	EFTA & Montenegro
2000	USA & Jordan	*2012*	EU, Peru, Colombia & Ecuador[b]
2000	USA & Laos	*2013*	EFTA & Bosnia
2003	USA & Chile	*2013*	Switzerland & China
2003	USA & Singapore	*2014*	EU & Georgia
2003	USA & Australia	*2014*	EU & Moldova
2004	USA, Costa Rica, El Salvador, Guatemala, Honduras, Nicaragua & the Dominican Republic	*2014*	EU & Ukraine
2004	USA & Bahrain	*2016*	USA, Australia, Brunei, Canada, Chile, Japan, Malaysia, Mexico, New Zealand, Peru, Singapore & Vietnam[c]
2004	USA & Morocco	*2016*	EFTA & Georgia
2004	EFTA & Lebanon	*2016*	EU & Canada
2004	EFTA & Tunisia	*2018*	USA, Canada & Mexico
2004	EFTA & Chile	*2018*	EFTA & Turkey
2004	EFTA & Korea	*2018*	EFTA & Ecuador
2005	USA & Oman	*2018*	EFTA & Indonesia
2006	USA & Colombia	*2018*	EU & Singapore
2006	USA & Peru	*2018*	EU & Japan
2006	USA & Korea	*2019*	EU & Vietnam

[a] The EFTA-Egypt agreement requires that data must be protected from 'unfair commercial use' for at least five years, but as in Article 39.3 this term is not defined

[b] Ecuador joined the agreement in 2016

[c] Note that while the TPP was signed in 2016, the test data exclusivity provisions were suspended in 2017 following the withdrawal of the USA

between the US and various Pacific states, have had their test data exclusivity provisions suspended. Table 5.1 shows quite clearly that the US has led by far the largest number of trade agreements with test data exclusivity provisions, including virtually all early agreements. While the Europeans have become more active in negotiating test data exclusivity provisions in trade agreements from the mid-2000s onwards, the absolute number of agreements they have concluded somewhat overstates their influence as in many cases the countries with which these agreements were signed had already committed to test data exclusivity in a previous agreement, the benefit of which would have extended to European companies and individuals as a result of the principles of MFN and national treatment. This is illustrated most dramatically by both the EFTA and the EU agreements with a number of Central American countries; in both of these agreements, the provisions on the protection of submitted test data explicitly state that submitted test data will be protected through the terms of the pre-existing US deals with the Central American countries and the principles of MFN and national treatment.[10] Because these provisions add no additional requirements regarding submitted test data beyond those already agreed in earlier trade deals with the US, they are not included in the discussions below.

Even those EFTA/Swiss- and EU-negotiated deals which do contain substantive terms on test data exclusivity often merely replicate the terms of pre-existing agreements or national laws. The US, in contrast, has only negotiated such a 'subsequent' trade agreement once, in the case of Korea; even this deal can be distinguished from the subsequent deals struck by the Europeans as the test data exclusivity terms of the US-led agreement are considerably more restrictive than those of the earlier EFTA-led deal.[11] As we shall see, the US-negotiated terms on the protection of submitted test data are typically more comprehensive and restrictive than those negotiated by EFTA/Switzerland and the EU; however, an exception to this trend is that both EFTA and the EU have been able to negotiate much stronger conditions regarding the protection of submitted test data (often exceeding the terms of many US-led agreements) in their deals with developing countries in Europe and its immediate neighbourhood. These countries have close links to the larger developed economies of EFTA and EU member states, and in some cases aspire towards EU membership, strengthening the negotiating position of the Europeans in this region.

The following section discusses the test data exclusivity provisions of these agreements and how they have changed over time and across regions in detail. To supplement this discussion, a number of tables are presented below summarising key details relating to the test data exclusivity terms of these agreements; Tables 5.2, 5.3, 5.4, 5.5 and 5.6 summarise the key details of the US-led agreements, Tables 5.7, 5.8, 5.9 and 5.10 summarise the key details of the EFTA and Swiss-led agreements, and Tables 5.11 and 5.12 summarise the key details of the EU-led agreements.

The first key detail is the length of the 'basic' term of test data exclusivity protection. 'Basic' protection here refers to the test data exclusivity protection that would be afforded to data submitted with respect to a standard application for a new drug, rather than more specialised forms of exclusivity which accrue to new clinical information or data associated with biologics. In some cases, this is expressed as

[10] EFTA-Central American FTA, Annex XIX Article 5; EU-Central American Association Agreement (2012).

[11] EFTA-Korea FTA (2004) Annex XIII Article 3; US-Korea FTA (2007) Article 18.9.

Table 5.2 Key details of test data exclusivity provisions in US-led trade agreements 1991–1993

Agreement & Year	Sri Lanka, 1991	Bulgaria, 1991	Albania, 1992	NAFTA, 1992	Ecuador, 1993	Jamaica, 1994
Basic term	5 years	5 years	5 years	5 years	5 years	5 years
Term for NCI	None	None	None	None	None	None
Protection for biologics	Not mentioned	Not mentioned	Not mentioned	Not mentioned	Not mentioned	Not mentioned
Indirect reliance prohibited?	No	No	No	No	No	No
Foreign data protected?	Yes	Yes	Yes	Yes	Yes	Yes
Is public health mentioned?	No	No	No	No	No	No
Are exceptions other than disclosure mentioned?	No	No	No	No	No	No
Is linking TDE to patent term prohibited?	No	No	No	No	No	No

Table 5.3 Key details of test data exclusivity provisions in US-led trade agreements 1994–1999

Agreement & Year	Latvia, 1994	Trinidad & Tobago, 1994	Cambodia, 1996	Nicaragua, 1998	Vietnam, 2000	Jordan, 2000
Basic term	5 years	5 years	5 years	5 years	5 years	Not specified[a]
Term for NCI	None	None	None	None	None	3 years
Protection for biologics	Not mentioned	Not mentioned	Not mentioned	Not mentioned	Not mentioned	Not mentioned
Indirect reliance prohibited?	No	No	No	No	No	No
Foreign data protected?	Yes	No	Yes	No	No	Yes
Is public health mentioned?	No	No	No	No	No	No
Are exceptions other than disclosure mentioned?	No	No	No	No	No	No
Is linking TDE to patent term prohibited?	No	No	No	No	No	No

[a] It is worth noting that Jordan had previously indicated that it would provide 5 years of test data exclusivity to NCEs during its accession to the WTO; see Sect. 5.4, below

Table 5.4 Key details of test data exclusivity provisions in US-led trade agreements 2000–2003

Agreement & Year	Laos, 2003	Chile, 2003	Singapore, 2003	Australia, 2004	CAFTA-DR, 2004	Bahrain, 2004
Basic term	5 years	5 years	5 years	5 years	5 years	5 years
Term for NCI	None	None	None	3 years	None	3 years
Protection for biologics	Not mentioned	Not mentioned	Not mentioned	Not mentioned	Not mentioned	Not mentioned
Indirect reliance prohibited?	No	Yes	Yes	Yes	Yes	Yes
Foreign data protected?	No	No	Yes	Yes	Yes	Yes
Is public health mentioned?	No	Yes	No	No	In side letter	In side letter
Are exceptions other than disclosure mentioned?	No	No	No	No	No	No
Is linking TDE to patent term prohibited?	No	No	Yes	Yes	Yes	Yes

Table 5.5 Key details of test data exclusivity provisions in US-led trade agreements 2004–2006

Agreement & Year	Morocco, 2004	Oman, 2006	Colombia, 2006	Peru, 2007	Panama, 2007	Korea, 2007
Basic term	5 years	5 years	5 years	5 years	5 years	5 years
Term for NCI	3 years	3 years	Explicitly excluded	Explicitly excluded	Explicitly excluded	3 years
Protection for biologics	Not mentioned	Not mentioned	Not mentioned	Not mentioned	Not mentioned	Not mentioned
Indirect reliance prohibited?	Yes	Yes	No	No	No	Yes
Foreign data protected?	Yes	Yes	Yes[a]	Yes[b]	Yes[c]	Yes
Is public health mentioned?	In side letter	In side letter	Yes	Yes	Yes	Yes
Are exceptions other than disclosure mentioned?	No	No	No	No	No	No
Is linking TDE to patent term prohibited?	Yes	Yes	Yes	Yes	Yes	Yes

[a] Where a Party relies on a marketing approval granted by the other Party, and grants approval within six months of the filing of a complete application for marketing approval filed in the Party, the reasonable period of exclusive use of the data submitted in connection with obtaining the approval relied on shall begin with the date of the first marketing approval relied on

[b] As with Colombia

[c] As with Colombia

Table 5.6 Key details of test data exclusivity provisions in US-led trade agreements 2007–2018

Agreement & Year	TPP, 2016[a]	USMCA, 2018
Basic term	5 years	5 years
Term for NCI	3 years[b]	3 years[c]
Protection for biologics	8 years or 5 years[d]	10 years[e]
Indirect reliance prohibited?	Yes	Yes
Foreign data protected?	Yes	Yes
Is public health mentioned?	Yes	Yes
Are exceptions other than disclosure mentioned?	No	No
Is linking TDE to patent term prohibited?	Yes	Yes

[a] The test data exclusivity provisions of the TPP were suspended in 2017 and remain suspended as of the time of writing

[b] Alternatively, a party may provide at least 5 years protection to new pharmaceutical products that contain a chemical entity that has not been previously approved in that Party. In addition, this provision only applies to NCI submitted in relation to non-biologic products

[c] Subsequently removed by the 2019 Protocol of Amendment to USMCA

[d] A party may provide 5 years protection as an alternative to 8 years protection if they can use 'other measures', including market circumstances, to deliver a 'comparable outcome in the market'

[e] Subsequently removed by the 2019 Protocol of Amendment to USMCA

concurrent periods of data exclusivity *per se* and market exclusivity. In a small number of agreements, the basic term of protection is undefined.

The second key detail is what term of protection (if any) is afforded to new clinical information submitted regarding a previously approved product. In some cases, this takes the form of a new exclusivity period, while in others such protection provides an extension to the existing term of protection associated with the product in question.

The third key detail is what protection (if any) is *explicitly* afforded to data submitted with respect to biologics. Explicit protection for biologic test data is a relatively new requirement in trade agreements, given that abbreviated approval pathways for biologics are themselves relatively new (see Sect. 2.5). Biologic products may have a separate period of protection or simply be included in the 'basic' term of protection.

The fourth key detail is whether the agreement explicitly prevents 'indirect' reliance on submitted test data. In Chap. 4, it was argued that TRIPS does not prevent reliance on the fact of originator approval if the underlying data itself is not accessed. A number of trade agreements have explicitly stated that such indirect reliance is impermissible.

The fifth key detail is whether protection is extended to data submitted in foreign jurisdictions. As noted in Chap. 4, TRIPS does not require the protection of data which has not been submitted to the relevant national government. A number of trade agreements explicitly require protection for test data submitted in a foreign jurisdiction.

The six key detail is whether an explicit reference is made to the parties' right to protect public health or to the Doha Declaration. Such references to public health and

Table 5.7 Key details of test data exclusivity provisions in EFTA-led trade agreements 2004–2008

Agreement & Year	Lebanon, 2004	Tunisia, 2004	Chile, 2004	Korea, 2005	Egypt, 2007	Colombia, 2008
Basic term	6 years	5 years	5 years	Not specified	5 years	5 years
Term for NCI	None	None	None	None	None	Explicitly excluded
Protection for biologics	Not mentioned	Not mentioned	Not mentioned	Not mentioned	Not mentioned	Not mentioned
Indirect reliance prohibited?	No	No	Yes	No	No	No
Foreign data protected?	No	No	No	No	No	Yes[a]
Is public health mentioned?	No	No	Yes	No	No	Yes
Are exceptions other than disclosure mentioned?	No	No	No	No	No	No
Is an alternative to TDE permitted?	Yes[b]	Yes[c]	No	Yes[d]	Yes[e]	No

[a] Where a Party relies on a marketing approval granted by another Party, and grants approval within six months of the filing of a complete application for marketing approval filed in the Party, the reasonable period of exclusive use of the data submitted in connection with obtaining the approval relied on shall begin on the date of the first marketing approval

[b] Data may be relied upon before the end of the exclusivity period if the first applicant is 'adequately compensated'

[c] As with Lebanon

[d] As with Lebanon

[e] Data must be protected from 'unfair commercial use' during the relevant term, but as in Article 39.3 this term is not defined

the Doha Declaration do not, in and of themselves, create additional rights for the parties, but provide some interpretive value.

The seventh key detail is whether any exceptions to test data exclusivity other than the ability to disclose submitted test data are explicitly provided for. Such explicit exceptions are rare, although as discussed below, the absence of such explicit exceptions does not mean they are prohibited.

Lastly, the final row of the charts deals with a provision unique to the test data exclusivity provisions negotiated by each of the leading parties. In the case of the US, this is the presence or absence of a prohibition on linking the term of protection to that of a patent associated with the product (as was formerly the case in some EU countries).[12] Such a policy obviously robs test data exclusivity of much of its

[12] Adamini et al. (2009), p. 989.

Table 5.8 Key details of test data exclusivity provisions in EFTA-led trade agreements 2009–2011

Agreement & Year	Albania, 2009	Serbia, 2010	Peru, 2010	Ukraine, 2010	Hong Kong, 2011	Montenegro, 2011
Basic term	8 years	8 years	5 years	3 years data exclusivity & 5 years market exclusivity (concurrent)	8 years	8 years data exclusivity & 10 years market exclusivity (concurrent)
Term for NCI	None	None	None	1-year extension to market exclusivity	None	1-year extension to market exclusivity
Protection for biologics	Not mentioned	Not mentioned	Not mentioned	Not mentioned	Included in basic term	Included in basic term
Indirect reliance prohibited?	No	No	No	No	No	No
Foreign data protected?	No	No	Yes[a]	No	No	No
Is public health mentioned?	No	No	Yes	No	No	No
Are exceptions other than disclosure mentioned?	No	No	No	No	No	No
Is an alternative to TDE permitted?	No	No	No	No	No	No

[a] Permits Peru to make use of the concurrent rule; see US-Peru TPA (2006) Article 16.10.2(c)

effectiveness by essentially ruling out the possibility of test data exclusivity continuing to prevent generic market entry after a patent expires or is revoked.

In the case of EFTA/Switzerland, this is the presence or absence of the possibility of protecting submitted test data through a means other than test data exclusivity. A number of early EFTA-led agreements contain such a provision with respect to pharmaceutical test data.

In the case of the EU, this key detail is the presence or absence of a commitment to 'align' legislation concerning data protection for medicinal products with that of the EU at a later date. Such a provision commits a party to adopting the EU's standards of test data exclusivity, amongst the highest in the world—this is typically

Table 5.9 Key details of test data exclusivity provisions in EFTA-led trade agreements 2012–2018

Agreement & Year	Bosnia, 2013	Georgia, 2016	Turkey, 2018	Ecuador, 2018	Indonesia, 2018
Basic term	8 years data exclusivity & 10 years market exclusivity (concurrent)	6 years	6 years[a]	3 years data exclusivity & 5 years market exclusivity (concurrent)	Not specified
Term for NCI	1-year extension to market exclusivity	1-year extension to market exclusivity	None	None	None
Protection for biologics	Included in basic term	Included in basic term	Included in basic term	None mentioned	None mentioned
Indirect reliance prohibited?	No	No	No	No	No
Foreign data protected?	No	No	No	No	No
Is public health mentioned?	No	No	No	Yes	Yes
Are exceptions other than disclosure mentioned?	No	No	No	Yes[b]	No
Is an alternative to TDE permitted?	No	No	No	No	No

[a] Turkey may start counting the exclusivity period from the date of the first marketing approval in the Turkey-EU Customs Union Area

[b] Test data exclusivity shall not prevent a Party from adopting measures in response to the abuse of intellectual property rights or unreasonably trade restrictive practices

because the agreement in question is seen as a prelude to eventual accession to the EU.

Not all aspects of the test data exclusivity provisions of a trade agreement can be easily summarised in a table; a number of additional details, including whether the agreement only requires protection for data that meets some or all of the requirements set out in Article 39.3, provisions on the disclosure of submitted test data and whether data exclusivity *per se* or market exclusivity must be granted are also discussed below.

Table 5.10 Key details of test data exclusivity provisions in Swiss-led trade agreements

Agreement & Year	Japan, 2009	China, 2013
Basic term	Not specified[a]	6 years
Term for NCI	None	None
Protection for biologics	None mentioned	Included in basic term
Indirect reliance prohibited?	No	No
Foreign data protected?	No	No
Is public health mentioned?	No	Yes
Are exceptions other than disclosure mentioned?	No	No
Is an alternative to TDE permitted?	No	No

[a] Article 121 specifies only that the data should be protected for 'a certain period of time' before acknowledging that at the time of the Agreement's entry into force such a period is stipulated as being 'no less than six years by the relevant laws of each Party'

Table 5.11 Key details of test data exclusivity provisions in EU-led trade agreements 2010–2015

Agreement & Year	Korea, 2010	Peru & Colombia. 2012[a]	Georgia, 2014	Moldova, 2014
Basic term	5 years	5 years	6 years	5 years data exclusivity & 7 years market exclusivity (concurrent)
Term for NCI	None	Explicitly excluded	1-year extension to basic term	1-year extension to market exclusivity
Protection for biologics	Included in basic term	Included in basic term for CO & EU; explicitly excluded for PE & EC	Unclear	Unclear
Indirect reliance prohibited?	No	No	No	Yes
Foreign data protected?	No	Yes	No	No
Is public health mentioned?	Yes	Yes	Yes	Yes
Are exceptions other than disclosure mentioned?	No	Yes[b]	No	No
Commitment to align legislation?	No	No	Yes	Yes

[a] Ecuador acceded to the agreement between the EU, Peru and Colombia in 2016

[b] The parties may exceptions for reasons of public interest, situations of national emergency or extreme urgency, when it is necessary to allow access to those data to third parties

Table 5.12 Key details of test data exclusivity provisions in EU-led trade agreements 2016–2019

Agreement & Year	Ukraine, 2014	Canada, 2016	Singapore, 2018	Japan, 2018	Vietnam, 2019
Basic term	5 years	6 years data exclusivity & 8 years market exclusivity (concurrent)	5 years[a]	Not specified[b]	5 years
Term for NCI	None	None	None	None	None
Protection for biologics	Unclear	Included in basic term	Not mentioned[c]	Unclear[d]	Unclear
Indirect reliance prohibited?	No	No	No	No	No
Foreign data protected?	No	No	No	No	No
Is public health mentioned?	Yes	Yes	Yes	Yes	Yes
Are exceptions other than disclosure mentioned?	No	No	No	No	No
Commitment to align legislation?	Yes	No	No	No	No

[a] Footnote 2 of page 234 of the Agreement specifies that the Parties will initiate discussions on the possible extension of this term after 5 years from the Agreement's entry into force. Footnote 3 of page 234 specifies that the term will be measured from the date of first application in Singapore and date of first approval in the EU

[b] Article 14.37 specifies only that the data should be protected for 'a certain period of time' before acknowledging that at the time of the Agreement's entry into force such a period is stipulated as being 'no less than six years by the relevant laws and regulations of each Party'

[c] Footnote 1 of page 232 of the Agreement specifies that each party will define the term 'pharmaceutical product' through their domestic legislation

[d] Footnote 1 of page 395 of the Agreement clarifies that for the EU 'pharmaceutical products' refers to medical products as defined in Regulation 469/2009, but does not clarify what the term means for Japan

5.3.1 *Discussion of US-Led Trade Agreements*

As discussed above, the US has been the major proponent of test data exclusivity in trade agreements, negotiating by far the largest number of such agreements. Some of these agreements are 'treaties' (all agreements signed before 2000, with the exception of NAFTA), while some are more comprehensive 'Free Trade Agreements' (all agreements signed after 2000, with the exception of the bilateral trade agreements with Vietnam and Laos). This distinction is purely a matter of domestic US law; for the purposes of international law, all US trade agreements are equally valid.

The US-led agreements are typically more comprehensive than the European-led agreements, covering issues such as indirect reliance on submitted data and the protection of foreign data not dealt with by the Europeans. The test data exclusivity provisions found in US-led agreements are also remarkably consistent—Drahos explains the general consistency of US trade agreements with reference to America's domestic politics; US trade agreements must receive domestic legislative approval ('only' a two-thirds supermajority in the Senate in the case of treaties, the approval of Congress as a whole in the case of FTAs), and US trade negotiators are aware that once an agreement has been approved, subsequent agreements with provisions modelled on its terms are much more likely to succeed domestically.[13] This creates a strong incentive for standardisation of terms in US-led agreements. In addition, the economic dominance of the US places US negotiators in a stronger bargaining position compared to EFTA and the EU; it would consequently be expected that US negotiators would have to compromise or amend their template provisions less frequently than other actors.

While consistent, the test data exclusivity provisions of US-led trade agreements can be divided into several distinct phases. The first US-led agreements with provisions on test data exclusivity were signed even before TRIPS itself, although as previously mentioned these provisions were clearly closely modelled on the bracketed test data protection provision of the 1990 Brussels Draft of TRIPS.[14] As noted above, all early US-led agreements with test data exclusivity provisions were bilateral IP treaties with the notable exception of NAFTA—in line with general US trade policy at the time, which focussed on bilateral treaties (often referred to as 'investment', 'trade relations' or 'intellectual property' treaties) rather than full FTAs. These treaties typically only specify a basic five-year term of test data exclusivity for new chemical entities and the prohibition of disclosure of submitted test data except under certain circumstances.

The next phase of US-negotiated test data exclusivity provisions began with the full FTAs signed from the early 2000s onwards; the test data exclusivity provisions in these agreements are typically more comprehensive, for example requiring protection for new clinical information and prohibiting indirect reliance. References to public health and the Doha Declaration begin to appear in this period as well, initially in the form of side letters issued by the USTR but later incorporated into the text of the agreement.

Three FTAs signed with Latin American countries (Peru, Colombia and Panama) in 2006 and 2007 are notably less restrictive than their predecessors; this reflects the so-called 'New Trade Policy (NTP)'[15] that House Democrats imposed on President George W Bush as part of negotiations over the renewal of so-called 'trade promotion authority' (TPA) necessary to conclude a number of FTAs.[16] In addition to matters relating to labour law, the environment, investment, government procurement and port security, the NTP set out that the period of test data exclusivity in US-led trade agreements should not generally extend beyond the period of

[13] Drahos (2011), p. 794.

[14] Lehman (1993), p. 408.

[15] USTR (2007).

[16] TPA is a 'fast-track' authority for the President to negotiate FTAs which Congress can then approve or reject (but not amend), and has regularly been bestowed on US presidents since the 1970s. Fergusson (2015), p. 27.

protection for the same product in the US, that the FTAs should contain clarifications that the parties may implement exceptions to the rules for protecting test data if necessary to protect public health, and should affirm the parties' mutual commitment to the Doha Declaration.[17] These are reflected to a greater or lesser extent in the NTP deals, which explicitly do not require protection for new indications, do not restrict indirect reliance and provide that the term of test data exclusivity may be measured from its approval in the other party under certain circumstances.

The US signed no further FTAs between 2008 and 2015. During this period, the Obama administration focused on larger multilateral deals, eventually leading to the signing of the 12-country Trans-Pacific Partnership in 2016. In 2018, the US signed the United States-Mexico-Canada Agreement (USMCA); a new trade agreement designed to replace NAFTA.[18] While some commentators at the time had suggested that the NTP would serve as a 'baseline' for future US deals,[19] both the TPP and the USMCA initially contained some of the highest levels of test data exclusivity found in a FTA. The TPP required, for the first time in a US-led trade agreement, an explicit requirement to provide test data exclusivity to data submitted in association with biologics. The USMCA increased the level of test data exclusivity that had been required by NAFTA to levels similar to those of the TPP. However, the high standards of test data exclusivity in both agreements have proved short lived; in 2017 President Donald Trump withdrew the US from the TPP; as a result, the remaining 11 signatories of the original agreement revived the trade deal as the 'Comprehensive and Progressive Agreement for Trans-Pacific Partnership' (CPTPP), suspending a number of provisions which the non-American parties to the agreement had opposed, including those on test data exclusivity.[20] In 2019, following opposition to ratifying the original text of the USMCA by the Democrat-controlled US Congress due to concerns over the impact of the agreement on drug prices, labour rights and the environment (the same issues raised by the NTP),[21] a Protocol of Amendment to the USMCA removed the provisions requiring protection for biologics and NCI.[22]

---

[17] USTR (2007).

[18] Agreement Between the United States of America, the United Mexican States, and Canada (2018).

[19] Fergusson (2015), p. 27.

[20] Comprehensive and Progressive Agreement for Trans-Pacific Partnership (2018), Article 2; Annex Article 7(e–f).

[21] Labonté et al. (2020).

[22] Protocol of Amendment to the Agreement Between the United States of America, the United Mexican States, and Canada (2019) 3(D)(III); 3(E).

5.3.1.1 Term and Scope of Protection

Perhaps the most striking example of the consistency of the US-led agreements is the near-uniformity of the term of protection for NCEs—five years of protection in all cases with the exception of the FTA with Jordan, which had committed itself to five years of test data exclusivity protection for NCEs during its accession to the WTO in any case (see Sect. 5.4, below).[23] This, of course, reflects the domestic term of protection for NCEs in the US under the Hatch-Waxman Act.

Most of the US-led agreements signed before 2003 formulate the term as some variation of 'a reasonable period *normally not less* than five years taking account of the nature of the data and the person's efforts and expenditures in producing them'; this language also features in the NTP deals. This theoretically permits an occasional period of under five years; other agreements mandate at least five years protection, which does not. Both formulations permit the grant of terms in excess of five years. However, as discussed in Chap. 6, virtually all jurisdictions with which the US has concluded a trade agreement with test data exclusivity terms simply provide a term of at least five years.

While in most US-led trade agreements the term of protection begins with its approval in the national territory, the NTP deals permit parties to begin the period of exclusivity for a product from the date of its approval in the other party if they themselves process the originator approval for that product in six months of receiving it; this is sometimes referred to as the 'concurrent period' rule.[24] While this is obviously binding on both the US and the other party, in practice the provision is clearly intended as an incentive for the Peruvian, Panamanian and Colombian drug regulatory authorities to process originator drug applications in a timely manner in exchange for a shorter period of exclusivity;[25] this reflects the agreement in the NTP that the period of test data exclusivity in developing countries should not extend beyond the period of protection for the same product in the United States, along with incentives to encourage the other party to process marketing approval applications 'in a timely manner.'[26]

Protection of new clinical information submitted for the approval of a pharmaceutical product containing a previously approved chemical entity has become a common feature of US FTAs since 2004—with the exception of the NTP deals (all of which explicitly *exclude* data submitted with respect to 'a pharmaceutical product that contains a chemical entity that has been previously approved in the territory of

[23] US-Jordan FTA (2000) Article 22; WTO, *Report of the Working Party on the Accession of the Hashemite Kingdom of Jordan to the World Trade Organization*, WT/ACC/JOR/33 (3 December 1999), para 215.

[24] US-Peru TPA (2006) Article 16.10, US-Colombia TPA (2006) Article 16.10 and US-Panama TPA (2007) Article 15.10.

[25] Roffe and Vivas-Eugui (2007), p. 15.

[26] USTR (2007).

the Party')[27] and the CAFTA-DR agreement, all US-led FTAs signed since 2004 have included such a provision, requiring at least three years of protection in all cases; again, this reflects the domestic US legal situation, although these were ultimately removed from both the TPP and USMCA. The basic five-year term of protection for NCEs in most US-led agreements applies to products which do not contain a previously approved chemical entity, a negative test—this alternative provision effectively flips the requirement for protection to a more easily satisfied positive requirement to simply contain at least one chemical entity that has not been previously approved, even if other chemical entities within the product have been previously approved.

While most of the US bilateral treaties[28] and NAFTA require protection against *reliance* on the submitted test data during the exclusivity period, i.e., data exclusivity *per se*, most US-led FTAs only require the parties not to *approve* an abbreviated application based on the submitted test data during the exclusivity period, i.e. market exclusivity. The only exceptions to this amongst the later US-led FTAs are the NTP agreements—unusual, given that the intention of the NTP was to make the test data exclusivity provisions of these agreements *less* restrictive than other US-led FTAs.[29]

5.3.1.2 Biologics

Protection for data submitted in association with biologics only featured as a major issue in the two most recent US-led FTAs, the TPP and USMCA. The US had originally pushed for 12 years of protection for data submitted in association with biologics in the TPP, but the final agreement gave parties the option of providing either eight years of protection, or five years supplemented through 'other means' to deliver a 'comparable outcome in the market,' recognising that 'market circumstances also contribute to effective market protection.'[30] This was an obvious diplomatic fudge, the meaning of which was never clarified during the negotiations themselves. It has been suggested that had the US remained in the TPP, it would have sought to 'clarify' what this meant with the parties which did not provide eight years of protection through side letters and bilateral negotiation;[31] not a dissimilar strategy to the US approach to Article 39.3. The US was more successful regarding

[27] US-Peru TPA (2006) Article 16.10, US-Colombia TPA (2006) Article 16.10 and US-Panama TPA (2007) Article 15.10.

[28] The one exception appears to be the Latvia Trade Relations and Intellectual Property Rights Agreement (1994) Article VIII(4)(b).

[29] This may have been an accidental consequence of reverting to the (generally) less restrictive test data exclusivity provisions of the bilateral treaties of the 1990s when the NTP agreements were amended in June 2007; the pre-2007 drafts of the agreements use the more typical prohibition on using the data to approve an abbreviated application before the end of the exclusivity term. See e.g., Article 16.10 of the January 6 Draft of the US-Peru Trade Promotion Authority.

[30] TPP (2016) Article 18.51.1.a-b.

[31] Artecona and Plank-Brumback (2016), p. 38.

negotiating a longer term of test data exclusivity protection in the USMCA, which initially required at least ten years of exclusivity for biologics prior to its amendment in 2019.[32] In contrast to small molecule drugs, both agreements explicitly stated that the parties were not required to protect information submitted regarding previously approved biologics.[33]

All other US-led FTAs are silent on the issue of whether data submitted with respect to biologics is protected, and it seems likely that biologics are beyond the scope of these agreements given that most use the phrase 'new chemical entity', a term which within the US refers exclusively to small molecule drugs as discussed at Sect. 4.4.2.1 (the term 'new active moiety' is typically used to refer to both new small molecule drugs and new biologic drugs).[34] This silence on the issue of biologics is presumably a result of these agreements being negotiated prior to the widespread adoption of abbreviated approval pathways for biologics; the US itself had no domestic legislation on biosimilars and biologic test data until the 2009 Biologics Price Competition and Innovation Act.

5.3.1.3 Article 39.3 Criteria

Over time, US-led agreements have moved away from the TRIPS formula of only requiring protection for test data that is undisclosed, the result of considerable effort and submitted in association with a new chemical entity. The earliest agreements tend to include all three (although a number of these agreements omit the requirement to be associated with a new chemical entity)—unsurprising, given that the test data exclusivity provisions of these agreements were modelled so closely on the Brussels Draft of TRIPS. However, only a requirement for newness appears in virtually all recent US-led agreements.

5.3.1.4 Additional Requirements

Over time, US-led agreements have increasingly included a number of additional measures seemingly aimed at preventing policies that would undermine the protection afforded by test data exclusivity; indirect reliance on the fact of approval rather than use of the submitted data itself, reliance on foreign data, and limiting the term of test data exclusivity to a patent associated with the pharmaceutical product in question. Aside from the NTP deals, all US-led FTAs since 2003 have explicitly prevented indirect reliance on evidence of marketing approval, and all US-led FTAs since 2004 have prohibited the limiting of the test data exclusivity term to that of an associated patent.

---

[32] USMCA (2018) Article 20.F.14.

[33] TPP (2016) Chapter 18, Footnote 59, USMCA (2018) Chapter 20, Footnote 4.

[34] Shaikh (2016), p. 82.

The provisions on protection for foreign data have undergone a slightly more complicated evolution, although again the general direction is one of increasing protection aside from the NTP agreements. Most early US trade agreements state that data submitted in the other party of the agreement is to be protected for a reasonable period from the date of approval in that party, although a small number of agreements between 1994 and 2003 are silent on the issue.[35] Since then, the requirement to protect foreign data has been a feature of all US-led trade agreements. The 2004 agreements with Australia and Singapore both specify that foreign data cannot be relied upon until five years (for NCEs) or three years (for new clinical information) from the date of foreign or domestic approval, whichever is later; a restrictive term, to be sure, but one that would at least eventually permit foreign reliance if the originator never sought approval in Singapore or Australia.[36] With the exception of the NTP deals, all other US-led FTAs specify that the data cannot be relied upon until five years after its *domestic* approval; this would appear to make reliance on foreign data impossible before the same data has been submitted domestically, essentially rendering reliance on foreign data pointless as the test data exclusivity protection for both domestic and foreign data would end simultaneously. This also suggests that if the data is never submitted in the relevant jurisdiction, an abbreviated application will be impossible—only the CAFTA-DR agreement contains a provision to address such a situation, adding the qualification that in order to obtain this protection, a party may require that the individual or corporation providing the information in the other territory must seek approval in the territory of the party within five years of obtaining marketing approval in the other territory.[37] The NTP agreements are somewhat unclear on the issue of foreign reliance as the concurrent rule does not explicitly state that foreign data is generally protected rather than protected only when the six-month deadline for originator approval is met.[38] However, it seems likely that it is; if not, the concurrent rule would incentivise the Latin American countries to process such applications *more* slowly than usual and reduce the entire provision to absurdity. It therefore seems likely that the NTP agreements require protection of foreign data from the date of domestic approval *except* when the concurrent rule applies.

There is little evidence that any of the practices blocked by these 'additional requirements' were widespread amongst those countries with which the US has concluded FTAs; indeed, in the case of reliance on foreign data several of the US-led agreements make it clear in footnotes that neither party permits this practice and these provisions are merely aimed at preventing such a policy being established in

---

[35] US-Trinidad and Tobago IPR Agreement (1994); US-Nicaragua IPR Agreement (1998) Article 9; US-Vietnam Bilateral Trade Agreement (2000) Article 9; US-Laos Bilateral Trade Relations Act (2003); US-Chile FTA (2003) Article 17.10.

[36] US-Singapore FTA (2003) Article 16.8; US-Australia FTA (2004) Article 17.10.

[37] CAFTA-DR (2004) Article 15.10.

[38] US-Colombia TPA (2006) Article 16.10; US-Peru TPA (2006) Article 16.10; US-Panama TPA (2007) Article 15.10.

the future.[39] These provisions seem to be reactions to particular incidents such as the Canadian judgment in the 1999 case of *Bayer v Attorney General* [40] that found indirect reliance on submitted data to be legal under Canadian law (discussed at Sect. 4.4.1) and the practice of some European countries of tying the term of exclusivity to the term of the patent over a product under the old Directive 87/21/EEC (both Canada and the EU have since amended their legislation in such a way that these practices are no longer possible).[41]

5.3.1.5 Exceptions

Almost none of the US-led trade agreements contain explicit exceptions to test data exclusivity (although the TPP contained several country specific exceptions permitting certain parties to retain pre-existing flexibilities around test data exclusivity; see Sect. 5.3.1.6). However, they also contain few, if any, explicit restrictions on providing exceptions. A few of the US-led trade agreements prevent the disclosure of the submitted test data (already unambiguously prohibited by Article 39.3),[42] but most of these agreements also include the flexibilities included in Article 39.3; that data may be disclosed if necessary to protect the public or if steps are taken to protect the data against unfair commercial use (although several agreements signed between the mid-1990s and mid-2000s permit disclosure *only* 'where necessary to protect the public'; a TRIPS-plus restriction, although one that would still permit the disclosure of submitted data in order to facilitate the compulsory licensing of a pharmaceutical if needed).[43] This is not redundant, as restricting the use of these flexibilities would not reduce the minimum level of intellectual property protection provided for in TRIPS. Additionally, it is worth noting that both the US-Australia FTA and CAFTA-DR agreement further require that governments continue to provide test data exclusivity for submitted test data even if it is subsequently disclosed by a government. Spina Alì takes the view that the FTAs with Singapore and Australia impose restrictions on the compulsory licensing of submitted test data because both these agreements state in their respective articles on patent law that when a compulsory license is issued in the case of a national emergency, the party may not require the patent owner to transfer/provide undisclosed information or technical 'know how' related to a patented invention without the consent of the patent owner; however, this view neglects the fact that submitted test data by its very definition has already been

[39] See, for example, the Australian and Moroccan FTAs, in which a footnote explains that neither party currently permits marketing pharmaceutical products on the basis of foreign approval); US-Australia FTA (2004) Footnote 17–18; US-Morocco FTA (2004) Footnote 15-12, 15-13.

[40] *Bayer v The Attorney General of Canada* 84 CPR (3d) 129.

[41] Canada, Food and Drug Regulations (as amended) C.08.004.1(2); EU, Directive 2004/27/EC.

[42] NAFTA, the US-Jordan FTA, US-Chile FTA, CAFTA-DR, US-Colombia TPA, US-Peru TPA and US-Panama TPA.

[43] The agreements with Trinidad and Tobago, Nicaragua, Vietnam, Laos, Chile and the CAFTA-DR.

transferred to the competent authorities within a jurisdiction and as such will be unaffected by prohibitions on data transfer.[44] The US-led trade agreements are therefore largely silent on the issue of exceptions to the test data exclusivity provisions.

Some commentators, including Correa, see the silence of the US agreements (and, as discussed below, many of the EFTA and EU FTAs) as *restricting* the ability of the various parties to enacte flexibilities and exceptions to test data exclusivity—essentially, the view that in the absence of provisions enabling exceptions to the test data exclusivity right, any exception is a breach of the agreement.[45] Against this, Spina Alì offers the counterargument that in the case of such silence, restrictions cannot be read into the agreements.[46] Strengthening this point is the fact that many of the US-led trade agreements affirm the rights of the parties to take measures to protect public health in line with the TRIPS Agreement and Doha Declaration. These affirmations have evolved over time; while those US-led agreements signed in the 1990s and early 2000s contain no such affirmation (unsurprising, given that they were signed prior to the Doha Declaration), from the FTA with Chile onwards references to the rights of parties to take TRIPS-compliant flexibilities with regards to intellectual property have been common. In the FTAs with Bahrain, Morocco and Oman, as well as CAFTA-DR, this affirmation does not appear in the text of the agreement but rather a side letter issued by the USTR, which states that the obligations of the IP chapter of the agreement do not affect the ability of the parties to take necessary measures to protect public health , 'in particular concerning cases involving HIV/AIDS, tuberculosis, malaria and other epidemic', recognising the Doha Declaration, stating the intellectual property chapter does not prevent effective utilisation of the TRIPS/Health solution and promising that if 'an amendment to TRIPS enters into force and a party's application of a measure in conformity with that amendment' violates the IP chapter, the parties would immediately consult to adapt the chapter as appropriate.[47] The NTP agreements all contain a provision in the intellectual property chapter acknowledging Doha and stating that the parties may take actions to protect public health 'by promoting access to medicines for all'—which notably does not restrict such actions to those necessary to protect public health. In addition, they contain a specific provision in the test data exclusivity article itself stating that nothing in that article will prevent the parties taking action in accordance with TRIPS. Both the general recognition of the right of the parties to protect public health and the test data exclusivity specific provision on public health

[44] Spina Alì (2018), p. 751. Spina Alì also takes the view that this prohibition is not required as indicated by the word 'may' although this interpretation also seems dubious (while the word 'may' does indicate a choice, the phrase 'may not' is commonly used as an absolute refusal (as in 'you may not leave the country').

[45] Correa (2006), p. 88.

[46] Spina Alì (2018), p. 751.

[47] US-Oman FTA, Side Letter on Public Health (2006); US-Bahrain FTA, Side Letter on Public Health (2004); US-Morocco FTA, Side Letter on Public Health (2004).

have been carried into the Korea FTA as well as the TPP and USMCA,[48] and now appears to be part of the standard US trade-agreement template.

These public health provisions do not create flexibilities themselves; rather, they simply confirm that the general flexibilities under the TRIPS Agreement remain permissible. This of course moves the issue to what is actually permissible under TRIPS—but as discussed at Sect. 4.4.3, the TRIPS Agreement gives members wide discretion as to implementing their obligations with regard to submitted test data, and at the very least permits waivers of test data exclusivity or compulsory licensing of submitted test data provided that the right holder is fairly compensated. However, the absence of explicit exceptions is still troubling. As already discussed with respect to Article 39.3, unclear obligations raise the cost of taking regulatory action, not least because they often enable the other party to make a *prima facie* case that the action they oppose breaches the obligation. Peru has regularly been criticised over its test data exclusivity regulations by the USTR's Special 301 Report, seemingly due to flexibilities and exceptions in the domestic Peruvian test data exclusivity law—despite the inclusion of a provision acknowledging that the parties understand that the obligations of the intellectual property chapter of the US-Peru TPA 'do not and should not prevent a Party from taking measures to protect public health by promoting access to medicines for all' and that 'this Chapter can and should be interpreted and implemented in a manner supportive of each Party's right to protect public health and, in particular, to promote access to medicines for all.'[49]

5.3.1.6 Concluding Remarks on Test Data Exclusivity Provisions in US-Led Trade Agreements

As can be seen from the above, while test data exclusivity provisions in US-led trade agreements have remained largely consistent, they have gone through a number of distinct stages of evolution. The test data exclusivity terms in the agreements of the 1990s tended to require 'only' five years of exclusivity, prohibition on disclosure and protection of foreign data for as long as it was protected in the foreign jurisdiction—however, requirements to protect new clinical information, prohibitions on indirect reliance on data, protection for foreign data from the date of domestic approval and prohibitions on linking the term of protection to that of associated patents all became common in the FTAs the US began concluding in the early-to-mid 2000s. The NTP deals stepped back from many of these more restrictive terms and included the concurrent rule, a genuinely useful adaption to test data exclusivity rights for developing countries. However, the two most recently signed US-led trade agreements both reverted back to the restrictive language of the pre-NTP deals and indeed incorporated longer terms of protection for data submitted with respect to biologics at the time of their signing, even if this was subsequently

[48] US-Korea FTA (2007); TPP (2017) and USMCA (2018).

[49] US-Peru TPA (2006) Article 16.13.2(a).

wholly suspended (in the case of the TPP) and partially removed (in the case of the USMCA). The one exception to this trend of increasing restrictiveness is the now ubiquitous inclusion of provisions safeguarding the TRIPS and Doha flexibilities regarding public health; however, while these provisions provide some interpretive value, they still leave doubt as to exactly what flexibilities and exceptions are permitted regarding test data exclusivity under US-led agreements. The reprimanding of FTA partners which utilise such flexibilities for supposedly inadequate protection of submitted test data in Special 301 Reports perhaps suggests that these public health statements are largely seen as symbolic but empty concessions by the US.[50]

It should be noted that the TPP did contain a number of country-specific exceptions regarding test data exclusivity (as well as other intellectual property rights); annex 18-B of the agreement specified that nothing in the test data exclusivity provisions would prevent Chile from maintaining a pre-existing article of its law on test data exclusivity which suspends test data exclusivity protection in certain circumstances and denies test data exclusivity to any product which has been approved in a foreign country for more than 12 months at the time of the submission of its application for approval in Chile;[51] annex 18-C permitted Malaysia to continue to require an applicant to commence the process of obtaining marketing approval for pharmaceutical products within 18 months of the date that the product is first granted marketing approval in any country in order to be eligible for test data exclusivity protection,[52] and annex 18-D permitted Peru to continue to use the concurrent period rule which first appeared in the US-Peru TPA.[53] This suggests a willingness by the US to retain existing flexibilities around test data exclusivity in specific cases, but an unwillingness to extend these to other parties going forward; an anonymous TPP negotiator has claimed that proposals related to ‘time windows’ for all parties were made during the negotiations, but in the end taken out and only retained for Malaysia and Chile in the annexes of the TPP.[54]

The impact on the globalisation of test data exclusivity of the two most recently signed US-led FTAs, the TPP and USMCA, is in some ways limited. The test data exclusivity provisions of the TPP have now been suspended, and in any case the parties to the agreement largely consisted of countries with which the US had already

---

[50] See e.g., USTR (2016).

[51] TPP (2016) Annex 18-B. The article in question is article 91 of Law 19.039 on Industrial Property, which suspends test data exclusivity when the owner has exploited that data in a manner contrary to fair competition, for reasons of extreme urgency, when the pharmaceutical product with which the data is associated is subject to a compulsory license, when the product in question has not been commercialised in Chile after 12 months of its registration or when the application for market authorisation in Chile is filed 12 months after the first international market authorisation.

[52] TPP (2016) Annex 18-C.

[53] TPP (2016) Annex 18-D.

[54] Spina Alì (2017), p. 269.

concluded trade agreements.[55] The USMCA is in many respects a renegotiation of NAFTA, which already contained test data exclusivity requirements, and the more restrictive provisions relating to biologics and new clinical information have now been removed. However, it must be recalled that the failure of the TPP was entirely unrelated to its provisions on test data exclusivity, and that the amendment of the test data exclusivity provisions of the USMCA was the result of domestic political wrangling in the US. In both cases, the US successfully negotiated considerable increases in test data exclusivity standards over previous agreements with the other parties. If the US continues to negotiate further trade agreements with test data exclusivity provisions, the restrictiveness of such provisions seems more likely to be dictated by domestic US politics than resistance by negotiating partners.

5.3.2 Discussion of EFTA and Swiss-Led Agreements

Despite being smaller by far than the US or EU, the EFTA states have concluded a significant number of FTAs that include test data exclusivity provisions (or in some cases test data exclusivity *adjacent* provisions); 17 in total, with Switzerland having negotiated a further two by itself. However, as noted above many of these agreements are subsequent to earlier US or (less commonly) EU agreements, and often do not go beyond the requirements of the previous agreement or the existing practice of the other party regarding submitted test data.

The reduced political and economic clout of EFTA has also resulted in test data exclusivity terms that are, generally speaking, less restrictive than those in US-led agreements. Several of the early EFTA-led trade deals with test data exclusivity terms explicitly permit the parties to protect the submitted test data through a liability model as an alternative to providing exclusivity. As has already been noted, the EFTA-led agreements made with developing countries in Europe and its immediate geographic neighbourhood have tended to contain more restrictive test data exclusivity obligations. However, test data exclusivity obligations in EFTA-negotiated deals with countries outside of this area tend to be limited in scope (the relatively restrictive test data exclusivity terms of the EFTA agreement with Hong Kong are a notable exception).[56] While Switzerland has successfully negotiated test data exclusivity terms with both of Asia's largest economies, these provisions essentially restate the existing practices of both Japan and China regarding test data exclusivity (although the Chinese agreement does state that biologic data must also be protected, which China's earlier commitment to provide test data exclusivity made during its

[55] Brunei, Japan and New Zealand being the only countries with which the US had not concluded a previous agreement with test data exclusivity provision; Japan of course has provided *de facto* data exclusivity since 1968 and New Zealand has had a test data exclusivity law since 1994 (New Zealand, the Medicines Amendment Act 1994).

[56] EFTA-Hong Kong FTA (2011) Annex XII Article 4.

accession to the WTO did not).[57] Test data exclusivity terms in EFTA/Swiss-led agreements are also less comprehensive than US agreements, typically specifying only the term of protection.

Despite this, test data exclusivity terms in EFTA-led agreements do seem to be becoming more restrictive over time; the EFTA agreements with a number of Balkan countries require upwards of a decade of protection. The most recently concluded EFTA-led agreement with provisions on test data exclusivity at time of writing is an FTA with Indonesia, a huge, non-European country which had made no previous commitments regarding test data exclusivity and which previously had no domestic test data exclusivity laws. While the provisions on the protection of submitted pharmaceutical test data are amongst the vaguest of any of the FTAs discussed in this section, this nonetheless represents a considerable development in EFTA's promotion of test data exclusivity through trade agreements. It remains to be seen what impact this will have on Indonesia's domestic laws in practice, and whether this foreshadows increased promotion of test data exclusivity by EFTA outside of Europe and its immediate geographic neighbourhood.

5.3.2.1 Alternatives to Test Data Exclusivity

Perhaps the most interesting feature of the EFTA agreements is that several of the early agreements provide for the possibility of protecting submitted test data through a means other than test data exclusivity. While the agreements with Lebanon, Tunisia and Korea all contain provisions stating that submitted test data should be protected through test data exclusivity, they also provide the alternative of protecting submitted test data through a compensation-based regime in which subsequent applicants can rely on submitted data at any point, provided that the applicant compensates them 'adequately' (what constitutes adequate compensation is left undefined in all three agreements).[58] This is essentially a liability-based cost-sharing approach to protecting submitted test data of the sort proposed by Reichman.[59]

While it does not mention a cost-sharing scheme, the EFTA-Egypt FTA also seems to envisage the possibility that submitted test data might be protected through a means other than test data exclusivity; the FTA specifies that the parties will protect submitted test data against disclosure and unfair commercial use 'until it is no longer confidential, or for a period not exceeding five years, whichever comes first,' but does not go into any specifics as to how this should be achieved. The fact that a time period is specified distinguishes this from the vague commitments to respect Article

---

[57] China-Switzerland FTA (2013) Article 11.11.

[58] EFTA-Korea FTA (2005), Annex XIII Article 3; EFTA-Lebanon FTA (2004) Annex V Article 4; EFTA-Tunisia FTA (2004) Annex V Article 4.

[59] See further Reichman (2009).

39.3 found in some other EFTA (and indeed EU) trade agreements,[60] and suggests the parties view Article 39.3 as requiring more than protection against misappropriation, but the provision does not explicitly require test data exclusivity. It is unclear what protection Egypt does provide to submitted test data—its national law is also ambiguous,[61] and the USTR has repeatedly urged Egypt to clarify how it protects submitted pharmaceutical test data through the Special 301 Report.[62]

No EFTA-led agreements with test data exclusivity obligations signed after 2007 permit cost-sharing as an alternative means of protecting pharmaceutical test data. However, it is worth noting that at least ten post-2007 EFTA-led agreements permit the possibility of a compensatory regime for data submitted to gain marketing approval for agricultural products.[63]

5.3.2.2 Term and Scope of Protection

In contrast to the US FTAs, the EFTA and Swiss-led agreements show considerable variance regarding the required term of protection. Both the earliest and most recent EFTA-led agreements specify no term at all—the EFTA-Korea FTA requires only that the data be protected for 'an adequate number of years' as determined by 'the relevant law and regulations of the Parties,'[64] and the FTA with Indonesia states that the parties shall 'process subsequent [pharmaceutical] applications and grant marketing approval only after a period of time defined in the domestic laws and regulations,'[65] with the period being again unspecified (it is worth noting that the equivalent provisions for agricultural products explicitly mandate a ten-year period of test data exclusivity).[66] In addition, the Swiss agreement with Japan merely requires both parties to protect submitted test data for a 'certain period of time', noting that at the time of the agreement's entry into force such a period is stipulated as being 'no less than six years by the relevant laws of each Party'; as the stipulation comes from the national laws and regulations of the parties rather than the agreement itself, this seems to impose little by way of an international obligation.[67]

---

[60] See, for example, the EFTA-Philippines FTA (2016) Annex XVIII Article 8.

This simply restates the requirements of Article 39.3 before stating that the parties will work to address the issue is a dispute arises in the future—no reference to time-limited rights are made.

[61] Egypt, Intellectual Property Law No. 82 (2002).

[62] For recent examples, see USTR (2017, 2018, 2019).

[63] These are the FTAs with Colombia, Albania, Ukraine, Ecuador, Serbia, Bosnia, Hong Kong, Montenegro, Georgia and Peru.

[64] EFTA-Korea FTA (2004), Annex XIII Article 3.

[65] EFTA-Indonesia FTA (2018), Annex XVII, Article 6(2)(b).

[66] EFTA-Indonesia FTA (2018), Annex XVII, Article 6(1)(b). The EFTA-Indonesia FTA has yet to be ratified as of the time of writing, and it remains to be seen how Indonesia implements this provision in practice.

[67] Switzerland-Japan FTA (2009) Article 121.

Other EFTA and Swiss-led deals with countries outside of Europe and its immediate neighbourhood do specify actual terms of protection, but these typically represent the pre-existing practice or commitments of the other Party; this is the case in the agreements with Ecuador,[68] Colombia,[69] China[70] and Turkey.[71]

In trade agreements made with other countries in Europe and its immediate vicinity, on the other hand, EFTA-led agreements impose some of the longest terms of protection found in any FTA. The term of protection is eight years of data exclusivity *per se* in all EFTA-led agreements with Balkan countries;[72] in the cases of the agreements with Bosnia and Montenegro this is concurrent with a further ten years of market exclusivity.[73] In addition, the agreements with a number of European countries require a one-year extension to the term of protection if, during the initial period of protection, an authorisation for one or more new therapeutic indications which are held to bring a 'significant clinical benefit' is obtained by the marketing authorisation holder.[74] This closely matches the so-called '8 + 2 + 1' test data exclusivity term used by the EEA members of EFTA.[75]

Outside of Europe and its immediate vicinity, EFTA/Swiss-led deals do not require protection for subsequently submitted data; indeed, the agreement with Colombia explicitly states that the parties do not need to apply the test data exclusivity provision to a pharmaceutical product which contains a chemical entity that has been previously approved in the territory of the Party[76] (a similar term is found in the earlier Colombian deal with the US).[77]

5.3.2.3 Biologics

Provisions explicitly requiring test data exclusivity for data submitted regarding biologics appear in EFTA-led trade deals much earlier than in US-led trade deals. As

[68] EFTA-Ecuador FTA (2018), Annex XVI Article 6.

[69] EFTA-Colombia FTA (2008), Article 6.11.

[70] China-Switzerland Free Trade Agreement (2013), Article 11.11.

[71] EFTA-Turkey FTA (2018), Annex XX Article 6.

[72] EFTA-Albania FTA (2009), Annex V Article 5; EFTA-Serbia FTA (2010) Annex VI Article 5; EFTA-Montenegro FTA (2011), Annex VI Article 6; EFTA-Bosnia FTA (2013), Article VII Article 6.

[73] EFTA-Bosnia FTA (2013), Article VII Article 6; EFTA-Montenegro FTA (2011), Annex VI Article 6.

[74] EFTA-Bosnia FTA (2013), Article VII Article 6; EFTA-Montenegro FTA (2011), Annex VI Article 6; EFTA-Ukraine FTA (2010), Annex XIII Article 5; EFTA-Georgia FTA (2016), Annex XV Article 6.

[75] That is, Norway, Iceland and Lichtenstein. Switzerland applies a similar system of eight years data exclusivity *per se* concurrent with ten years market exclusivity, although it also provides a separate period of between three and 10 years of protection for new indications.

[76] EFTA-Colombia FTA (2008) Article 6.11.

[77] US-Colombia TPA (2006) Article 16.10.

discussed at Sect. 5.3.3.2, this is also true of the EU; this likely reflects the earlier adoption of abbreviated approval pathways for biosimilars and test data exclusivity rights for biologic data by the Europeans. Five EFTA-led trade agreements (all made with developing countries in Europe and its immediate vicinity with the exception of the agreement with Hong Kong) explicitly require protection for data associated with biologics,[78] as does the Switzerland-China FTA.[79] The EFTA-led agreement with Ecuador appears to exclude data submitted in association with biologics from the scope of protection, although this is not explicit.[80] Unlike the US-led agreements, EFTA-led agreements which require protection for biologic test data simply state biologic products may also benefit from the 'basic' term of protection—this reflects the domestic approach of the EFTA states to biologic test data protection.

5.3.2.4 Article 39.3 Criteria

The EFTA deals have been less inclusive of the Article 39.3 criteria than US-led agreements. Many EFTA-led agreements simply require that the data be 'undisclosed', although most agreements since 2011 have also included a requirement that the origination of the data have involved considerable effort. Those deals which require all three of the Article 39.3 criteria have largely been countries far outside Europe and are seemingly modelled on earlier US test data exclusivity provisions.[81]

5.3.2.5 Additional Requirements

As noted above, the EFTA/Swiss-led agreements are considerably less comprehensive than those of the US. None of the EFTA-led agreements prohibit tying test data exclusivity to the term of associated patents, for example. The only EFTA-led agreements which deal with foreign approvals are those with Peru and Colombia.[82] These agreements repeat the concurrent period rule which appears in the US-led

[78] EFTA-Bosnia FTA (2013), Article VII Article 6; EFTA-Montenegro FTA (2011), Annex VI Article 6; EFTA-Georgia FTA (2016), Annex XV Article 6; EFTA-Turkey FTA (2018), Annex XX Article 6.

[79] China-Switzerland FTA (2013), Article 11.11; EFTA-Hong Kong FTA (2011), Annex XI Article 4.

[80] The agreement states that data submitted regarding the marketing approval of pharmaceutical or agricultural chemical products which utilise 'chemical or biological entities' must be protected from disclosure, test data exclusivity is only required for data submitted regarding 'pharmaceutical or of agricultural chemical products which contain new chemical entities.' EFTA-Ecuador FTA (2018) Annex XVI Article 6.

[81] The agreements with Chile, Colombia, Ecuador, Peru, Korea and Egypt. Note that all aside from Korea and Egypt had a previous agreement with the US.

[82] EFTA-Colombia (2008), Article 6.11; EFTA-Peru FTA (2010), Article 6.11.

FTAs with those countries (an approach also taken by the later EU-led agreement with those countries);[83] these provisions were presumably inserted at Peru and Colombia's request in order to safeguard the flexibility secured in their FTAs with the US.[84] The EFTA agreement with Tunisia states that the term of protection should not exceed the term of protection in the country of origin or export;[85] this is presumably motivated by the same concerns as motivated the concurrent period rule.

Unlike US-led agreements, EFTA/Swiss agreements have little to say on the topic of indirect reliance. Only the Chilean FTA prohibits 'indirect' reliance on submitted test data, and even in this case, this appears to be because the test data exclusivity provisions of the EFTA-Chile deal are largely modelled on the test data exclusivity provisions of the US-Chile deal, which was signed 20 days before it.[86]

5.3.2.6 Exceptions

The EFTA/Swiss-led agreements are generally silent on the issue of exceptions, although a small number do contain explicit exceptions to test data exclusivity. The agreements with three—Peru, Colombia and Ecuador—all state that the test data exclusivity provisions in those agreements 'shall not prevent a Party from adopting measures in response to the abuse of intellectual property rights or unreasonable trade restrictive practices,' and that, in addition, the parties may take measures to protect public interest or public health in situations of national emergency or extreme urgency in accordance with the Doha Declaration, TRIPS and any further amendments to TRIPS.[87] The agreement with Chile contains a general provision that nothing in the agreement shall be construed as to prevent the adoption or enforcement by any Party of measures necessary to protect human, animal or plant life or health, which would presumably include exceptions to test data exclusivity.[88] In all cases, these references echo references to flexibilities or public health found in earlier FTAs (signed with the US in the case of Peru, Colombia and Chile and with the EU in the case of Ecuador).[89]

---

[83] Trade agreement between the EU and Peru and Colombia (2012), Article 231.

[84] As noted elsewhere, a similar caveat appears in the EU deals with Colombia and Peru as well as in Annex 18-D of the TPP.

[85] EFTA-Tunisia FTA (2004) Annex V Article 4.

[86] The EFTA provision reads 'each Party shall not permit third persons . . . to market a product based on this new chemical entity, on the basis of the approval granted to the person submitting such information', while the US version reads 'the Party shall not permit third parties . . . to market a product based on this new chemical entity, on the basis of the approval granted to the party submitting such information.' EFTA-Chile FTA (2004) Annex XII Article 4; US-Chile FTA (2004) Article 17.10.

[87] EFTA-Peru FTA (2010) Article 6.11, EFTA-Colombia FTA (2008) Article 6.11 and EFTA-Ecuador FTA (2018) Article XVI Article 6.

[88] EFTA-Chile FTA (2003) Article 21(b).

[89] US-Peru TPP (2006); US-Colombia TPA (2006) and US-Chile FTA (2004); Trade Agreement between the EU and Peru, Colombia and Ecuador (2016).

The Agreements with Georgia and Indonesia contain brief provisions stating that the terms of the intellectual property annex are 'without prejudice to the Doha Declaration on the TRIPS Agreement and Public Health',[90] while the agreements with Korea and Chile cite the Doha Declaration as a restriction, requiring that compulsory licenses will not go beyond the terms of the Declaration—in practice, both framings have the same effect.[91] The other EFTA/Swiss agreements do not provide for exceptions to test data exclusivity or mention public health.

Some EFTA-led agreements include a prohibition on the disclosure of submitted test data, but all such agreements permit its disclosure when necessary to protect the public or where reasonable steps are taken to protect it from unfair commercial use in line with Article 39.3.[92]

5.3.2.7 Concluding Remarks on Test Data Exclusivity Provisions in EFTA/Swiss-Led Agreements

As with the US-led agreements, the test data exclusivity terms in the EFTA-led agreements have become more restrictive with time—moving from a policy of permitting alternatives to test data exclusivity to requiring some of the longest terms of protection of any trade agreement discussed in this chapter, particularly with developing countries in Europe and its immediate neighbourhood. EFTA and Switzerland have had significantly less influence regarding the protection of submitted test data outside of Europe, although this may now be changing considering the 2018 FTA with Indonesia. Still, the test data exclusivity terms of that agreement are vague, and other recent EFTA trade negotiations have failed to produce commitments to provide test data exclusivity; for example, the 2016 EFTA-Philippines FTA specifies only that both countries will meet their Article 39.3 obligations and that if an issue pertaining to this arises, the Parties shall work together to address the issue, establishing a mechanism to finding a 'mutually agreeable measure' if necessary.[93]

What explains the prolific number of FTAs with test data exclusivity provisions signed by EFTA/Switzerland, especially when compared to the smaller number of trade agreements with test data exclusivity terms concluded by the much larger EU? Part of the reason almost certainly lies with the fact that although the US and EU both have a larger domestic research-based pharmaceutical industry in absolute terms, the research-based pharmaceutical industry of EFTA forms a larger share of the overall economy. The research-based pharmaceutical industry is especially important for Switzerland—despite being a medium-sized European country,

[90] EFTA-Georgia FTA (2016) Annex XV Article 6; EFTA-Indonesia FTA (2018) Annex XVII Article 6.

[91] EFTA-Korea FTA (2005) Annex XIII Article 3; EFTA-Chile FTA (2004) Annex XII Article 4.

[92] The agreements with Tunisia, Chile, Montenegro, Bosnia, Georgia, Turkey and Indonesia.

[93] EFTA-Philippines FTA (2016), Annex XVIII Article 8.

Switzerland hosts several of the world's largest pharmaceutical companies.[94] Switzerland has a larger GDP than the other three members of EFTA combined, and thus dominates the club economically. As a result, Swiss pharmaceutical businesses presumably find it easier to enrol Swiss and EFTA officials to advocate higher standards of intellectual property for pharmaceutical products in trade deals. The fact that EFTA and Swiss negotiators have often ended up negotiating only weak or vague protections for submitted test data reflects the fact that, while easier to enrol, the negotiating power of the EFTA countries is considerably weaker than that of the US or EU.

5.3.3 *Discussion of EU-Led Agreements*

The EU has signed only nine trade agreements with test data exclusivity terms, the majority of which have been subsequent to a US or EFTA/Swiss-led agreement. Like EFTA, the EU has been able to negotiate more restrictive terms on test data exclusivity with developing countries in Europe and the immediate vicinity; in the case of the EU, these are Georgia, Moldova and Ukraine.[95] In addition to having relatively restrictive terms on test data exclusivity to begin with, these agreements all also contain provisions stating that the non-EU party will undertake to 'align' its legislation concerning submitted test data protection for medicinal products with that of the EU at a later date to be decided by the committee governing the treaty (a number of commitments to align appear in other areas of these agreements as well).[96] This presumably will require the full adoption of the EU's test data exclusivity provisions. All three countries are pursuing membership of the EU, although for various reasons this is unlikely to take place in the immediate future. It is unclear when this alignment will take place.

5.3.3.1 Term and Scope of Protection

The EU-led agreements with Georgia and Moldova set the term of protection at six years and five years of data exclusivity *per se* respectively, in both cases concurrent with at least seven years market exclusivity which may be extended by one year if during the period of data exclusivity *per se* the right holder 'obtains an authorisation for one or more new therapeutic indications considered to be of significant clinical

[94] A 2011 report found that the pharmaceutical industry contributes almost 6% of Switzerland's overall GDP; Vaterlaus et al. (2011).

[95] EU-Georgia Association Agreement (2014) Article 286; EU-Moldova Association Agreement (2014) Article 48 and EU-Ukraine Association Agreement (2014) Article 222.

[96] E.g., EU-Georgia Association Agreement (2014) Article 187; EU-Moldova Association Agreement (2014) Article 315 and EU-Ukraine Association Agreement (2014) Article 57.

benefit in comparison with existing therapies.' These provisions closely reflect the EU's own test data exclusivity laws, which provide concurrent periods of data exclusivity *per se* and market exclusivity and may extend the term of exclusivity when new data is submitted.[97] Most other agreements set the term of protection at five years and do not mention further protections for subsequent data. While the Canadian agreement does contain obligations to provide both a longer period of exclusivity and extensions for subsequent data, these reflect the existing Canadian test data exclusivity laws of the time.[98]

Some recent EU agreements seem to reflect a desire on the part of the EU negotiators to negotiate a longer term of protection; the agreement with Singapore, which sets the term of protection at a minimum of five years, contains a footnote stating that the parties will initiate discussions on the possible extension of this term five years from the agreement's entry into force, seemingly pushing a point of contention downstream,[99] while the agreement with Japan replicates the language of the Swiss-Japan agreement, requiring both parties to protect submitted test data for a 'certain period of time' before noting that at the time of the agreement's entry into force such a period is stipulated as being 'no less than six years by the relevant laws and regulations of each Party.'[100]

5.3.3.2 Biologics

As with EFTA and Switzerland, the test data exclusivity provisions negotiated by the EU often explicitly protect biologic data, and, as with the EFTA-led agreements, the EU-led agreements which require protection for data submitted with respect to biologics protect it through the same term of protection as other pharmaceutical products, rather than a separate, longer term.

The agreements with Canada, Moldova and Korea all state in footnotes that biologic drugs are included in the scope of protection.[101] Protection for biologic data is less clear in other EU-led agreements; while the deals with Ukraine, Georgia and Vietnam do not *explicitly* state that biologic data is to be protected, they do require protection for data submitted with respect to 'medicinal products'—a term which, on its most obvious reading, would appear to include any biologic which is also a medicinal product.[102] In the cases of Ukraine and Georgia, at least, the

[97] Council Directive 2001/83/EC on the Community code relating to medicinal products for human use [2001] Article 10.

[98] See Canada, Food and Drug Regulations (as amended) C.08.004.1.

[99] EU-Singapore FTA (2018) Article 10.33.

[100] EU-Japan Economic Partnership Agreement (2018) Article 14.37.

[101] EU-Canada Comprehensive Economic and Trade Agreement (2016) Article 20.29; EU-Colombia-Peru-Ecuador (2012) Article 231; EU-Korea (2010) FTA Article 10.36.

[102] EU-Georgia Association Agreement (2014) Article 187; EU-Ukraine Association Agreement (2014) Article 57; EU-Vietnam Free Trade Agreement (2019) Article 12.41.

commitment to eventual full alignment with the EU regime suggests that test data exclusivity for biologic data is envisaged. The agreement between the EU and Peru and Colombia states that the EU and Colombia will protect data submitted in association with biologic drugs through test data exclusivity, while Peru will protect such data against disclosure only per Article 39.2 of TRIPS rather than through providing test data exclusivity (this 'exception' was also extended to Ecuador upon its accession to the agreement).[103]

The agreements with Singapore and Japan are also unclear on the issue of protection for biologic data, and imply that the EU was unsuccessful in convincing these countries to commit to the protection of biologics—the Singaporean agreement specifies that each member shall define the term 'pharmaceutical product' through its own legislation,[104] while the Japanese agreement states that while the term 'pharmaceutical product' refers to medical products as defined in Regulation 469/2009 for the purposes of the EU,[105] it does not specify what the term refers to in the case of Japan.[106]

5.3.3.3 Article 39.3 Criteria

EU-led agreements only rarely make reference to the Article 39.3 criteria. Only the agreement with Canada requires protection only for data which meets all three criteria,[107] and some agreements with other European countries simply omit them all together.[108]

5.3.3.4 Additional Requirements

As with the EFTA agreements, the EU-led FTAs cover few of the other matters addressed in US-led FTAs. None of the EU-led FTAs contain provisions preventing parties from limiting the term of test data exclusivity to the term of patents associated with the pharmaceutical product in question. Furthermore, most of the EU-led agreements do not deal with the issue of foreign data, with the exception of the

[103] Trade Agreement between the EU and Peru, Colombia and Ecuador (2012) Article 231.

[104] EU-Singapore FTA (2018) Article 10.33.

[105] Regulation 469/2009, the most recent version of the SPC regulation, defines medicinal products at Article 1(a) as 'any substance or combination of substances presented for treating or preventing disease in human beings or animals and any substance or combination of substances which may be administered to human beings or animals with a view to making a medical diagnosis or to restoring, correcting or modifying physiological functions in humans or in animals'—a definition that includes virtually as biologic drugs.

[106] EU-Japan Economic Partnership Agreement (2018) Article 14.37.

[107] EU-Canada Comprehensive Economic Trade Agreement (2016), Article 20.29.

[108] EU-Georgia Association Agreement (2014) Article 286; EU-Moldova Association Agreement (2014). Article 48 and EU-Ukraine Association Agreement (2014) Article 222.

Peru-Colombia-Ecuador FTA; this agreement explicitly acknowledges that reliance on foreign data is permitted, but that in such cases 'the period of exclusive use of the data submitted in connection with obtaining the approval shall begin from the date of the first marketing approval relied on, when the approval is granted within six months from the filing of a complete application'—a rewording of the 'concurrent period' rule that appears in the US FTAs with Peru and Colombia.[109] Again, it seems likely that this provision was inserted at the request of the South American countries rather than the EU in order to preserve existing flexibilities.

Only the agreement with Moldova explicitly prohibits 'indirect' reliance on submitted data, stating that 'no person or entity... shall be allowed to rely directly or indirectly on such data.'[110] It is unclear why the agreement with Moldova alone takes this approach.

5.3.3.5 Exceptions

The Peru-Colombia-Ecuador treaty contains one of the few explicit exceptions to test data exclusivity found in any of the trade agreements; the deal permits the parties to regulate exceptions 'for reasons of public interest, situations of emergency or extreme urgency, when it is necessary to allow access to those data to third parties' and 'measures in response to the abuse of intellectual property rights or practices which unreasonably restrain trade.'[111]

All EU-led FTAs which include test data exclusivity provisions contain a separate provision recognising or acknowledging the Doha Declaration, and all but the agreement with Georgia specify that the intellectual property chapter should be interpreted and implemented in a way consistent with the Declaration. Only the agreements with Canada and Vietnam expressly state that data may be disclosed to protect public health or when steps are taken to protect data from unfair commercial use, as set out in Article 39.3, although the universal inclusion of the references to the Doha Declaration would suggest that such an exception, present in TRIPS, is still permissible.[112]

5.3.3.6 Concluding Remarks on Test Data Exclusivity Provisions in EU-Led Agreements

While the EU has negotiated provisions which impose restrictive test data exclusivity obligations on its European neighbours, outside of Europe the EU-led agreements

[109] Trade Agreement between the EU and Peru, Colombia and Ecuador (2012) Article 231.

[110] EU-Moldova Association Agreement (2014) Article 315(2).

[111] Trade Agreement between the EU and Peru, Colombia and Ecuador (2012) Article 231.

[112] EU-Canada Comprehensive Economic Trade Agreement (2016) Article 20.29; EU-Vietnam Free Trade Agreement Article 12.41.

have had little influence on test data exclusivity beyond the issue of biologics, with test data exclusivity provisions typically only echoing those of previous agreements or the existing practice of the other party. In some cases, the EU has failed to negotiate even this—the EU-Japan Economic Partnership does not even contain a specific exclusivity period, despite the fact that Japan has had *de facto* test data exclusivity since the 1980s and had been prepared to agree to such terms in the TPP less than two years prior. This may be the product of the well-documented difficulties in achieving consensus amongst the EU's many member states—the EU-Canada Comprehensive Economic and Trade Agreement was famously almost thwarted by the Belgian regional Walloon parliament (albeit for issues unrelated to test data exclusivity); it is presumably easier to achieve consensus regarding test data exclusivity (and indeed other contentious issues) within the US government and between the four national governments of EFTA than between the member states of the EU.

However, the EU-led agreements with Ukraine, Moldova and Georgia hint at an easily-overlooked manner by which the EU has contributed to the globalisation of test data exclusivity. Accession to the EU requires a new member state to be bound by and give effect to the full EU *acquis communitaire*, including the EU's rules on test data exclusivity. As such, enlargement of the EU has been an important means by which test data exclusivity laws have globalised within Europe. In 1986, the year that Directive 87/21/EEC was passed, the EC (as it was then) had only 12 members.[113] Two, Spain and Portugal, had joined that very year, and, as previously discussed, the fact that neither country provided patents over pharmaceuticals may partly have motivated the EU's adoption of test data exclusivity rights in the first place.[114] Post-1986, 16 countries have acceded to the EU and consequently adopted the EU's rules on test data exclusivity (one country, the UK, has also withdrawn from the EU; however, it has retained the EU approach to test data exclusivity).[115] In addition, the EU's rules on test data exclusivity extend to members of the European Economic Area (EEA) which are not EU members—presently there are three such states, Norway, Iceland and Lichtenstein (which are also members of EFTA). The EU has not expanded for the purpose of spreading test data exclusivity rights, of course; still, it is important to understand that accession to the EU is by far the most common reason that European jurisdictions have adopted test data exclusivity provisions in the post-TRIPS period.

---

[113] Those members were Belgium, France, West Germany, Italy, Luxembourg, the Netherlands, Denmark, Ireland, the UK, Greece, Portugal and Spain; Adamini et al. (2009), p. 989.

[114] Ibid.

[115] UK, European Union (Withdrawal) Act 2018 Section 3(1).

5.3.4 Concluding Remarks on Test Data Exclusivity and Trade Agreements

In his 2016 study, Shaikh concluded that 'no clear trend' regarding the restrictiveness of test data exclusivity obligations in trade agreements emerged from his analysis, and that on average the test data exclusivity provisions of FTAs have only become 'very slightly' less access-oriented.[116] This is in a sense accurate; the test data exclusivity terms of the European-led agreements in particular show little over-all consistency, and the obligations of US-led agreements became somewhat less restrictive in the late-2000s. However, this does not represent the whole picture. The US appears to have moved away from the more liberal approach to the protection of submitted test data in the NTP era, although the amendments to the USMCA show that imposing higher levels of test data exclusivity still remains controversial in Congress. Furthermore, while many of the European-led agreements on test data exclusivity are less restrictive, these often merely replicate pre-existing rules from other agreements or domestic laws; as such, they have virtually no impact on how submitted test data is protected in practice, while appearing to make the test data exclusivity provisions found in FTAs less restrictive on average. In addition, the US bilateral intellectual property treaties of the 1990s (which Shaikh did not include in his study) were considerably less restrictive regarding the protection of submitted test data than more recent US-led agreements. When these factors are taken into account, test data exclusivity provisions have quite clearly become significantly more restrictive over time; trade agreements now frequently impose obligations explicitly requiring protection for biologics, protection for new clinical information or indications, significantly longer terms of protection and, in the case of US agreements, general prohibitions on certain TRIPS-compatible approaches to test data exclusivity. Explicit exceptions to test data exclusivity periods are extremely uncommon, and, aside from the early EFTA-led agreements, alternative means of protection for submitted test data are not accommodated.

The one exception to this trend is the increase in references to the Doha Declaration and the rights of parties to take actions to protect public health, which have become a common feature of recent US and EU-led agreements, often appearing in the article on test data exclusivity itself. However, Correa is of the opinion that the public health statements and references to the Doha Declaration have little practical effect and are unlikely to provide a sufficient legal basis to derogate from the obligations established by the test data exclusivity provisions of the agreement.[117] Certainly, few of the states which have concluded agreements with such references have gone on to implement domestic public health exceptions to test data exclusivity, and those which have done so have nevertheless been the subject of US ire in the Special 301 Report. The references to Doha and public health would thus appear to

[116] Shaikh (2016), pp. 142–143.

[117] Correa (2006), p. 81.

be examples the more general trend of principles being used in a symbolic manner in order to engender quiescence in the globalisation of regulation.[118]

While the test data exclusivity provisions of trade agreements negotiated in the past decade have been mostly led by Europeans, it would be a mistake to conclude that the Europeans have usurped the US as the chief globalisers of test data exclusivity, especially given the low impact many European-negotiated obligations regarding test data exclusivity have in practice. Furthermore, both of the most recent US-negotiated trade agreements contain the strictest test data exclusivity provisions of any US-led deal so far, even if domestic US politics led to the suspension and amendment of the test data exclusivity provisions of the TPP and USMCA respectively. Still, the Europeans have negotiated extremely restrictive test data exclusivity terms in the agreements with their developing neighbours and have been particularly successful in securing protection for biologic test data. Of course, these developed country actors are not competitors in this area. Indeed, the reverse is true—as we have already seen, the principles of MFN and national treatment mean that the concessions on test data exclusivity achieved by either the US, EU or EFTA/ Switzerland will apply to the others as well (indeed, to all other WTO members). Subsequent trade agreements made by these actors therefore 'ratchet-up' standards of test data exclusivity protection, as they have for other intellectual property rights; the first agreement sets a minimum standard of protection, with subsequent agreements then raising that standard.[119] This is particularly useful when the trade representatives of one actor cannot raise a standard internationally because of pressures at home, as was the case for the US regarding biologics prior to the enactment of the BPCIA and regarding test data exclusivity generally during the NTP period; the US established basic standards of test data exclusivity which the Europeans then ratcheted up. As a result, US firms enjoyed higher protection for submitted test data abroad without having to first achieve consensus on the issue at home.

Furthermore, the repetition of identical test data exclusivity provisions in multiple agreements is not entirely inconsequential; to borrow another metaphor from the world of engineering, they provide regulatory redundancy. For example, if the US abandoned NAFTA, as it threatened to do in 2018, Canada would still have been obliged to provide test data exclusivity as a result of its treaty with the EU. Agreeing to identical test data exclusivity provisions with multiple other parties significantly increases the diplomatic, political and economic costs of ratcheting-down the protection of submitted test data—likely well past the point of viability for most states—because every party must agree to a renegotiation. If a state chooses to simply revoke the regulatory measures in breach of its obligations, the cost is potentially the entire value derived from all relevant trade agreements.

The patterns in the test data exclusivity provisions of FTAs can also be explained with reference to the other parties to the agreements. As has been noted, test data

[118] Braithwaite and Drahos (2000), p. 30.

[119] Ibid, p. 519.

exclusivity obligations tend to be especially restrictive in agreements between developing countries in Europe, such as Bosnia and Ukraine, and EFTA and the EU. In addition, Peru, Chile, Ecuador and Colombia seem particularly adept at negotiating less-restrictive measures regarding test data exclusivity across agreements made with all three developed country actors.[120] The experience of the countries demonstrates that it is possible for states to both negotiate flexibilities regarding the protection of submitted test data and to retain those flexibilities in subsequent agreements.[121]

Japan has also been surprisingly reluctant to commit to test data exclusivity in trade agreements, refusing to even commit to a specific term of protection in its agreements with Switzerland and the EU, despite possessing a large domestic research-based pharmaceutical industry and having had provisions equivalent to test data exclusivity in place since before the TRIPS Agreement came into force. This, along with Japan's historic reluctance to push for test data exclusivity, may be changing; a 2015 leak of the intellectual property chapter of the Regional Comprehensive Economic Partnership (RCEP), a trade agreement between 15 states in Asia and Oceania,[122] showed that Japan (and South Korea) had proposed five years of test data exclusivity.[123] However, this proposal was opposed by all other parties to the negotiations,[124] and the final version of the RCEP signed in 2020 requires only that parties protect undisclosed information in accordance with Article 39(2) of TRIPS.[125]

Resistance to test data exclusivity obligations is still apparent at the international level, despite the increasing restrictiveness of trade agreements on the matter. The issue of test data exclusivity protection for biologics held up the talks over the TPP for some time, and resulted in an ambiguous compromise.[126] Test data exclusivity provisions have also seen resistance in other major trade agreements under negotiation; in 2013, the European Commission's Trade Commissioner publicly stated that the EU would not require India to introduce any kind of test data exclusivity as part of the EU-India trade agreement.[127] Similarly, the protection of submitted test data does not appear in the EU-Mercosur FTA agreed in principle in 2019.[128]

---

[120] Shaikh (2016), p. 167.

[121] Of course, this must be contrasted against the position of most other South American countries which simply do not have any test data exclusivity provisions at all.

[122] Brunei, Cambodia, Indonesia, Laos, Malaysia, Myanmar, the Philippines, Singapore, Thailand, Vietnam (all members of the Association of Southeast Asian Nations, ASEAN), China, Japan, South Korea, Australia and New Zealand. India had been party to the negotiations, but withdrew in 2019.

[123] Yu (2017), p. 713.

[124] Ibid, p. 713.

[125] Regional Comprehensive Economic Partnership Agreement (2020) Article 11.56.

[126] Yu (2018), p. 28.

[127] European Commission (2013).

[128] European Commission (2019).

On the other hand, a number of upcoming trade agreements seem likely to contain test data exclusivity provisions. The agreed texts of the upcoming EU Free Trade Agreement with New Zealand and the modernised trade agreement with Mexico both contain provisions on test data exclusivity (explicitly covering biologics in the case of the agreement with Mexico).[129] Furthermore, future trade agreements with test data exclusivity provisions may come from actors other than the US, EFTA and EU. Since its withdrawal from the EU in 2020, the UK has been free to negotiate its own trade agreements; as a country with a large research-based pharmaceutical industry, the UK is likely to push for test data exclusivity provisions in future agreements. A draft of the UK-India Free Trade Agreement leaked in 2022 did in fact contain provisions requiring six years of test data exclusivity for both pharmaceuticals containing new chemical entities and biologics.[130]

5.4 Test Data Exclusivity and Accession to the World Trade Organisation

While trade agreements have been the most common method by which countries outside of the US, EFTA and EU have committed to test data exclusivity rules, other methods have also played a role. Accession to the WTO is perhaps the second most important of these—as we shall see, this further demonstrates the role that Article 39.3 has played in facilitating the globalisation of test data exclusivity post-TRIPS.

Membership of the WTO is open to 'any state or customs territory having full autonomy in the conduct of its trade policies.'[131] Before acceding to the WTO, the prospective member must agree to the existing WTO treaties and bring their domestic law in line with the obligations these impose. During the accession process, existing WTO members have the right to negotiate with the acceding member over 'rules', (including intellectual property rights), followed by bilateral negotiations over goods and services between the applicant and each member interested in conducting such negotiations; Abbot and Correa note that this distinction is relatively unimportant in practice because nothing prevents individual countries from raising rules issues in bilateral discussion.[132] The results of these multilateral and bilateral negotiations are reflected in the Report of the Working Party (WPR) on the accession of the relevant country, although the identities of the countries that have negotiated them are not revealed. Because of the WTO practice of consensus voting,[133] this means that a single existing member may effectively veto the

[129] EU-New Zealand FTA Article 18.44; Modernisation of the Trade part of the EU-Mexico Global Agreement Chapter 41 Article X.51.

[130] UK-India Free Trade Agreement Draft Intellectual Property Chapter (2022) Article F2.

[131] Marrakesh Agreement Establishing the World Trade Organization (1994) Article XII(1).

[132] Abbott and Correa (2007), p. 2.

[133] Marrakesh Agreement Establishing the World Trade Organization (1994) Article IX.

application of a prospective member if it is unsatisfied with the terms of the accession. The measures to which the acceding party formally agrees in the Report are officially 'commitments' and are legally binding on the acceding member.[134] Even if a country does not formally commit to a measure, it may still indicate that it has adopted such a measure in order to appease members of the working party; while this obviously provides more legal flexibility in future, the immediate domestic outcome within the party remains the same.

Post-1995, 36 countries have acceded to the WTO.[135] The Working Party Reports of these countries show that at least 11 countries have made either a legally binding commitment to provide test data exclusivity or given a non-binding indication that they had already or would shortly adopt such a law—these countries are listed in Table 5.13. In addition to these countries, other states have indicated that they have passed some kind of legislation to protect submitted test data, but do not reveal the exact nature of this protection in their working party report.[136] It is possible—perhaps even probable—that many of these countries have made unrecorded concessions regarding the protection of test data during the WTO accession process, although these would not be legally binding commitments under WTO rules.

The link between test data exclusivity and Article 39.3 is explicit in most Reports. The wording of the issue in the Report of the Working Party on the Accession of China provides a typical example:

> Some members requested that China specifically provide in its law and regulations that it would protect against unfair commercial use of undisclosed test or other data submitted in support of applications for marketing approval of pharmaceutical or of agricultural chemical products which utilize new chemical entities [a paraphrased version of Article 39.3], by providing that no person other than the person that submitted such data may, without the permission of the person initially submitting the data, rely on such data in support of an application for product approval for a period of at least six years from the date on which marketing approval to the person that submitted the data had been granted.
>
> [In response to this, the representative of China confirmed that China would indeed provide the exact protections specified.][137]

Despite its obvious ambiguity (as discussed at length in the preceding chapter), Article 39.3 has demonstrably strengthened the ability of certain developed countries

[134] Abbott and Correa (2007), p. 4.

[135] WTO, Protocols of accession for new members since 1995, including commitments in goods and services https://www.wto.org/english/thewto_e/acc_e/completeacc_e.htm#list Accessed 26 January 2023.

[136] Yemen, for example, stated that its law on the protection of undisclosed information would be 'redrafted to comply with Article 39.3 of the TRIPS Agreement by according protection of undisclosed information submitted to the competent authorities for the marketing approval of chemical, pharmaceutical or agricultural products' but did not explain what this would mean in practice. WTO, *Report of the working party on the accession of Yemen to the World Trade Organization,* WT/ACC/YEM/42 (26 June 2014), para 240.

[137] WTO, *Reporting Party Report on the accession of China*, WT/ACC/CHN/49 (1 October 2001), para 282–284.

Table 5.13 Indications of or commitments to the adoption of test data exclusivity provisions in WTO Working Party Reports

Acceding country	Year of WTO accession	Relevant Working Party Report paragraph(s)	Term of exclusivity discussed
Jordan	2000	215	At least 5 years (indicated)[a]
China	2001	284	At least 6 years (committed)[b]
Cambodia	2004	205–206	At least 5 years (committed)[c]
Saudi Arabia	2005	261	At least 5 years (indicated)[d]
Vietnam	2007	437	5 years (indicated)[e]
Tonga	2007	167–168	At least 5 years (committed)[f]
Ukraine	2008	433	At least 5 years (committed)[g]
Montenegro	2012	240–241	At least 5 years (indicated)[h]
Russia	2012	1295	At least 6 years (committed)[i]
Vanuatu	2012	121–122	5 years (committed)[j]
Kazakhstan	2015	1079	6 years (committed)[k]

[a] WTO, *Report of the working party on the accession of the Hashemite Kingdom of Jordan to the World Trade Organization,* WT/ACC/JOR/33 (3 December 1999)

[b] WTO, *Report of the working party on the accession of China*, WT/ACC/CHN/49 (1 October 2001)

[c] WTO, *Report of the working party on the accession of Cambodia,* WT/ACC/KHM/21 (15 August 2003)

[d] WTO, *Report of the working party on the accession of the Kingdom of Saudi Arabia to the World Trade Organization,* WT/ACC/SAU/61 (1 November 2005)

[e] WTO, *Report of the working party on the accession of Viet Nam,* WT/ACC/VNM/48 (27 October 2006)

[f] WTO, *Report of the working party on the accession of Tonga to the World Trade Organization,* WT/ACC/TON/17 (2 December 2005)

[g] WTO, *Report of the working party on the accession of Ukraine to the World Trade Organization,* WT/ACC/UKR/152 (25 January 2008)

[h] WTO, *Report of the working party on the accession Montenegro to the World Trade Organization,* WT/ACC/CGR/38 (5 December 2011). Term taken from Law on Protection of Undisclosed Information (Official Gazette of Republic of Montenegro, Nos. 16/2007 and 73/2008), which Montenegro indicated it had adopted in the Working Party Report. Montenegro also indicated that an exception permitting the competent authority to disclose the submitted data in certain circumstances at Article 9.3.1 of the law had been amended to be TRIPS compliant

[i] WTO, *Report of the working party on the accession of the Russian Federation to the World Trade Organization* WT/ACC/RUS/70 (17 November 2011)

[j] WTO, *Report of the working party on the accession of Vanuatu to the World Trade Organization,* WT/ACC/VUT/17 (11 May 2011)

[k] WTO, *Report of the working party on the accession of the Republic of Kazakhstan*, WT/ACC/KAZ/93 (23 June 2015)

to compel other jurisdictions to adopt test data exclusivity rights. If a prospective member of the WTO fails to provide test data exclusivity or develop its own system (which, as discussed at Sect. 4.5, is made difficult by the unclear nature of Article 39.3), developed countries can then raise the entirely legitimate argument that the prospective member has not met its obligations regarding the protection of submitted test data. In the absence of another proven model for the protection of submitted test data, acceding countries therefore adopt test data exclusivity laws as demanded by the US and European countries. Ultimately, acceding members find themselves providing the very standards of test data exclusivity rejected from Article 39.3 in order to comply with Article 39.3—indeed, in some cases providing a *higher* standard of protection, as evidenced by the commitments of China, Russia and Cambodia to provide 6 years of test data exclusivity.

The commitments and indications made regarding the protection of test data in WPRs are less detailed than the provisions of the FTAs discussed above, and none specify matters such as protection for biologic data or protection for new clinical information. However, the fact that the WTO accession process was used to extend test data exclusivity to China is by itself enough to make it one of the most significant factors by which test data exclusivity has been globalised.[138] Commitments or indications regarding test data exclusivity have become more common with time; of the 18 states which have acceded to the WTO since 2004, only 7 did not make a commitment or indication regarding test data exclusivity.[139]

5.5 The Globalisation of Test Data Exclusivity and the Role of Coercion

The globalisation of test data exclusivity though trade agreements and accession to multilateral organisations might be characterised as a series of bargains between the US, EU and EFTA and the various other states involved. Even if test data exclusivity rights and other forms of increased intellectual property standards do not directly benefit these states, accepting such rights was still an aspect of a bargaining process in which they received other concessions. However, as Drahos observes, while economic theory suggests that voluntary deals between parties should be 'pareto' improvements (i.e. improvements that do not make another party worse off), when the difference in bargaining power between two parties is especially great, the risk of

[138] WTO, *Report of the working party on the accession of Ukraine to the World Trade Organization*, WT/ACC/UKR/152 (25 January 2008).

[139] These are Nepal, Laos, Yemen, Liberia, Afghanistan, Seychelles, Samoa and Cape Verde. The absence of test data exclusivity obligations for these states probably reflects that fact that they are largely either LDCs and thus exempted from compliance with the TRIPS requirements on pharmaceuticals until 2033 or are tiny island nations. However, it is worth noting that Cambodia (and LDC) and Vanuatu (both an LDC and tiny island nation) have both made commitments to provide test data exclusivity during their accessions to the WTO.

domination of one party by the other calls this assumption into question.[140] Coercion has played an important role in the globalisation of test data exclusivity post-TRIPS, as it has for other intellectual property rights. In at least one case this has been military coercion; following the 2003 invasion of Iraq, the Coalition Provisional Authority (the US-controlled occupation government) passed a reform of Iraq's intellectual property laws which, *inter alia*, introduced a five-year period of test data exclusivity for pharmaceuticals.[141]

While this would appear to have been the only occasion on which test data exclusivity has been introduced to a jurisdiction at rifle point, economic coercion has played a more significant role. As has been discussed, criticisms over inadequate protection of submitted test data first appeared in the Special 301 Report in 1995, the year TRIPS entered into force.[142] Australia's listing on the Watch List in 1996 over failure to provide 'adequate' protection for test data prompted the Australian government to adopt test data exclusivity provisions shortly thereafter.[143] By 2004, the reports on over 25 Priority Watch List or Watch List countries mentioned concerns regarding the protection of submitted test data.[144]

As has already been noted, the Special 301 Report has been used to rebuke states for making use of flexibilities related to test data exclusivity that are ostensibly in the spirit of the guarantees on public health found in those agreements; this has probably discouraged the use of similar flexibilities by other countries. The US aggressively chastised Israel regarding its failure to provide test data exclusivity for pharmaceutical test data and other intellectual property measures relating to pharmaceuticals, making it clear that Israel would be removed from the Priority Watch List once it complied with these measures; Israel did so in 2012.[145] Special 301 was also used to coerce Russia into providing increased intellectual property protection, including for submitted test data, during the negotiations over Russia's accession to the WTO; as the 2010 Report documents, this ultimately led to Russia enacting and implementing a test data exclusivity law.[146]

Perhaps surprisingly given its general ineffectiveness in negotiating obligations to provide test data exclusivity in trade agreements, the EU has also made use of bilateral pressure backed by threats of economic coercion to promote the globalisation of test data exclusivity. The EU's Trade Barrier Regulation (TBR) establishes a system under which EU companies, associations of companies and Member States may lodge complaints with the Commission regarding alleged breaches of international trade rules, which may then launch an investigation; such an investigation may

[140] Drahos (2003), p. 85.

[141] Coalition Provisional Authority Order Number 81, 'the Patent and Industrial Designs Laws and Regulations (No. 65 of 1970).'

[142] USTR (1995b).

[143] USTR (1996), p. 11.

[144] USTR (2004).

[145] USTR (2011), p. 29.

[146] USTR (2010), p. 23.

lead to a WTO case and eventually to retaliatory measures from the EU such as increased tariffs.[147] Of the 24 examination procedures initiated since the Regulation came into force in 1996, two have involved allegations that other states were in breach of Article 39.3 as a result of providing inadequate protection for submitted test data. In the first investigation, against Korea in 2000, the data protection issue was not pursued on the grounds that no case of unfair use of confidential data was reported in the context of the investigation.[148] However, a 2004 investigation against Turkey took the issue of the protection of submitted test data much more seriously. While the Turkish authorities claimed that Article 39.3 did not require a proprietary right allowing originators to exclude other parties from making reference to submitted test data in abbreviated drug approvals, the European Commission made the argument that providing data exclusivity for a certain period of time is the 'envisaged way' to comply with Article 39.3.[149] Ultimately, Turkey agreed to provide six years of data exclusivity.[150] This again demonstrates how the ambiguity of Article 39.3 has been exploited to promote test data exclusivity in the post-TRIPS period.

5.6 Explaining the Globalisation of Test Data Exclusivity

During the TRIPS negotiations, it was suggested by some within the US government that if developing countries agreed to the TRIPS Agreement, the US would ease off on negotiating intellectual property standards bilaterally.[151] This has quite obviously not occurred, least of all with respect to the protection of submitted test data. Including the developed country proponents of test data exclusivity, at least 78 countries with almost half of the world's population (and almost all of its pharmaceutical market) have made some kind of international commitment to providing test data exclusivity. The only regions in which few countries have made such indications/commitments are Eastern South America, sub-Saharan Africa and Central and South Asia. As we have seen in this chapter, multiple mechanisms and tactics have been used to achieve this result, with states often being subject to pressure from several actors making use of different tactics.

A key part of this strategy for promoting test data exclusivity laws through trade negotiations has been the forum shifting of discussions around intellectual property rights from the multilateral level to the bilateral level. In the case of the push for

[147] European Council Regulation (EC) 3286/94 of 22 December 1994 laying down Community procedures in the field of the common commercial policy in order to ensure the exercise of the Community's rights under international trade rules, in particular those established under the auspices of the World Trade Organization [1994].

[148] Commission decision of 25 October 2000 suspending the examination procedure concerning obstacles to trade in pharmaceutical products on the market of the Republic of Korea (2000).

[149] European Commission (2004), p. 41.

[150] Kennedy (2017), p. 95.

[151] Drahos (2001), p. 792.

TRIPS-plus protection for submitted test data (and indeed TRIPS-plus standards of intellectual property protection generally), negotiating further agreements within the WTO was unfavourable for proponents of those measures because it enabled coordination amongst the individually weaker developing countries (such as the coordination that led to the Doha Declaration). Trade agreements, on the other hand, are the result of bilateral negotiations (or negotiations between a small group of countries), while the WTO accession process gives individual members the opportunity to negotiate bilaterally with prospective members as well as the ability to essentially veto their accession.[152] As Correa has observed, this has served to amplify the power asymmetries between developed and developing countries,[153] and leads to a much more conducive environment for promulgating Western-developed standards of intellectual property.

In 2009, Reichman warned that if nothing intervened in the transmission of test data exclusivity rights to new jurisdictions, this new intellectual property right would become a likely candidate for permanent multilateral recognition.[154] Such a multilateral decision has not yet come to pass, but test data exclusivity has certainly become extremely widely globalised, even relative to other TRIPS-plus intellectual property rights; patent linkage terms are a common feature of US-led trade agreements, but do not feature in agreements led by the EU or EFTA states, while commitments to provide patent term extensions for pharmaceuticals do not appear in WTO Working Party Reports. As discussed at Sect. 4.5, Article 39.3 has played an important role in this globalisation. Some members of the WTO may have come to believe that the article does in fact require test data exclusivity or that at the very least it is the 'envisaged way' of doing so, in line with the arguments of the US and EU.[155] Even for members which do not hold this view, however, developing and defending an alternative approach to Article 39.3 would be a difficult and costly prospect. Faced with legitimate arguments that they are not in compliance with TRIPS during trade negotiations, adopting test data exclusivity laws comes to be seen as the only viable option.

[152] Abbott and Correa (2007), p. 3.

[153] Correa (2004), p. 81; see also Sell (2010).

[154] Reichman (2009), p. 8.

[155] As we shall see in the next chapter, there are certainly states which adopted test data exclusivity laws soon after the end of the TRIPS negotiations despite the absence of carrots or sticks and their own lack of a research-based pharmaceutical industry—New Zealand, for example, passed its test data exclusivity law in 1994.

5.7 Conclusion

The most significant means by which test data exclusivity rights have globalised post-TRIPS are trade agreements negotiated by the US, EU and EFTA/Switzerland, although other instruments such as accession to the WTO have also played a role. Commitments to provide test data exclusivity have become increasingly common with time, and the protection required for submitted test data has become more expansive and restrictive, especially in trade agreements; terms of protection have become longer, and exclusivity periods for new clinical information and biologic data are increasingly required, and explicit exceptions to test data exclusivity remain almost unheard of outside of anaemic references to parties' rights to take action in line with the Doha Declaration.

The fact that test data exclusivity has chiefly globalised in this way is concerning for a number of reasons. Firstly, if an intellectual property right is chiefly developed and globalised as a result of international negotiations in which geopolitical factors and power dynamics play a significant role, there is little reason to believe that it will bear any particular relationship to the public good. In addition, trade negotiations are especially prone to the collective action problems highlighted by Olson in *the Logic of Collective Action*,[156] as they take place between a comparatively small group of negotiators to which organised interests have relatively easy access, but which diffused publics are effectively excluded from, aside from the ability to potentially veto the deal at the ballot box. Furthermore, such a system of globalisation has a very low capacity for error-correction—that is, changing or amending aspects of provisions which turn out to be less beneficial or more costly than initially envisioned. Trade agreements are renegotiated very rarely and typically with great difficultly, and abandoning a trade agreement over a single provision is rarely cost effective.

The obligations to provide some form of protection to submitted test data in the TRIPS Agreement have enabled developed countries to make legitimate arguments for other WTO members (or states with ambitions of WTO membership) to take action in this area, and then insist that this protection take the form of test data exclusivity. Faced with the choice of enduring the financial, political and diplomatic costs of developing an original solution to Article 39.3 (and potentially defending that solution at the DSB), other countries are strongly incentivised to adopt test data exclusivity.

In spite of this, however, the commitments to test data exclusivity made through trade-based methods are often vague, and typically leave signatories significant discretion regarding the form of test data exclusivity in their jurisdiction, especially regarding the presence of flexibilities and limitations. The next chapter examines various approaches to the implementation of the protection of submitted test data at the national level.

---

[156] Olson (1965), p. 9.

References

Abbott FM, Correa C (2007) World Trade Organization accession agreements: intellectual property issues. Quaker United Nations Office (QUNO)

Adamini S, Maarse H, Versluis E, Light DW (2009) Policy making on data exclusivity in the European Union: from industrial interests to legal realities. J Health Polit Policy Law 34(6): 979–1010

Artecona R, Plank-Brumback RM (2016) Access to medicines and incentives for innovation: the balance struck in the Trans-Pacific Partnership (TPP) on intellectual property (patent and data exclusivity) protection for pharmaceutical products. ECLAC

Braithwaite J, Drahos P (2000) Global business regulation. Cambridge University Press, Cambridge

Correa C (2004) Bilateralism in intellectual property: defeating the WTO system for access to medicines. Case West Reserve J Int Law 36:79

Correa C (2006) Protecting test data for pharmaceutical and agrochemical products under free trade agreements. In: Roffe P, Tansey G, Vivas-Eugui D (eds) Negotiating health: intellectual property and access to medicine. Earthscan, London, pp 81–96

Drahos P (2001) BITs and BIPs: bilateralism in intellectual property. J World Intellect Prop 4:791

Drahos P (2003) When the weak bargain with the strong: negotiations in the World Trade Organization. Int Negot 8(1):79–109

European Commission (2004) Report to the Trade Barriers Regulation Committee – TBR proceedings concerning Turkish practices affecting trade in pharmaceutical products

European Commission (2013) Q&A on Access to Medicines for EU-India Free Trade Agreement Negotiations

European Commission (2019) EU-Mercosur trade agreement: The Agreement in Principle and its texts

Fergusson R (2015) Trade promotion authority (TPA) and the role of Congress in trade policy. Congressional Research Service

Holzer S (2012) Regulatory data protection of medicinal products from a Swiss perspective. Bio-Sci Law Rev 12(5):184–191

Kennedy M (2017) WTO Dispute Settlement and the Trips Agreement: applying intellectual property standards in a trade law framework. Cambridge University Press, Cambridge

Labonté R, Gleeson D, McNamara CL (2020) USMCA 2.0: a few improvements but far from a 'healthy' trade treaty. Glob Health 16:1–4

Lehman BA (1993) Intellectual property under the Clinton administration. Georgetown J Int Law Econ 27:395

Olson M (1965) The logic of collective action. Harvard University Press, Cambridge

Reichman JH (2009) Rethinking the role of clinical trial data in international intellectual property law: the case for a public goods approach. Marquette Intellect Prop Law Rev 13(1):1

Roffe PR, Vivas-Eugui D (2007) A shift in intellectual property policy in US FTAs? Bridges 11(5): 15–16

Sell SK (2010) TRIPS was never enough: vertical forum shifting, FTAs, ACTA, and TPP. J Intellect Prop Law 18:447

Shaikh OH (2016) Access to medicine versus test data exclusivity: safeguarding flexibilities under international law. Springer, Berlin

Spina Alì G (2017) Article 39 (3) TRIPS: understanding the obligations, exploiting the flexibilities. The University of Hong Kong

Spina Alì G (2018) The 13th Round: Article 39 (3) TRIPS and the struggle over "Unfair Commercial Use". J World Intellect Prop 21(3–4):201–242

't Hoen E (2002) TRIPS, pharmaceutical patents, and access to essential medicines: a long way from Seattle to Doha. Chic J Int Law 3:27

USTR (1995a) The Protection of Undisclosed Test Data in Accordance with TRIPs Article 39.3

USTR (1995b) 1995 Special 301 Report

USTR (1996) 1996 Special 301 Report

USTR (2004) 2004 Special 301 Report
USTR (2007) A new trade deal for America
USTR (2010) 2010 Special 301 Report
USTR (2011) 2011 Special 301 Report
USTR (2016) 2016 Special 301 Report
USTR (2017) 2017 Special 301 Report
USTR (2018) 2018 Special 301 Report
USTR (2019) 2019 Special 301 Report
Vaterlaus S, Suter S, Fischer B (2011) The importance of the pharmaceutical industry for Switzerland. Interpharma/BAK Economics AG
Yu PK (2017) The RCEP and Trans-Pacific intellectual property norms. Vand J Transnat'l L 50:673
Yu PK (2018) Data exclusivities in the age of big data, biologics, and plurilaterals. Tex A&M Law Rev Arguendo 6:22–33

Chapter 6
Approaches to the Implementation of the Protection of Submitted Test Data

Abstract This chapter provides an examination of how different jurisdictions have implemented the protection of submitted pharmaceutical test data. The chapter first considers how submitted test data is protected in jurisdictions which do not provide test data exclusivity rights, before moving to consider differing approaches to test data exclusivity itself through an analysis of the test data exclusivity provisions of 27 jurisdictions.

The analysis in this chapter firstly shows that jurisdictions that do not provide test data exclusivity generally protect submitted test data either through the general provisions protecting undisclosed information in that jurisdiction, or through a submitted test data specific law that protects only against misappropriation. Secondly, while the specifics of test data exclusivity laws tend to vary slightly in a number of regards, they are also remarkably consistent, even considering the need to conform to international obligations in free trade agreements *et cetera*. However, a number of countries have adapted this intellectual property right in a manner that better takes into account their own regulatory context; these adaptations provide lessons on how to better implement the protection of submitted test data.

6.1 Introduction

Having explored the origins of test data exclusivity and its globalisation in previous chapters, this chapter provides an examination of the different approaches to the protection of submitted test data across different jurisdictions. This examination shows that most, if not all, jurisdictions appear to fall into one of two categories; those which protect submitted pharmaceutical test data only against misappropriation (either through that jurisdiction's general laws on undisclosed information or a submitted test data specific law), and those which provide test data exclusivity. It does not appear that any jurisdiction makes use of an 'alternative' means of protecting submitted pharmaceutical test data.

Amongst those jurisdictions which provide test data exclusivity, the provisions of their national laws vary to a degree; however, many aspects of these laws are remarkably similar. This often goes even beyond the similarities that would be

A. Buick, *Intellectual Property Rights in Pharmaceutical Test Data*,
https://doi.org/10.1007/978-3-031-29436-5_6

expected due to the fact that most national laws on test data exclusivity are a response to specific international obligations. A number of jurisdictions, however, have implemented exceptions and limitations to their test data exclusivity laws that serve to safeguard public health and promote access to medicine while still protecting submitted test data; these exceptions and limitations may also prove useful in other jurisdictions seeking to balance the protection of submitted pharmaceutical test data with the wider public interest.

6.2 Non-exclusivity Based Approaches to the Protection of Submitted Test Data

With the exceptions of LDCs, all full members of the WTO have an obligation to protect certain types of submitted test data from unfair commercial use as a result of Article 39.3 of the TRIPS Agreement. As was discussed in Chap. 4, arguments over what exactly this requires range from no more than the protection of submitted test data from misappropriation to the implementation of test data exclusivity.[1] In Chap. 4, this book concluded that entirely unrestrained, uncompensated use of submitted test data in abbreviated applications likely constitutes unfair commercial use per Article 39.3 of TRIPS, but that Article 39.3 does not require members to provide test data exclusivity, and that a range of mechanisms could be used to provide submitted test data with protection from unfair commercial use—including direct funding of clinical trials, compulsory liability regimes and additional tax levies on generic drugs. It was also concluded that Article 39.3 provides those states which *do* provide test data exclusivity with a range of flexibilities, including permitting 'indirect' reliance, reliance on foreign approvals and freedom to impose objective as opposed to relative standards of novelty. It might have been expected that the ambiguity of Article 39.3 and the wide discretion it grants to WTO members would have led to a wide range of approaches to the protection of submitted test data. However, this is not the case. As argued in Chaps. 4 and 5, the ambiguity of Article 39.3 has paradoxically led to the widespread globalisation of a very specific form of protection for submitted test data.

Those jurisdictions which do not provide test data exclusivity are split into two categories; those which provide no explicit protection for submitted test data and those which provide some kind of explicit protection against misappropriation per Correa's argument regarding Article 39.3. A number of jurisdictions have specific laws addressing the protection of submitted test data which nevertheless leave their actual approach unclear; in practice, these jurisdictions are likely to follow one of the approaches mentioned above. There is no evidence that any of the alternative mechanisms of protection for submitted test data discussed at Sect. 2.5 are currently used by states, at least with respect to pharmaceutical test data.

[1] See, for example, Correa (2002) and USTR (1995) for two extremes here.

6.2.1 Jurisdictions with No Regulatory Framework for the Protection of Submitted Test Data

Amongst those jurisdictions which do not provide test data exclusivity, the absence of any specific measures on the protection of submitted test data is by far the most common approach. This is perhaps a surprising state of affairs almost three decades since the TRIPS Agreement came into force; having no specific framework in place to protect submitted test data is almost certainly a violation of TRIPS even under the least restrictive interpretations of Article 39.3.[2] However, it should be recalled that as of 2023, some 35 members of the WTO are LDCs,[3] and therefore under no obligation to comply with Article 39.3 until 2034 at the earliest (although as discussed at Sect. 5.4, at least two LDCs who have acceded to the WTO since the mid-2000s have committed themselves to providing test data exclusivity prior to 2034).[4] In addition, the continued lack of specific measures on the protection of submitted test data by non-LDC jurisdictions has been enabled by the absence of dispute settlement proceedings regarding Article 39.3 since the end of the inconclusive US-Argentina spat in the early 2000s; for those jurisdictions for which trade relations with the developed country proponents of test data exclusivity are not important enough to warrant non-reciprocal coordination over test data exclusivity, or for states which have the wherewithal to resist developed country pressure regarding the protection of submitted test data in trade negotiations, the ambiguity of this approach has facilitated this lack of action.

6.2.2 Jurisdictions Which Protect Submitted Test Data Only Against Misappropriation

A small number of jurisdictions do not place limitations on the ability of subsequent applicants to make reference to previously submitted test data, but do explicitly protect submitted test data against misappropriation—essentially, they adhere to Correa's interpretation of Article 39 discussed in Chap. 4.[5] Argentina is a central example; the Argentine data protection law states that submitted test data will be protected from 'dishonest commercial use' and from 'disclosure', but also makes it

---

[2]For example, Carlos Correa's argument that Article 39.3 requires little more than that submitted test data be protected against misappropriation; Correa (2002).

[3]WTO, Least Developed Countries. https://www.wto.org/english/thewto_e/whatis_e/tif_e/org7_e.htm. Accessed January 26, 2023.

[4]WTO, *Extension of the transition period under Article 66.1 of the TRIPS Agreement for Least Developed Country members* (29 June 2021) IP/C/88. As we saw in the previous chapter, both Cambodia and Vanuatu committed to providing test data exclusivity in their Working Party Reports despite their LDC status.

[5]See further Correa (2002).

clear that the Public Health Authority can approve or authorise the marketing of 'similar products' without the need for the submission of full clinical trial data.[6] The wording of this law suggests that it was drafted with the specific intention of rebuking the claim that Article 39.3 requires formal exclusivity protection—hardly surprising, given the confrontation between the US and Argentina over the subject. Brazil also provides similar protection for test data submitted regarding pharmaceutical drugs for human use,[7] although it does provide test data exclusivity for veterinary drugs and agrichemicals.[8]

Other jurisdictions may also fall into a similar position to Argentina and Brazil, even if this is not explicitly set out in national legislation. Most jurisdictions have general laws pertaining to the protection of trade secrets and other confidential information and in some cases, these may also extend to submitted test data. However, this is not guaranteed; India, for example, has both general common law principles of trade secrecy and an official secrets act, but its courts have never dealt with a case in which the government has actually disclosed submitted test data and academic commentators have expressed doubt as to whether either set of rules would extend to submitted test data.[9]

6.2.3 *Jurisdictions with Ambiguous Provisions on the Protection of Submitted Test Data*

A number of other jurisdictions have legislation clearly designed to implement Article 39.3, but which nevertheless leaves their approach to the protection of submitted test data deeply unclear. These laws often simply repeat the vague wording of Article 39.3 itself, stating that submitted test data will be protected against 'unfair commercial use' without explaining what exactly this entails.[10] In practice, no jurisdiction with a system for abbreviated drug approvals can be 'agnostic' on the question of whether there are limitations on the ability of subsequent applicants to make reference to originator data because test data exclusivity operates as an automatic function of a jurisdiction's drug approval system; either a subsequent applicant will be met by limitations when they try to refer to previously submitted test data, or they will not. In some jurisdictions, this will ultimately be a matter of policy on the part of the national drug regulatory authority or another non-legislative institution. In several cases, this derogation of the implementation of

[6] Argentina, Law on the Confidentiality of Information and Products, No. 24,766, Article 5 (2011).

[7] Torronteguy et al. (2022), p. 68.

[8] Brazil, Law 10603/02.

[9] Basheer (2006), p. 37; Sharma (2007), p. 109.

[10] See, for example, Philippines, Republic Act No 8293 1997 (as amended), Article 72.4; Thailand, trade secrets act 2545 (as amended), Section 15.

the protection of submitted test data to regulatory institutions is explicit in the legislation; the relevant law of the Philippines, for example, states –

> That, in order to protect the data submitted by the original patent holder from **unfair commercial use provided in Article 39.3** of the Agreement on Trade-Related Aspects of Intellectual Property Rights (TRIPS Agreement), the **Intellectual Property Office, in consultation with the appropriate government agencies, shall issue the appropriate rules and regulations necessary therein**[11] [emphasis added]

This highlights the importance of drug regulatory authorities and other regulatory bodies in the protection of submitted test data. Such a derogation of policy is in some ways problematic; in addition to issues of transparency, it is not obvious that a non-legislative body is an appropriate institution to determine the scope and limitations of a novel intellectual property right. Nothing in the literature suggests that any of the jurisdictions which have derogated the protection of submitted test data to national organisations in this way have implemented an alternative system for its protection.

6.2.4 *Does It Matter if These Approaches Do Not Conform with Article 39.3?*

For the most part, these approaches to the protection of submitted test data do not comply with the interpretation of Article 39.3 this book set out in Chap. 4. However, given the absence of DSB proceedings regarding Article 39.3, the *legal* consequences of this noncompliance seem largely hypothetical, even for non-LDC members of the WTO. Many of these jurisdictions have been in a state of probable non-compliance with Article 39.3 for years or even decades with little to no consequences; it might therefore appear that there is little to no benefit in attempting to provide increased protection for submitted test data outside of the context of reciprocal coordination in a trade deal, where the jurisdiction in question is at least likely to receive some concessions in return.

Still, this does not mean that lack of compliance with Article 39.3 has no consequences at all. Indeed, lack of compliance with Article 39.3 may make it more likely that a jurisdiction will adopt test data exclusivity in the long term. As discussed in the previous chapter, there has been a clear trend of jurisdictions with no specific framework for protecting submitted test data committing to providing test data exclusivity over the past two decades; virtually all large economies which have acceded to the WTO since 2004 have committed to providing test data exclusivity, and developed countries continue to successfully promulgate test data exclusivity through trade agreements. This is illustrated by the agreement between EFTA and Indonesia, in which Indonesia—a huge jurisdiction which did not previously appear to have any legislative provisions specifically dealing with the protection of

[11] Philippines, Republic Act No. 8293 1996 (as amended), Article 72.4.

submitted test data—committed to 'process subsequent applications and grant marketing approval only after a period of time defined in the domestic laws and regulations.'[12]

As was argued in Chaps. 4 and 5, Article 39.3 has played an important role in this trend. Jurisdictions with no framework on the protection of submitted test data are open to the criticism that they have done nothing to conform with their international obligations under Article 39.3; those that wish to enter into trade agreements or accede to the WTO are thus in a weak position to reject demands that they protect submitted test data, and have little alternative but to adopt test data exclusivity as the solution to their Article 39.3 obligations.

The position of those jurisdictions such as Argentina which provide protection only against test data exclusivity is somewhat more secure. While the interpretation that Article 39.3 requires no more than protection against misappropriation has flaws as discussed in Chap. 4, in the absence of an authoritative interpretation of Article 39.3 by the DSB this remains a legitimate approach to an inarguably ambiguous treaty provision and thus enables states in this position to more easily resist pressure to adopt the US and European models of test data exclusivity. It is, however, regrettable that *no* jurisdiction appears to have implemented an alternative means of protecting pharmaceutical originator data from 'unfair' abbreviated drug approvals other than test data exclusivity. It is precisely this absence of other viable models for the protection of submitted test data that has incentivised the adoption of test data exclusivity rights. Even the large jurisdictions that have so far held out against test data exclusivity may not be able to do so indefinitely, as the recent experience of Indonesia shows.

6.3 Test Data Exclusivity at the National Level

As previously mentioned, at least 50 jurisdictions, including virtually all major pharmaceutical markets, provide test data exclusivity as the primary means of protecting submitted test data. The number of jurisdictions which provide test data exclusivity has grown steadily since the late 1980s, with the majority of this globalisation of test data exclusivity being the result of commitments made in trade agreements or during accession to the WTO, as recounted in the previous chapter. This growth seems to have slowed in recent years, partly because of the dearth of new US-led trade deals with the exception of the TPP (the test data exclusivity provisions of which are now abandoned) and USMCA (a renegotiation of NAFTA), but also because few major pharmaceutical markets without test data exclusivity remain. The globalisation of test data exclusivity has moved from a focus on expansion to new jurisdictions to a focus on the ratcheting up of standards of protection in international agreements.

[12] EFTA-Indonesia FTA (2018), Annex XVII, Article 6.

As the analysis below reveals, it is quite correct to speak of these different test data exclusivity provisions across this diverse range of jurisdictions as a single, coherent intellectual property right. While these test data exclusivity provisions vary in how they are formulated and expressed, they all share a common feature; these test data exclusivity rights provide for a time-limited period during which the ability of subsequent applicants to use the abbreviated drug approval system is restricted following the approval of an originator drug. However, beyond this core feature, the test data exclusivity provisions of these jurisdictions vary across a range of details, including term length, the sorts of submitted test data which are protected and the presence of limitations and exceptions to the test data exclusivity right. In the next section, this book provides a more in-depth examination of the specifics of test data exclusivity at the national level.

6.4 National Approaches to Test Data Exclusivity

This section examines the test data exclusivity provisions of 27 select jurisdictions (including the EU and EEA, which cover a further 30 countries)[13] in order to provide an insight into how test data exclusivity has developed as it has been globalised across different legal systems. After setting out the methodology of this survey, this section gives an overview and general observations of the test data exclusivity provisions of these jurisdictions before discussing these test data exclusivity laws in more detail.

In particular, this section analyses the term and scope of basic test data exclusivity protection, the criteria for protection and any systems in place to assess this pre-grant or challenge it post-grant, the protection available for 'other' forms of submitted test data such as data submitted regarding new indications or biologics, the approach to the disclosure of submitted test data and any exceptions to test data exclusivity provided.

6.4.1 Methodology

The 27 jurisdictions examined in this section are: the Commonwealth of Australia,[14] Kingdom of Bahrain,[15] Canada,[16] People's Republic of China,[17] Republic of

[13]The EU/EEA rules on test data exclusivity have also been retained by the UK following its withdrawal from the EU in 2020; UK, European Union (Withdrawal) Act 2018, Section 3.

[14]Australia, Therapeutic Goods Act 1989.

[15]Bahrain, Law No. (7) of 2003 On Trade Secrets.

[16]USA, Food and Drug Regulations (as amended).

[17]China, Regulations for Implementation of the Drug Administration Law of the People's Republic of China (2002).

Chile,[18] Republic of Colombia,[19] Republic of Costa Rica,[20] the EU and EEA (referred to as the EU throughout this section),[21] Republic of El Salvador,[22] Japan,[23] Hashemite Kingdom of Jordan,[24] Republic of Kazakhstan,[25] Malaysia,[26] Republic of Mauritius,[27] New Zealand,[28] Sultanate of Oman,[29] Republic of Peru,[30] Russian Federation,[31] Kingdom of Saudi Arabia,[32] Republic of Serbia,[33] Republic of Singapore,[34] Swiss Confederation,[35] Republic of China (Taiwan),[36] Republic of Trinidad and Tobago,[37] Republic of Türkiye,[38] the USA[39] and Socialist Republic of Vietnam.[40] In all cases, a copy of the relevant legislation or implementing regulations governing test data exclusivity from an official source (generally WIPOlex or the national legislation database) has been consulted. In the majority of cases an English version of the legislation was available, either because English is a national language of the jurisdiction or because an English translation had been provided by

[18] Chile, Law No. 19.039 on Industrial Property (as amended).

[19] Colombia, Decree 2085 of 2002.

[20] Costa Rica, Executive decree 34927 of 28/11/2008, Regulations on the Undisclosed Information Act.

[21] EU, Regulation 726/2004 and Directive 2001/83.

[22] El Salvador, Law on the Promotion and Protection of Intellectual Property, Decree No. 604 (1993) as amended by Article 103 of Legislative Decree No. 912 (2005).

[23] Japan, Pharmaceutical Affairs Law 1960.

[24] Jordan, Law on Unfair Competition and Trade Secrets, 2000.

[25] Kazakhstan, Law of the Republic of Kazakhstan No. 365-V on Amendments and Additions to Certain Legislative Acts of the Republic of Kazakhstan with regard to the Accession to the World Trade Organization (2015).

[26] EU, Directive on Data Exclusivity (Directive No. 2 of 2011), issued under Regulation 29 of the Control of Drugs and Cosmetics Regulations 1984.

[27] Mauritius, The Protection against Unfair Practices (Industrial Property Rights) Act 2002.

[28] New Zealand, Medicines Act 1981 as amended by the Medicines Amendment Act 1994.

[29] Oman, Royal Decree 67/2008 Promulgating the Law on Industrial Property Rights.

[30] Peru, Legislative Decree 1072 of 2008 and Supreme Decree 002-2009-SA.

[31] Russian Federation, Federal law 61-FZ on circulation of medicines (2010), as amended by Federal Law 429-FZ (2014).

[32] Saudi Arabia, Regulations for the Protection of Confidential Commercial Information (2005).

[33] Serbia, law on medicinal products and medicinal devices (2010).

[34] Singapore, Medicines Act, 1975.

[35] Switzerland, Federal Act on Medicinal Products and Medical Devices (Therapeutic Products Act, TPA) 2000.

[36] Taiwan, Pharmaceutical Affairs Act.

[37] Trinidad and Tobago, Protection Against Unfair Competition Act 27/1996, as amended by Act No. 18 of 2000, Intellectual Property (Misc Amendments).

[38] Turkey, Regulation on Authorization of Pharmaceutical Products for Human Use (2005).

[39] USA, Drug Price Competition and Patent Term Restoration Act of 1984, 21 USC § 355 and Biologics Price Competition and Innovation Act of 2009 (BPCIA), 42 USC §262.

[40] Vietnam, Intellectual Property Law and Circular No. 17/2011/TT-BNNPTNT 2011.

the jurisdiction in question;[41] in the few cases where an English translation was not readily available, the machine translation function of WIPOlex was relied upon.

In selecting a diverse range of jurisdictions, this analysis aims to represent a wide range of countries of various sizes, levels of development and geographical location, and covers a population of almost three billion people. A notable omission from the list of countries surveyed is the absence of African countries (other than Mauritius); this is both because few African countries appear to have test data exclusivity laws (unsurprising, given both that a majority of African countries are classed as LDCs and thus exempt from Article 39.3 of TRIPS, and that the US, EU and EFTA have signed few trade deals with African countries) and because of difficulties locating authoritative text for the national laws of those African countries known to have committed to providing test data exclusivity in FTAs, such as Morocco and Tunisia.[42]

The previous chapter's discussion of the test data exclusivity provisions found in FTAs was able to present precise comparisons of the different provisions; such an approach regarding the terms of trade agreements is relatively straightforward, as these are often based on a similar model, cover similar general points and (in the case of terms negotiated by the US, EU and EFTA) typically have an official English language translation. This is not the case regarding national laws. As such, this section takes a more general approach to discussing the broad trends found in the different national laws.

This method does have limitations. The analysis of the text of test data exclusivity laws inevitably misses the nuances added by judicial interpretation, other relevant laws within the jurisdiction which may pertain to the test data exclusivity regulations and the practices of the regulatory institutions that administer test data exclusivity. In addition, while care has been taken to ensure accuracy during the data collection process, it is possible (indeed, probable) that some of the records of national legislation are inaccurate, mistranslated or simply out of date. In the case of China, a proposed reform to the national test data exclusivity law is under consideration at the time of writing; China's National Medical Products Administration (NMPA) released a proposed amendment to the country's drug laws that would create a 12 year term of protection for data submitted in association with biologics, as well as introducing exclusivity for paediatrics and orphan drugs in 2018 (because this remains unimplemented at the time of writing, the analysis in this section considers only China's current test data exclusivity law).[43]

As these limitations show, this section would undoubtably be an unequivocal failure if its purpose was to provide a definitive and accurate overview of the test data

[41]It should be noted that in the cases where a jurisdiction for which English is not an official language has provided such a translation, it is typically valid for the purposes of guidance only.

[42]It is unclear whether this is because these countries are simply in breach of their international obligations or simply because copies of the legislation are not easily available. Shaikh was also unable to obtain copies of these laws during his study of national test data exclusivity laws; Shaikh (2016), p. 195.

[43]NMPA (2018).

exclusivity laws of the jurisdictions surveyed. This, however, is not its purpose. Instead, the goal of this section is to provide an understanding of the differing approaches that have been taken to implementing international obligations regarding the protection of submitted test data.

6.4.2 General Observations

Before discussing specific aspects of test data exclusivity amongst the jurisdictions surveyed in more detail, there are a number of general observations and insights that can be made. These relate to the role that both non-reciprocal coordination in trade negotiations and modelling have played in the expansion of test data exclusivity, as well as the differences in the approaches of developed and developing countries to test data exclusivity.

Most of the jurisdictions in this analysis have made a specific commitment to provide test data exclusivity at the international level, as discussed in the previous chapter. Amongst the jurisdictions surveyed, only Mauritius and Taiwan have not made a commitment to provide test data exclusivity in a trade agreement or by the terms of their WTO accession, and it should be noted that formal trade agreements with Taiwan are essentially impossible for a jurisdiction which wishes to retain formal relations with the People's Republic of China due to the so-called 'One China' doctrine. Of course, it should be noted that in at least some of these cases, national measures on test data exclusivity precede any international commitment to provide such rights; for example, Australia adopted its test data exclusivity provisions in the late 1990s, years before the conclusion of its FTA with the US. Furthermore, the only agreement signed by both New Zealand and Malaysia with test data exclusivity provisions was the TPP, the test data exclusivity provisions of which were suspended following the US withdrawal from the agreement. Still, the near ubiquity of international commitments to provide test data exclusivity amongst the jurisdictions analysed in this section demonstrates the connection between international trade and the spread of test data exclusivity, as well as the fact that the freedom of most jurisdictions with test data exclusivity provisions to legislate on the issue is now constrained to some extent at least by international commitments.

As was noted in the previous chapter, these international commitments tend to be vague; while they require more specific protection than Article 39.3, they still leave jurisdictions with wide discretion as to how to implement the test data exclusivity rules. In his 2016 study, Shaikh observed that many national test data exclusivity laws were in fact more restrictive than necessary to comply with the terms of any relevant FTAs,[44] and unsurprisingly this survey of national laws confirms that many jurisdictions do not take advantage of the flexibilities afforded to them in implementing test data exclusivity provisions. Of course, some jurisdictions have

[44] Shaikh (2016), p. 207.

multiple international obligations regarding test data exclusivity, some more restrictive than others; for example, while Jordan's FTA with the US does not specify how long the term of test data exclusivity for data submitted regarding NCEs must be,[45] Jordan committed to a 5-year term during its earlier accession to the WTO.[46] However, many jurisdictions have implemented test data exclusivity in more restrictive terms than required by *any* of their international obligations. This both includes jurisdictions which do not implement measures on which the relevant international obligation is silent, such as exceptions for compulsory licensing, but also in some cases flexibilities that have been specifically negotiated in a trade agreement; Colombia, for example, does not appear to apply the so-called 'concurrent rule' in its national test data exclusivity provisions despite its inclusion in its FTAs with both the US and EU—it is unclear whether this is the result of fear of retaliation, lobbying at the national level, a lack of awareness of the issue by the drafters of the implementing legislation, or if the policy is implemented by a measure other than the national legislation.[47] Interestingly, in some cases the national legislation of the jurisdictions surveyed appears to provide *less* protection than required by their international agreements—for example, both Jordan and Australia committed to providing 3 years of exclusivity to new clinical information in their FTAs with the US,[48] but neither appears to do so in their national laws.[49]

The fact that national laws on test data exclusivity are often more restrictive than the terms of associated international obligations, or in some cases possibly not in conformity with those international obligations, demonstrates the fact that while trade policy has been perhaps the primary means by which test data exclusivity has globalised, other mechanisms have been important in determining the precise details on national test data exclusivity laws. Modelling has clearly played a large role in the globalisation of test data exclusivity. In many cases this modelling is general; for example, the fact that the most common term by far is 5 years, even amongst countries which have not committed to providing specifically this term of protection, reflects the modelling of the US approach to test data exclusivity, as does the decision by many jurisdictions to follow the approach of the EU and extend test data exclusivity protection to biologic drugs. However, in some cases the modelling is extremely specific; the test data exclusivity laws of New Zealand and Singapore, for example, are exceptionally similar—indeed, identical in places.[50] Modelling tends to be stronger between spatially, culturally or linguistically proximate

[45] US-Jordan FTA (2000), Article 22.

[46] WTO, *Report of the working party on the accession of the Hashemite Kingdom of Jordan to the World Trade Organization,* WT/ACC/JOR/33 (3 December 1999).

[47] US-Colombia TPA (2006); EU-Colombia-Peru-Ecuador FTA (2012); Republic of Colombia, Decree 2085 of 2002.

[48] US-Jordan FTA (2000), Article 22, US-Australia FTA (2004), Article 17.10.

[49] See Jordan, Law No. 15 of 2000 on Unfair Competition and Trade Secrets; Australia, Therapeutic Goods Act, 1989 (as amended).

[50] New Zealand, Medicines Act 1981 as amended by the Medicines Amendment Act 1994; Singapore, Medicines Act, 1975 (as amended).

jurisdictions,[51] and this is generally borne out in the jurisdictions surveyed—the EU's approach has been closely modelled by Switzerland and Serbia; Peru, Colombia and Chile all place extremely similar limitations on the test data exclusivity rights in their national laws; and as already mentioned, the laws of Singapore and New Zealand—both small, wealthy, English-speaking countries—are virtually identical. In other cases, modelling has different motivations. The proposed amendments to China's laws on test data exclusivity mentioned at Sect. 6.4.1 are explicitly modelled on the American Hatch-Waxman Act, despite the significant dissimilarities between the US and China; in this case, the modelling appears to be motivated by the desire by China's leadership for the country to become an 'innovator' rather than a 'imitator' economy.[52]

While jurisdictions vary along these regional and cultural lines, by far the biggest division between the approaches to test data exclusivity between the jurisdictions featured in this section is the differing approaches of developed and developing countries. For example, two distinct patterns of formulation of test data exclusivity provisions are apparent amongst those countries surveyed; test data exclusivity is formulated either as an aspect of the drug approval system or as a free-standing intellectual property right. While this does not by itself influence the substantive test data exclusivity provisions of a jurisdiction, it is indicative of a wider trend. Developed countries tend to adopt the former approach to a greater or lesser degree. The US and EU, for example, do not explicitly state that submitted test data is protected for a particular period; instead, test data exclusivity is the result of the period of time before an applicant can make use of an abbreviated drug application which references the originator product.[53] Other jurisdictions do make explicit reference to a specific test data exclusivity period but do so in their legislation on medicine. Japan takes the 'drug approval system' approach to the extreme; as discussed in previous chapters, Japan restricts access to the abbreviated approval system through a 'post-marketing surveillance period' in which other versions of a new drug may not be approved.[54]

Developing countries, on the other hand, tend to express test data exclusivity as a separate intellectual property right concerned with the protection of the submitted

[51] Braithwaite and Drahos (2000), p. 583.

[52] See further Yu (2019).

[53] USA, 21 USC § 355; EU Council Directive 2001/83/EC on the Community code relating to medicinal products for human use [2001].

[54] Japan, Pharmaceutical Affairs Law, Article 14-4. While post-market surveillance of pharmaceutical products is a standard practice in many jurisdictions, the link with exclusivity for the originator product is unusual. In theory, this is a public health measure designed to safeguard public health, but in practice, it operates virtually identically to standard test data exclusivity (Shaikh describes it as '*de facto* data exclusivity'; Shaikh (2016), p. 6). Indeed, it seems that over time the rationale behind the Japanese-style approach has shifted towards that of US-style test data exclusivity; a longer 'post-marketing surveillance period' is available for orphan drugs in Japan, for example, while in Korea independently generated data can be used to approve a product during the post-marketing surveillance period—both policies more in line with incentivising innovation than protecting public health.

data, although there are exceptions, particularly amongst the developing countries in Europe and the immediate area, such as Russia, Turkey and Serbia.[55] The fact that this approach predominates in developing jurisdictions reflects the fact that for the most part these jurisdictions adopted test data exclusivity in order to conform with international obligations under FTAs or WTO accession agreements, rather than developing the provisions themselves or directly modelling them from another developed country.

Jurisdictions which have adopted this second approach are significantly more likely to provide meaningful exceptions and limitations to test data exclusivity than those jurisdictions which adopt the first approach. It is unclear to what extent this is causation rather than mere correlation; perhaps formulating test data exclusivity as an intellectual property right highlights its status as a policy choice which imposes real costs to be mitigated in addition to its purported benefits, although it may also be the case that developing countries are more inclined to place pro-access to medicines restrictions on intellectual property rights to begin with.

It is certainly the case that developed countries tend to have significantly more restrictive test data exclusivity provisions in general, such as longer terms of protection and additional protections for NCI, paediatric formulations and biologics. This is unsurprising; developed countries are the most likely to host the research-based pharmaceutical companies who will be the immediate beneficiaries of increased IP protection for medicines, as opposed to developing countries for which increased IP protection for products developed and marketed by foreign research-based pharmaceutical companies represents a transfer of wealth out of the country.

Lastly, it should be observed that there is a significant amount of variation in the length of the test data exclusivity provisions of the jurisdictions surveyed; the various national laws range in length from a few sentences in the case of Russia,[56] to several pages of provisions in the case of Peru.[57] A long law is not necessarily a good law, of course, but a very short legislative provision might be expected to lack in nuance.

6.4.3 Basic Test Data Exclusivity Protection

This section firstly examines the term of the 'basic' test data exclusivity period in the surveyed jurisdictions, before moving to examine the nature of the basic test data exclusivity protection as well as the criteria for protection. 'Basic' test data

[55] Russia, Federal law 61-FZ on circulation of medicines (2010), Article 18, Serbia, Law on medicinal products and medicinal devices (2010), Article 31, Turkey, Regulation on Authorization of Pharmaceutical Products for Human Use (2005), Article 9.

[56] Russia, Federal law 61-FZ on circulation of medicines (2010), Article 18.

[57] Peru, Legislative Decree 1072 of 2008 and Supreme Decree 002-2009-SA.

exclusivity here refers to the general test data exclusivity protection available to an originator product, rather than more specialised forms of protection for data submitted in associated with new indications or biologic drugs.

6.4.3.1 Term

The length of the basic term of test data exclusivity varies between 5 and 10 years in the jurisdictions surveyed, although in some cases longer and shorter terms of protection are available for certain types of data such as that submitted concerning new indications or biologics (see below). By far the most common basic term of protection is 5 years—of the 27 countries surveyed, 18 grant a basic test data exclusivity period of 5 years.[58] Other jurisdictions surveyed apply a longer basic test data exclusivity period. China, Russia, Kazakhstan and Turkey all apply a 6-year period; Japan and Canada both apply a basic period of 8 years protection; while the EU, Switzerland and Serbia apply a 10-year period of protection.

In addition, some jurisdictions permit a grant of exclusivity longer or indeed shorter than this basic period. The laws of Trinidad and Tobago, Oman, Saudi Arabia and Mauritius state that the term of protection will be ‘at least’ or ‘a minimum’ of 5 years, theoretically permitting a longer term of protection, while on the other hand Malaysia treats the 5-year term as a ceiling, allowing a lower term to be granted.[59] Peru simply states that the term of protection will ‘normally’ be 5 years, suggesting that it may not be so in some abnormal circumstances.[60] It is unclear how frequently higher or lower terms of protection are actually granted; data from the Malaysian National Pharmaceutical Regulatory Agency and Peru’s Ministry of Health shows that in practice these jurisdictions, at least, have granted 5 years of protection to every NCE which qualified for test data protection between 2010 and 2018 (although often measured from the date of a foreign approval, as noted below).[61]

Prior to the amendment of the EU test data exclusivity regime in 2004, many European countries limited the test data exclusivity to that of the term of patents associated with the pharmaceutical product in question.[62] However, this practice is

---

[58] These are Australia, Bahrain, Chile, Colombia, Costa Rica, El Salvador, Jordan, Malaysia, Mauritius, New Zealand, Oman, Peru, Saudi Arabia, Singapore, Trinidad and Tobago, the USA and Vietnam.

[59] Trinidad and Tobago, Protection Against Unfair Competition Act 27/1996, as amended by Act No. 18; Oman, Royal Decree 67/2008: Promulgating the Law on Industrial Property Rights, Article 65; Saudi Arabia, Regulations for the Protection of Confidential Commercial Information (2005), Article 5; Mauritius, The Protection against Unfair Practices (Industrial Property Rights) Act 2002, Article 9; Malaysia, Directive on Data Exclusivity (Directive No. 2 of 2011), Article 4.6.

[60] Peru, Legislative Decree 1072 of 2008, Article 3.

[61] See Appendix A.

[62] EU, Council directive 87/21/EEC. Those countries which used a 6-year data exclusivity period could choose to limit its duration to that of the patent term. This was not possible if countries used the longer 10-year protection period.

now uncommon—unsurprising, given that as we saw in the previous chapter virtually all US-led FTAs from the mid-2000s onwards have explicitly prohibited this practice. Of the countries surveyed, only Turkey limits the term of exclusivity to the term of patents associated with the pharmaceutical product.[63]

Longer terms of test data exclusivity will, obviously, have a greater impact on the date of market entry of generic products, although it should be noted that this impact is likely to be greater in developing countries as discussed at Sect. 2.3.1.1. However, as noted above, most of the jurisdictions surveyed have a basic term of test data exclusivity protection at the lower end of the range of terms—5 or 6 years—with only a few jurisdictions providing significantly longer terms. That 5 years is the most common basic term of protection is unsurprising; while entirely arbitrary, 5 years was the original period of test data exclusivity protection for pharmaceuticals in the US Hatch-Waxman Act, and many jurisdictions have followed the US approach either as a result of a trade agreement with the US (of the 18 jurisdictions with a 5-year basic term, 11 have signed an FTA with the US committing to providing test data exclusivity for at least 5 years)[64] or as a result of modelling the US approach. As discussed in the previous chapter, those jurisdictions which provide 6 years of protection do so as a result of international obligations negotiated with developed countries—commitments made during the WTO accession process in the case of China, Russia and Kazakhstan, and a result of the settlement in the dispute with the EU in the case of Turkey.[65] Those jurisdictions with significantly longer terms of protection are largely developed countries such as Canada, Japan and the EU (while Serbia also provides 10 years of protection, this is clearly a result of the direct modelling of the EU approach, as discussed above).

Measuring the Term of Protection

In most of the jurisdictions surveyed, the term of protection runs from the date of domestic approval of the drug in question. There are some exceptions; New Zealand, Trinidad and Tobago and Mauritius appear to measure the term of exclusivity from the date on which the data is *submitted*,[66] which would obviously translate into a lower effective term of protection (Singapore measures the term of protection for confidential supporting information from the date of submission,[67] and of safety and efficacy data from the date of registration).[68]

---

[63] Turkey, Regulation on Authorization of Pharmaceutical Products for Human Use (2005), Article 5.

[64] Those countries are Australia, Bahrain, Chile, Colombia, Costa Rica, El Salvador, Oman, Peru, Singapore Trinidad and Tobago and Vietnam.

[65] European Commission (2004).

[66] New Zealand, Medicines Act 1981 as amended by the Medicines Amendment Act (1994) s23A; Trinidad and Tobago, Protection Against Unfair Competition Act 27/1996, as amended by Act No. 18 of 2000, Intellectual Property (Misc Amendments), Article 9; Mauritius, The Protection against Unfair Practices (Industrial Property Rights) Act 2002, Article 9.

[67] Singapore, Medicines Act 1975 (as amended) Regulation 26.

[68] Singapore, Medicines Act 1975 (as amended) Article Regulation 29.

A few jurisdictions measure the term from a *foreign* approval date; Peru applies the so-called 'concurrent rule' featured in its FTAs with the US and EU;[69] when the approval for an originator product is completed in 6 months, the term of exclusivity will be measured from the date of approval in a 'country with high sanitary monitoring' rather than the date of national registration[70] (interestingly, Colombia does not seem to have any domestic provisions on the matter despite its inclusion in both its trade deals with the US and EU,[71] although such provisions may be applied in practice). Malaysia measures the term of protection from the product's first approval in 'the country of origin or in any country recognized and deemed appropriate',[72] this applies regardless of how quickly Malaysia processes the originator application (while Peru's concurrent rule is the result of a compromise with the US in a trade agreement, Malaysia has no such agreement with the US). Turkey measures the term of protection from the first approval in the EU-Turkey Customs Union,[73] while Serbia measures its term of protection from the first approval in Serbia, the EU or 'countries that have the same or similar requirements'[74]—in practice, this will mean that the term is virtually always measured from the first approval in the EU, as a drug will rarely be registered in Turkey or Serbia before a western European country.

Impact of Measuring the Term of Protection from a Foreign Date of Approval Measuring the term of protection from the date of application will obviously reduce the effective period of exclusivity, as the approval process itself will take time. It is unclear if such a reduction in the effective test data exclusivity term is the intention of these jurisdictions. Measuring the term of protection from a foreign approval, however, *does* appear to be an intentional policy decision to prevent test data exclusivity acting as a perverse incentive to delay the launch of a product in the jurisdiction as discussed at Sect. 2.4.1.1, and indeed may serve as an incentive to launch the product more quickly in the jurisdiction in question. How significant an impact does measuring the term of protection from a foreign approval have in practice? Data on the approval of certain pharmaceutical drugs in Peru and Malaysia relating to the grant of test data exclusivity provide some insight here.[75]

Between January 2010 and June 2018, the Peruvian government granted test data exclusivity to 58 new chemical entities. While all products granted test data exclusivity in Peru were granted 5 years (60 months) of protection, the effective term of

[69] US-Peru TPA (2006), Article 16.10; Agreement between the EU and Peru and Colombia (2012), Article 231.

[70] Peru, Legislative Decree 1072 of 2008, Article 3.

[71] US-Colombia TPA (2006), Article 16.10; Agreement between the EU and Peru and Colombia (2012), Article 231.

[72] Malaysia, Directive on Data Exclusivity (2011), Article 4.6.

[73] Turkey, Regulation on Authorization of Pharmaceutical Products for Human Use (2005), Article 9.

[74] Serbia, Law on medicinal products and medicinal devices (2010), Article 31.

[75] Calculations based on data provided in Annex A.

protection in Peru was less than the potential full term for every product; the mean length of the test data exclusivity term for those pharmaceuticals for which it was granted between December 2009 and June 2019 was 38.4 months (64% of the potential full term).

Malaysia granted test data exclusivity to 32 new chemical entities between January 2012 and April 2019. As with Peru, all products which were granted test data exclusivity received a term of 5 years (60 months), but the effective term of protection in Malaysia was less than this in all cases, with a mean effective term of 38.6 months (64.4% of the potential full term). Malaysia also grants 3 years (36 months) of test data exclusivity to new chemical indications. Eight new chemical indications were approved between June 2012 and November of 2018; all were granted a nominal term of 3 years, but the mean effective term of protection in Malaysia was 22.5 months (62.5% of the potential full term).

These results represent the impact of measuring the term of test data exclusivity from a foreign approval in only two jurisdictions and over a relatively short period of time. However, they demonstrate that such a policy has a clear impact on reducing the term of test data exclusivity. It is notable that in both jurisdictions, the reduction in the total potential term of test data exclusivity was almost equal. Peru and Malaysia are both upper-middle income countries with a similar population, which may explain why the reductions are so similar between the two jurisdictions; other jurisdictions may find that such a policy has a different impact on the effective test data exclusivity period.

6.4.3.2 Data Exclusivity *Per Se* and Market Exclusivity

As previously discussed in Chap. 2, test data exclusivity can take the form of data exclusivity *per se* (that is, an abbreviated application which seeks to rely upon or use previously submitted data may not be processed at all during the exclusivity period) or market exclusivity (that is, such an application may be processed during the exclusivity period, but can only be approved once the period has ended). Market exclusivity is theoretically less restrictive than data exclusivity *per se*—regulators can still use the submitted originator data to process abbreviated applications during the exclusivity term, then approve them as soon as the protection term ends. In contrast, under data exclusivity *per se*, would-be generic competitors must wait till the term expires, then launch their applications, further delaying market entry—for example, while the test data exclusivity for new chemical entities in the US is 5 years of data exclusivity *per se*, because of the time taken to process ANDAs, the term of exclusivity is closer to 7.5 years in practice.[76]

Generally speaking, it is difficult to determine whether a jurisdiction provides data exclusivity *per se* or market exclusivity from the mere wording of the governing legislation; the law as written may only prohibit the *approval* of an abbreviated

[76] Shaikh (2016), p. 101.

application before the end of the exclusivity period, but the practice of the national regulatory authority may be to only accept abbreviated applications once the exclusivity period has ended, or indeed *vice versa*. However, a number of jurisdictions quite explicitly provide both a period of data exclusivity *per se* supplemented by a longer period of market exclusivity. Taiwan, Russia, Canada, the EU, Switzerland and Serbia all take this approach; Taiwan provides a 3-year period of data exclusivity *per se* concurrent with a 5 year period of market exclusivity, Russia 4 years of exclusivity *per se* concurrent with 6 years market exclusivity;[77] Canada 6 years exclusivity *per se* concurrent with 8 years market exclusivity and 8 years exclusivity *per se* concurrent with 10 years market exclusivity in the EU, Switzerland and Serbia.

The logic behind such an approach is to ensure that applications can be processed during the final period of exclusivity protection to allow the generic products to enter the market soon after test data exclusivity expires, in a similar manner to the so-called 'Bolar' or early working exemption to patent law which permits the use of patent pharmaceuticals in order to conduct tests necessary for regulatory approval;[78] this helps to ensure that originators do not end up with an effective exclusivity period significantly longer than that set out by the law. While this is to be welcomed from the perspective of promoting access to medicines, it should be noted that with the exception of Taiwan, most jurisdictions which take this approach have significantly longer periods of protection to begin with, in many cases exceeding the likely practical exclusivity period for a jurisdiction with 5 years of data exclusivity *per se*.

6.4.3.3 Qualification for Protection

As discussed at Sect. 2.4.1.4, one of the concerns around test data exclusivity is that because test data exclusivity protection is both easier to obtain and harder to challenge than patent protection, it risks undermining the checks and balances that intellectual property rights in pharmaceutical products are normally subject to. For a patent to be granted, the claimed invention must satisfy the strict criteria of novelty, inventive step and industrial application, which are assessed during a process of formal examination and which third parties can challenge through opposition and invalidation proceedings—such mechanisms reduce the chance that patents are granted inappropriately. Article 39.3 requires only the protection of submitted test data that is undisclosed, is associated with a new chemical entity, and if its origination involved considerable effort—and many jurisdictions do not even apply all of these criteria. Furthermore, test data exclusivity often arises automatically as a result of a pharmaceutical product being approved and many jurisdictions do not provide formal routes to challenge this protection.

---

[77] This differs for biologic drugs, as discussed below.

[78] See further Tridico et al. (2014).

With the exception of Russia,[79] all jurisdictions surveyed require that data be submitted with respect to a new pharmaceutical product in order to qualify for the basic term of protection, either directly (through an explicit requirement the data be submitted regarding a new drug) or indirectly (by only restricting access to the abbreviated application process for a period after the first approval of a drug in that jurisdiction).[80] As discussed in Chap. 4, there is some debate over whether this standard of novelty should be assessed against all existing pharmaceutical products ('global novelty') or assessed against only those products that have already been approved in the jurisdiction in question ('local novelty'). In practice, most of the jurisdictions surveyed apply a local novelty standard. However, a few jurisdictions vary from this approach to a greater or lesser degree. China appears to apply a standard of global novelty, only granting exclusivity to drugs that are new to the world,[81] a practice which the USTR's Special 301 Report has criticised for years[82] (the proposed new Chinese medicines law would move the country to a local novelty standard).[83] Taiwan, Chile, Vietnam and Malaysia all require that in order to receive test data exclusivity, a product must not have been registered in another jurisdiction for longer than a certain period prior to the application for marketing approval in that jurisdiction; for more than 3 years in the case of Taiwan, 18 months in the case of Malaysia and 12 months in the cases of Vietnam and Chile.[84] As with those jurisdictions which measure the term of exclusivity from the approval in a foreign jurisdiction, these measures serve to mitigate the issue that test data exclusivity may incentivise companies to delay launching a product in a particular jurisdiction in order to maximise the monopoly period discussed at Sect. 2.4.1.1.

Most jurisdictions also apply the requirement that data should be undisclosed to be eligible for protection. Only a minority of mostly developed countries do not make this requirement explicit in their test data exclusivity law,[85] although even in these cases secrecy may be a *de facto* requirement if the jurisdiction permits publicly available information to be used in abbreviated applications, as the US does through so-called 'paper-NDAs.'[86]

By far the least consistently applied of the 39.3 criteria is that the data be the product of 'considerable effort.' Of the 27 jurisdictions surveyed, only 12 jurisdictions—all developing countries—state that data must be the product of

[79] Russia, Federal law 61-FZ on circulation of medicines (2010), Article 18.

[80] For example, the US only grants test data exclusivity to the data associated with products approved through a new drug application—which must necessarily be new; 21 USC § 355.

[81] Balzano (2022).

[82] See, for example, USTR (2019).

[83] NMPA (2018).

[84] Taiwan, Pharmaceutical affairs act, Article 40-2; Malaysia, Directive on Data Exclusivity (2011), Article 4.2; Vietnam, Circular No 17/2011/TT-BNNPTNT 2011, Article 3; Chile, Law No 19.039 on Industrial Property (as amended), Article 91.

[85] These are: The US, EU, Switzerland, Turkey, Russia, Serbia, Japan, Canada and Taiwan.

[86] USA, 21 USC §355.

considerable effort to received protection.[87] It is unclear what impact this requirement has in practice. Firstly, data which does not require 'considerable' effort to generate will be significantly less valuable, given that it will necessarily be easier for competitors to generate themselves. Secondly, it is unclear how national drug regulatory bodies assess whether submitted data required 'considerable' effort to generate or not, or indeed whether any national regulatory authorities actually make this assessment at all. As such, it is unsurprising that many jurisdictions have omitted this criterion from their national laws.

In most of the jurisdictions surveyed, it appears that test data exclusivity protection arises automatically as a result of the submission or approval of the drug application, although Malaysia and Vietnam both require that an application for test data exclusivity must be made to receive protection; it is unclear whether this application process involves any substantive assessment or whether it is merely a formality.[88] More interestingly, Vietnam and Peru also explicitly provide for a mechanism to revoke test data exclusivity if it has been improperly granted. Vietnam provides that 'all organisations and individuals' may request the termination of test data exclusivity protection, including on the grounds that the data does not meet the requirements for protection.[89] Peru mandates the publication of details relating to the grant of test data exclusivity in *El Peruano*, the newspaper of record, within 15 days of the filing of the new drug application and permits any party with a 'legitimate interest' to oppose the grant of protection.[90] In addition, the Peruvian law provides that test data exclusivity protection can be cancelled '*ex officio* or at the request of a party' if an administrative procedure determines that the protection was improperly granted.[91]

It is likely that in at least some other jurisdictions it is possible to challenge grants of test data exclusivity through general systems of judicial review or other aspects of administrative law. However, the provision of specific measures to challenge test data exclusivity makes the revocation of improperly granted protection more likely. Furthermore, the Peruvian system of publication and potential opposition to the grant of test data exclusivity adds a degree of transparency to what can otherwise be an unhelpfully opaque system. Such mechanisms guard against the risks that test data exclusivity will undermine the checks and balances of the wider intellectual property system.

[87] El Salvador, Costa Rica, Colombia, Peru, Chile, Saudi Arabia, Jordan, Malaysia, Vietnam, Bahrain, Trinidad and Tobago and Mauritius.

[88] Malaysia, Directive on Data Exclusivity (2011), Article 4.2; Vietnam, Circular No 17/2011/TT-BNNPTNT 2011, Article 3.

[89] Vietnam, Circular No 17/2011/TT-BNNPTNT 2011, Article 11, 14.

[90] Peru, Regulation on Legislative Decree No. 1072 on the Protection of Test Data and Other Undisclosed Data Relating to Pharmaceuticals (approved by Supreme Decree No. 002-2009-SA) (2009), Article 7–8.

[91] Ibid, Article 20.

6.4.4 *Protection for Other Types of Submitted Test Data*

Article 39.3 of TRIPS requires only that data submitted with regards to new chemical entities be protected. However, some jurisdictions (mostly developed countries) also provide protection for 'other' types of data, such as new indications for previously approved active ingredients, data concerning paediatric studies or data submitted with respect to biologic drugs. While these jurisdictions are in a clear minority, such additional protection has become an increasingly common feature of trade agreements and may represent the next major area of expansion for test data exclusivity.

This section details the approaches of the jurisdictions surveyed to data submitted regarding non-novel small molecule drugs as well as data submitted regarding biologics.

6.4.4.1 Protection for Data Submitted Regarding Non-novel Uses of Small Molecule Drugs

A number of jurisdictions provide additional protection for new indications, paediatric indications and/or orphan drugs. These additional protections either take the form of extensions to the basic term of protection when this additional data is provided, or the form of an entirely separate test data exclusivity period covering the data in question.[92]

The EU, Serbia, the US and Canada all provide for exclusivity extensions. The EU and Serbia provide an extra year of market exclusivity for new therapeutic indications that are held to have 'significant clinical benefit' in comparison with existing therapies approved during the first 8 years of exclusivity.[93] Canada grants an additional 6 months of market exclusivity if an originator submits the results of clinical trials relating to use of the drug in paediatric populations.[94] The US also grants a 6 month extension for market authorisation holders who submit paediatric studies, although this applies to any exclusivity related to the drug in question, including associated patents or orphan drug exclusivity,[95] and as such is not a purely test data exclusivity provision.[96]

[92] These extensions of existing test data exclusivity rights or creations of new data exclusivity periods should not be confused with the similar but distinct concept of 'orphan exclusivity' that exists in jurisdictions such as the US and EU, discussed at Sect. 2.3.1.3. Whereas test data exclusivity provisions restrict the ability of subsequent applicants to reference originator data in an abbreviated approval, these provisions prohibit *any* other version of the same drug being approved for the disease in question (although approval for other purposes is still permitted).

[93] EU, Council Directive 2001/83/EC, Serbia, Law on medicinal products and medicinal devices (2010), Article 31.

[94] Canada, Food and Drug Regulations (as amended) C.08.004.1(2).

[95] USA, § 21 USC 301.

[96] Heled (2015), p. 327.

Grants of new exclusivity periods are more common amongst the jurisdictions surveyed. The US offers 3 years of market exclusivity to new chemical indications (NCIs).[97] Oman and Malaysia also provide 3 years of exclusivity to data submitted regarding NCIs;[98] similar to the requirements placed on data submitted regarding NCEs, Malaysia requires the application for the NCI to have been made within 12 months of the first international approval and that the data be the result of considerable effort.[99] Taiwan provides 2 years of data exclusivity *per se* concurrent with 3 years of market exclusivity for data submitted regarding NCIs, with the period of protection extended to 5 years when a domestic clinical trial is conducted regarding the new indication and is sought within 3 years of its first international approval.[100] Japan grants between 6 and 10 years of *de facto* exclusivity for orphan and paediatric drugs, and 4–6 years of exclusivity for new indications.[101] Switzerland grants 3 years of exclusivity for corresponding documentation on new indications, modes of administration, dosage forms or dosages, but this can be set at 10 years exclusivity if the new information is expected to bring a significant clinical benefit in comparison with existing therapies and if it is supported by extensive clinical trials. Switzerland also grants period of 10 years test data exclusivity for products 'specifically and exclusively' for paediatric use and of 15 years for 'important orphan medicinal products.'[102]

It is apparent that amongst the jurisdictions surveyed protection for other forms of data is significantly more varied than 'basic' test data exclusivity protection, ranging from 6-month extensions to an additional 15-year term. The jurisdictions that provide such protection are largely developed ones. Developing countries are significantly less likely to provide such protection—indeed, the national laws of Peru, Colombia, Chile and Costa Rica explicitly state that data submitted regarding new indications, doses, methods of administration *et cetera* of previously approved products will not be granted exclusivity.[103] The non-developed countries which provide such protection featured in this section have committed to providing such protection in an FTA (in the case of Oman),[104] or have closely modelled their law on that of the US or EU (in the cases of Malaysia, Taiwan and Serbia). It is worth noting

[97] That the protection is market exclusivity rather than data exclusivity *per se* was established in *Bristol-Myers Squibb Co. v Donna E. Shalala*, 91 F.3d 1493 (1996).

[98] Oman, Royal Decree 67/2008: Promulgating the Law on Industrial Property Rights, Article 65; Malaysia, Directive on Data Exclusivity (2011).

[99] Ibid.

[100] Taiwan, Pharmaceutical Affairs Act, Article 40-2.

[101] Japan, Pharmaceutical Affairs Law, Article 14-4.

[102] Switzerland, Federal Act on Medicinal Products and Medical Devices (Therapeutic Products Act) 2000 (as amended 2016), Article 11–12.

[103] Peru, Legislative Decree 1072 of 2008; Colombia, Decree 2085 of 2002, Article 1–5; Chile, Law No 19.039 on Industrial Property (as amended), Article 89; Costa Rica, Executive decree 34927 of 28 November 2008, Regulations on the Undisclosed Information Act, Article 12–15.

[104] US-Oman FTA (2006), Article 15.9.

that two jurisdictions featured in this section, Jordan[105] and Australia,[106] had committed to providing 3 years of test data exclusivity protection to NCI in their FTAs with the US, but do not appear to provide such protection in their statutory law; it is unclear if this is a case of noncompliance, or if this protection is provided in another area of the law or the policy of the national drug regulatory authority.

Both this diversity of approaches and the general absence of protection for other forms of submitted test data outside of the developed world reflects the fact that the measure is clearly TRIPS-plus; that additional data submitted regarding previously approved chemical entities need not be protected from unfair commercial use is one of the few unambiguous aspects of Article 39.3. However, as discussed in Chap. 5, a number of recent FTAs include provisions on the protection of NCI. This is an area in which test data exclusivity rights might be expected to expand in coming years.

6.4.4.2 Protection for Data Submitted Regarding Biologic Drugs

The question of whether test data submitted regarding biologics should be protected was largely academic for the first decade or so after TRIPS entered into force. As discussed at Sect. 2.5, the increased size of biologics and the more complicated processes involved in their manufacture make the creation of exact copies of an originator drug effectively impossible;[107] along with the relative novelty of biologic drugs, this meant that abbreviated processes for 'biosimilar' drugs simply did not exist in most major jurisdictions.

This changed in the mid-2000s, when, as detailed at Sect. 2.5.1, the first abbreviated approval pathways for biologics were created following a wave of expirations of patents over biologic products;[108] for the first time, the issue of how test data submitted regarding biologics should be protected, if at all, became relevant. As the first jurisdiction to create an abbreviated approval pathway for biologics, the EU was also the first to deal with the issue of how the data submitted in association with innovator biologics should be protected. The EU opted to use the same legislative

[105] US-Jordan FTA (2000), Article 22.

[106] US-Australia FTA (2004), Article 17.10. A footnote to the paragraph of the US-Australia FTA which requires 3 years of protection for NCI states that 'As an alternative to this paragraph, where a Party, on the date of entry into force of this Agreement, **has in place a system for protecting information** submitted in connection with the approval of **a pharmaceutical product that utilizes a previously approved chemical component** from unfair commercial use, the Party may retain that system, notwithstanding the obligations of this paragraph.' (Footnote 17–26, emphasis added). However, Australia's test data exclusivity law clearly states that test data exclusivity is only available when 'no other therapeutic goods consisting of, or containing, that active component were included in the Register', which would preclude new indications for previously approved products (Australian Therapeutic Goods Act (1989), section 25A(c)(i)).

[107] Matthews (2017), p. 106.

[108] EU, Directive 2001/83/EC, Article 10.

basis for the approval of biosimilars as for generic small molecule drugs; because test data exclusivity is an intrinsic aspect of the EU's abbreviated approval procedure as discussed above, biologics are therefore protected by the same system of 8 years of data exclusivity *per se* concurrent with 10 years market exclusivity (and the possibility of a year's extension to the market exclusivity period for significant new therapeutic indications) as traditional pharmaceuticals.[109]

The US, on the other hand, created an entirely new legislative basis for its biosimilar approval pathway in the form of the 2009 Biologics Price Competition and Innovation Act (BPCIA), meaning that the issue of test data exclusivity had to be considered separately. In the run up to the passage of the BPCIA, many different periods of exclusivity were discussed, including a proposal by Henry Waxman (one of the co-sponsors of the Hatch-Waxman Act itself) that would have given no exclusivity period to biologics,[110] and a proposal that would have required a 14-year exclusivity period.[111] Ultimately, the period of test data exclusivity for biologic products was set at 12 years after the date of the originator's approval in total,[112] split into a period of 4 years of data exclusivity during which the FDA cannot accept biosimilar applications, and a concurrent 12 year period of market exclusivity during which the FDA cannot grant approval to biosimilars.[113] As with other exclusivities in the US, both periods of protection can be extended by a further 6 months if further paediatric testing is submitted,[114] although unlike test data exclusivity for small molecule drugs, no additional protection is provided for new indications, formulations *et cetera*. Unlike small molecule drugs under the Hatch-Waxman Act, there is no 'novelty' requirement for a biologic to receive test data exclusivity; any product approved through a standard, non-biosimilar biologic application will receive exclusivity protection, even if an identical product has previously been authorised. This may be due to the difficulty of establishing whether a biologic drug has been previously approved, given the complexities of their structure—in practice, all biologic drugs are different, and therefore to some extent 'novel.' Additionally, it may be to deal with the issue of subsequent s262 (a) applications for second-to-market versions of biologic products which have previously been approved acting as 'back doors' for abbreviated applications. Shaikh suggests that such non-abbreviated follow on applications may be more common for biologics than for small molecule drugs because the higher cost of developing a biosimilar compared to a generic small molecule drug, as well as the smaller price difference between brand name and generic biologics compared to small molecule drugs, may incentivise companies to make original biologic

[109] EU, Directive 2001/83/EC, Article 10(1)–(5); Regulation 2309/93, Article 13(4); Regulation 726/2004, Article 14.11.

[110] Grabowski (2008), p. 479.

[111] Ibid.

[112] US, 42 USC § 262(k).

[113] US, 42 USC § 262(k).

[114] Matthews (2017), p. 107.

licensing applications (BLAs) for their own versions of products already on the market during the originator's exclusivity period, and because medical practitioners may be more confident about prescribing another biologic than a drug approved via the biosimilar pathway.[115]

The decision to distinguish the treatment of small molecule drugs and biologics in the US can be partly explained by historical factors; biologics are regulated under the 1944 Public Health Services Act rather than the 1938 Federal Food, Drug, and Cosmetic Act. This meant that biologics were not included within the scope of the Hatch-Waxman Act. However, the substantial difference in the test data exclusivity term between biologics and small molecule drugs was chiefly the result of a successful campaign by various interested parties in the US who argued that biologics required a much longer period of test data exclusivity protection than small molecule drugs in order to be commercially viable. As was discussed in Chap. 2, this is not obviously the case, and many have criticised the US decision to make biologic test data exclusivity so much longer than test data exclusivity for small molecule drugs—including the Obama administration, which attempted (unsuccessfully) to revise the exclusivity period for biologics down to 7 years.[116]

The approach of other jurisdictions to the protection of data submitted regarding biologics is less clear. Given that this is still a relatively novel issue, the question may simply not yet have arisen, especially amongst developing jurisdictions. For some jurisdictions, the issue will turn on the wording of the domestic legal provisions; for example, New Zealand law clearly defines the medications with regard to which test data exclusivity can arise as those which include a 'chemical or biological entity',[117] which leaves little doubt as to whether test data exclusivity would extend to data submitted with regards to biologics. In other cases, countries have committed to providing test data exclusivity for biologics in an FTA—the EFTA-Turkey FTA and the EU's FTAs with Colombia and Canada all contain commitments regarding the protection of biologic test data, as discussed in the previous chapter. Aside from these examples, such international commitments are uncommon, although this is likely to change in future as discussed in Chap. 5. Some jurisdictions appear to have rejected the notion of test data exclusivity for data submitted regarding biologics all together; the Biotechnology Innovation Organisation (BIO, the biotech counterpart to PhRMA) has previously lambasted Chile and Peru (as well as Mexico and Israel) for stating that they would not be providing test data exclusivity for data submitted with respect of biologics.[118] It is worth noting

[115] Shaikh (2016), p. 108.

[116] Matthews (2017), p. 110.

[117] New Zealand, Medicines Act (1981) as amended by the Medicines Amendment Act (1994), Article 23A.

[118] See, for example, USTR (2016, 2017, 2018).

both Chile and Peru later committed to providing test data exclusivity for biologics in the TPP (albeit with significant transition periods),[119] and Mexico committed to providing such protection in the USMCA;[120] while both these commitments were ultimately suspended or removed from their respective agreements, this does suggest that few countries will exclude biologic test data from the scope of their test data exclusivity laws in the longer term. Amongst the developed jurisdictions featured in this section, by far the most popular approach has been to extend the existing basic test data exclusivity protection to cover data submitted regarding biologics; Australia, Canada, Japan, New Zealand and Switzerland have all taken this approach.[121] This is perhaps to be expected, given that many jurisdictions have modelled other elements of the pioneering approach of the EU to the regulation of biosimilars.

Few countries appear to have adopted the US approach of a separate, longer period of protection for data submitted in association with biologics. Russia slightly varies its approach to test data exclusivity for biologics and small molecule drugs in that while small molecules drugs are granted 4 years of data exclusivity *per se* followed by 2 years of market exclusivity, biologics are granted 3 years of data exclusivity *per se* followed by 3 years of market exclusivity—however, the differences between these two approaches is minimal.[122] As already noted, the USMCA initially required a separate 10-year period of protection for biologics in contrast to a 5-year term for small molecule drugs,[123] and the now-suspended test data exclusivity provisions of the TPP required 8 years of protection for biologic data;[124] given the decisive role of the US in promoting test data exclusivity for small molecule drugs, a push for longer periods of protection for biologic data by the US may have a significant impact. Furthermore, the proposed Chinese law mentioned at Sect. 6.4.1 would provide for 12 years of exclusivity for innovative biologics, an approach explicitly modelled on that of the US—if China does implement this proposal, it will bring one of the world's largest pharmaceutical markets into line with the US approach.[125]

Matthews has compared the EU policy favourably to that of the US, stating that the EU's approach is 'simpler', and proves that differential treatment of test data exclusivity for small molecule drugs and biologics is not inevitable.[126] From the

---

[119] TPP (2016), Article 18.51.

[120] USMCA (2018), Article 20.49.

[121] Australia, Therapeutic Goods Act 1989 s25A; Canada, Food and Drug Regulations, Section C.08.004.1; Gitter (2013), pp. 231–232; Switzerland, Federal Act on Medicinal Products and Medical Devices (Therapeutic Products Act, TPA) 2000 (as amended 2016), Article 11–12.

[122] Russia, Federal law 61-FZ on circulation of medicines (2010), Article 18.

[123] USMCA (2018), Article 20.49.

[124] TPP (2016), Article 18.51. Note that the TPP also permitted parties to provide 5 years protection as an alternative to 8 years protection if they could use 'other measures', including market circumstances, to deliver a 'comparable outcome in the market.'

[125] NMPA (2018).

[126] Matthews (2017), p. 116.

perspective of promoting access to medicine, the EU approach is certainly preferable to that of the US; while the EU itself has amongst the longest term of test data exclusivity protection in the world, most jurisdictions have a much shorter period, as discussed above, and following the EU approach will mean faster market entry for biosimilars. However, the protection of test data submitted regarding biologics is also a TRIPS-plus measure; while there is evidence of resistance to the notion that data submitted with respect to biologics should receive a significantly greater period of protection, it is disappointing that the level of protection for submitted test data has been ratcheted up through its expansion to an entire set of data not covered by TRIPS with little debate as to the policy merits of this approach.

6.4.5 Disclosure of Submitted Test Data

Article 39.3 requires members to protect submitted test data against disclosure, except where 'necessary to protect the public' or where the data will be 'protected from unfair commercial use.' As discussed in Chap. 4, if a jurisdiction uses test data exclusivity to protect submitted test data from unfair commercial use, the jurisdiction is free to disclose the information as long as there is some mechanism in place to prevent unfair use of the data (for example, by preventing subsequent applicants relying on this information during the test data exclusivity term).

Despite this, however, most of the jurisdictions surveyed do prohibit the disclosure of submitted test data as part of their test data exclusivity legislation,[127] although most also permit the disclosure of the data under certain circumstances.[128] These circumstances are typically formulated along the same lines as exceptions to Article 39.3 itself; if the disclosure is necessary to protect the public or if steps are taken to protect the data from unfair commercial use.[129] The fact that many jurisdictions have implemented the 'necessary to protect the public' protection is interesting because, as was discussed in Chap. 4, this exception could potentially act as a means to bypass test data exclusivity in a public health emergency because data disclosed under such circumstances does not need to be protected from unfair commercial use. However, this is speculative, and there is no record in the literature of such an episode occurring.

Requirements that steps be taken to protect the data from unfair commercial use, on the other hand, are somewhat redundant as all jurisdictions involved have already

[127]The jurisdictions which do not explicitly prevent the disclosure of submitted test data in their test data exclusivity legislation are the EEA, Switzerland, Turkey, Serbia, USA, Canada, Australia, Colombia, Saudi Arabia and Malaysia.

[128]Russia, Bahrain and Taiwan do not.

[129]New Zealand, Singapore, Vietnam and Chile permit data to be disclosed only when necessary to protect the public. El Salvador, China, Oman, Jordan, Trinidad and Tobago, Costa Rica, Mauritius and Peru permit data to be disclosed to the public *or* when steps are taken to prevent the data from unfair commercial use. Japan prohibits data to be disclosed unless there is a 'valid reason' to do so.

taken such steps, often in the same provision; while the inclusion of specific measures to prevent such unfair commercial use would make sense, the logic of repeating the language of Article 39.3 here is unclear. In many cases, this is probably a result of similar wording being used in an international obligation such as an FTA or WTO WPR commitment that the national law is implementing. While not particularly impactful in and of itself, the superfluous prohibitions on disclosure of submitted test data unless protected against unfair commercial use in so many of the jurisdictions surveyed demonstrates the plodding manner in which test data exclusivity has been enacted at the national level in many cases. Due to either an unsophisticated understanding of their international obligations or a desire to err on the side of compliance, many national governments have implemented test data exclusivity in this redundant manner.

Interestingly, both the EU and the US provide for the disclosure of submitted test data. Under its 'policy on publication of clinical data for medicinal products for human use,' the EU's EMA actively publishes clinical data submitted under its centralised marketing procedure.[130] 'Unfair commercial use' of the information remains prohibited, and the EMA works with the submitter of clinical trial data to determine what information is 'commercially confidential information' (defined as any information submitted which 'is not in the public domain or publicly available and where disclosure may undermine the legitimate economic interest of the applicant') and redact it from the published reports.[131] There has been little to no discussion of the implications of Article 39.3 on the EMA policy, although given that the data and market exclusivity provided to originators is unaffected (as well as the additional steps the EMA takes to prevent the disclosure of 'commercially confidential information'), there is no reason to think that it would violate the article.[132] In December 2018, the EMA suspended the publication of clinical data as a result of the implementation of the third phase of its business continuity plan, the agency's strategy for handling the disruption caused by its relocation from London in the aftermath of the UK's withdrawal from the EU; as of early 2023, the publication of clinical data remained suspended due to ongoing business continuity linked to the COVID-19 pandemic.[133]

The US permits the disclosure of 'safety and effectiveness data' submitted in an NDA to the public upon request under certain circumstances. These are when an application was not approved and all appeals have been exhausted, and when an abbreviated application has or could be approved (essentially, when test data exclusivity and other exclusivities have expired). In all cases, the disclosure of the

[130] EMA (2019).

[131] Ibid.

[132] Shaikh (2016), p. 127.

[133] EMA, What Clinical Data EMA Publishes; https://www.ema.europa.eu/en/human-regulatory/marketing-authorisation/clinical-data-publication#timelines-for-publication-section. Accessed 26 January 2023.

information will be refused if 'extraordinary circumstances' are shown; these include situations in which the information in question still has 'competitive value.'[134]

6.4.6 *Exceptions to Test Data Exclusivity*

Exceptions are an important aspect of any intellectual property regime. Ideally, exceptions add nuance and flexibility to the right in question; at the very least they should mitigate the most egregious cases of harm that it might cause. This is especially relevant in the case of test data exclusivity, which imposes obvious costs in exchange for uncertain benefits. A number of jurisdictions provide exceptions to the test data exclusivity term. These exceptions all take the form of the temporary suspension or premature ending of test data exclusivity protection. This is due to the nature of exclusivity protection for submitted test data; the right simply restricts access to the abbreviated drug approval pathway, with the submitted data itself never being directly accessed by the prospective 'user'—as such, other types of intellectual property exceptions (such as fair dealing or experimental use) are not applicable (several jurisdictions frame the ability of the originator of the submitted data to permit its use during the exclusivity term as an 'exception', but this is not a true exception to exclusivity any more than a patent holder's ability to license their patent is an exception to patent protection).[135]

Several of the jurisdictions surveyed cease providing test data exclusivity if the associated product is not commercialised within the jurisdiction following its registration. Canada simply does not apply test data exclusivity if the 'innovative medical product' in question is not marketed in Canada.[136] Chile and Columbia both have provisions stating that exclusivity protection does not apply if the pharmaceutical product in question is not marketed within the national territory within a year of its registration.[137] Kazakhstan's legislation states that test data exclusivity will be suspended if 'the supply of a medicinal product is insufficient to meet the needs of the population within twelve months from the date of registration,'[138] while Saudi Arabia provides that the competent authority may permit third parties to use the submitted test data if the product has not been commercialised within Saudi Arabia within a 'reasonable period of time determined by the registration authority.'[139] While such provisions do not address the issue of test data exclusivity incentivising

[134] USA, 21 USC § 355(l)(1).

[135] These jurisdictions are Australia, Chile, Russia, Switzerland, China.

[136] Canada, Food and Drug Regulations (as amended) C.08.004.1(2).

[137] Chile, Law No 19.039 on Industrial Property (as amended), Article 91; Colombia, Decree 2085 of 2002, Article 1.

[138] Kazakhstan, Code of the Republic of Kazakhstan No 193-IV (2009), Article 71(21).

[139] Saudi Arabia, Regulations for the Protection of Confidential Commercial Information (2005), Article 6.

delayed releases, they do provide an incentive to actually bring the pharmaceutical in question to market, as well as guarding against situations where a drug is not being marketed but the entry of generic alternatives is also effectively blocked by test data exclusivity.

Most other exceptions concern extraordinary circumstances under which it may be in the public interest to suspend or end test data exclusivity. As has been discussed, one of the main concerns regarding test data exclusivity is that test data exclusivity provisions can frustrate the compulsory licensing of pharmaceutical products; if generics produced under compulsory license are unable to reference originator data through the abbreviated approval process, the ability to address national emergencies through compulsory licensing will be significantly undermined as products produced under compulsory license could not be marketed. A number of jurisdictions provide explicit exceptions to test data exclusivity whenever a compulsory licensed is issued; Peru, Chile, Malaysia, Kazakhstan and Vietnam all explicitly provide that test data exclusivity is suspended in the event that a compulsory license is issued regarding the associated pharmaceutical product.[140] Peru, Chile and Kazakhstan also provide that test data exclusivity does not apply in cases in which there is a breach of competition law relating to the submitted test data.[141] Anti-competitive practices are a potential risk with any state-sanctioned monopoly, and indeed the need to remedy competition abuses is one of the rationales behind the existence of compulsory licensing provisions.[142] While Peru, Chile and Kazakhstan all suspend test data exclusivity in cases where a compulsory license has been issued for any reason (including, presumably, competition abuses), the provision that test data exclusivity can be suspended for anti-competitive behaviour addresses situations in which no patent is present and test data exclusivity may be the only source of the monopoly in question.

A number of jurisdictions provide for exceptions to test data exclusivity for general reasons. New Zealand, Singapore and Colombia all permit the use of data were necessary to protect public health—a general provision that would presumably include use of the submitted data in cases in which a compulsory license had been issued for reasons of public health.[143] The exceptions of other jurisdictions are more general still. Peru and Kazakhstan also permit use of submitted test data for general 'emergency situations' in addition to protecting public health,[144] Saudi Arabia

[140] Peru, Supreme Decree 002-2009-SA; Chile, Law No 19.039 on Industrial Property (as amended), Article 91; Malaysia, Directive on Data Exclusivity (2011); Kazakhstan, Code of the Republic of Kazakhstan No 193-IV (2009), Article 71; Vietnam, Circular No 17/2011/TT-BNNPTNT 2011, Article 3.

[141] Peru, Legislative Decree 1072 of 2008; Chile, Law No 19.039; Kazakhstan, Code of the Republic of Kazakhstan No 193-IV (2009), Article 71.

[142] Dutfield (2008), pp. 107–112.

[143] New Zealand, Medicines Act 1981 as amended by the Medicines Amendment Act (1994) s23A; Singapore, Medicines Act 1975 (as amended), Article 19A; Colombia, Decree 2085 of 2002, Article 1–5.

[144] Peru, Legislative Decree 1072 of 2008; Kazakhstan, Kazakhstan, Code of the Republic of Kazakhstan No 193-IV (2009), Article 7.

permits use of submitted test data if 'required by a pressing necessity' and Vietnam will end test data exclusivity if 'necessary to protect the public health and to meet urgent needs of the society.'[145] Chile and Malaysia both have extremely wide general exceptions; Chile's exception can be granted if 'for reasons of public health, national security, non-commercial public use, national emergency or other circumstances of extreme urgency declared by the competent authority, it is justified to put an end to the protection',[146] while Malaysia's exclusivity provisions do not 'prevent the Government from taking any necessary action to protect public health, national security, non-commercial public use, national emergency, public health crisis or other extremely urgent circumstances declared by the government' or apply to the implementation of 'measures consistent with the need to protect public health and ensure access to medicines for all.'[147]

The developing jurisdictions surveyed are thus significantly more likely to have robust exceptions to test data exclusivity than developed jurisdictions. However, it should be noted that the US and EU both provide exceptions to test data exclusivity, albeit of a limited nature. The US will shorten the test data exclusivity period of an NCE from 5 years to 4 years whenever a patent associated with the drug in question is subject to a successful invalidity or noninfringement judgment.[148] The EU, on the other hand, has legislation in place to allow access to submitted test data in order to facilitate compulsory licensing under the WTO's 30 August 2003 decision to create a solution to the issues around compulsory licensing in countries with little domestic capacity raised in Paragraph 6 of the Doha Declaration.[149] The 30 August 2003 decision, which in 2017 became the first ever amendment to a WTO agreement when it became Article 31*bis* of the TRIPS Agreement,[150] provides a waiver to the requirement in Article 31(f) of TRIPS that any use of compulsory licensing be 'predominantly for the supply of the domestic market of the Member authorising such use,'[151] permitting countries to issue compulsory licenses with the aim of supplying the products produced under license to another country with limited or no manufacturing capacity in the pharmaceutical sector. Regulation 816/2006, passed in order to facilitate this decision, provides that applicants for compulsory licenses under the system may avail of the scientific opinion procedure of the EMA (or similar national procedures) in order to assess quality, safety, and efficacy of

[145] Saudi Arabia, Regulations for the Protection of Confidential Commercial Information (2005); Vietnam, Circular No 17/2011/TT-BNNPTNT 2011.

[146] Chile, Law No 19.039 on Industrial Property.

[147] Malaysia, Regulation 29 of the Control of Drugs and Cosmetics Regulations 1984, 4.7.

[148] USA, 21 USC § 355(c)(3)(f).

[149] WTO, *Declaration on the TRIPS Agreement and Public Health*, WT/MIN(01)/DEC/2 (20 November 2001).

[150] TRIPS Article 31*bis*.

[151] TRIPS, Article 31(f).

medicines for products intended exclusively for markets outside the EU, and that the EU's test data exclusivity rules shall not apply in such a situation.[152]

While these exceptions are extremely limited in scope, they do demonstrate that the two jurisdictions which have been the principle proponents of test data exclusivity do not reject exceptions to test data exclusivity in principle. It is therefore perplexing that these developed jurisdictions leave themselves vulnerable to abuses of test data exclusivity of the sort that more general exceptions are designed to guard against. The EU, at least, is aware of this issue; as has been discussed, the European Commission acknowledged in 2006 that EU law does not contain any provision allowing a waiver or suspension of the rules on test data exclusivity regarding domestic drug approvals.[153] Ellen 't Hoen, Pascale Boulet and Brook Baker suggested in 2017 that the EU should introduce a domestic test data exclusivity waiver based on that found in Regulation 816/2006,[154] a suggestion they have repeated in the context of the COVID-19 pandemic.[155]

It should be noted that some jurisdictions may have provisions that might function in a similar manner to an exception to test data exclusivity in practice. Taiwan, for example, permits the import and sale of medicines without the need to go through the normal regulatory channels in certain circumstances, including 'emergency public health circumstances,'[156] which could in theory avoid the issue of test data exclusivity frustrating a compulsory license as the need to reference originator data would be irrelevant (although from a public health perspective this seems less desirable than demonstrating the generic product's bioequivalence to the originator product). However, such 'general' legal principles that might provide a *de facto* exception to test data exclusivity suffer from the issue of being more complex and less legally certain.

A range of exceptions to test data exclusivity are present across the jurisdictions surveyed in this chapter. These are in some cases extremely robust, covering virtually all situations in which it would be desirable to suspend or terminate the test data exclusivity right. However, in some cases, such as the US, Canada or the EU, the limitations to test data exclusivity are extremely narrow. Furthermore, almost half of the jurisdictions surveyed seem to provide no specific exceptions to test data exclusivity at all, raising the issue that compulsorily licensing the patents over pharmaceuticals in cases of national emergency may be entirely ineffectual during long portions of the patent term. The absence of exceptions or limitations to test data exclusivity laws is especially common in developed countries, despite the

[152] EU Regulation 816/2006 on compulsory licensing of patents for the manufacture of pharmaceutical products for export to countries with public health problems outside the EU, Article 18(1)–(2).

[153] European Commission (2006).

[154] 't Hoen et al. (2017).

[155] Perehudoff et al. (2021), p. 3.

[156] Taiwan, Pharmaceutical Affairs Act, Article 48-2.

fact that they are amongst the least likely to be subject to international pressure to provide stricter protection to submitted test data.

6.5 Conclusion

During the Uruguay Round, the requirement to provide test data exclusivity was rejected in favour of a vague, general requirement to provide some kind of protection to submitted test data. Despite this, almost three decades since the TRIPS Agreement came into force, those jurisdictions which provide specific protection for pharmaceutical test data per Article 39.3 do so in a very similar manner.

As has been discussed, many of those jurisdictions with no specific provisions on the protection of submitted test data are likely not in conformity with even the least restrictive interpretations of Article 39.3. In the absence of a renewed interest in Article 39.3 at the DSB, however, this situation is unlikely to change soon.

The analysis of the national test data exclusivity laws of the 27 jurisdictions surveyed in this chapter reveals a number of details about the approaches taken to test data exclusivity across jurisdictions. Firstly, it is accurate to speak of test data exclusivity as a coherent intellectual property right. Test data exclusivity provisions across all jurisdictions share as their core feature the ability of the right holder to prevent subsequent applicants from making use of the abbreviated approval pathway for a time limited period following the approval of the originator product. Furthermore, test data exclusivity provisions are similar in other details as well. The typical test data exclusivity law amongst the jurisdictions surveyed is a relatively short term of protection (typically 5 years) that covers only data submitted regarding a new drug, but also lacks any notable limitations or exceptions; one that provides somewhat limited protection but also has little flexibility or nuance. A significant number of jurisdictions are exceptions to this trend. The developed jurisdictions surveyed such as the EU, US, Japan, Canada and Switzerland have significantly more restrictive test data exclusivity terms. These jurisdictions cover a large percentage of the population of the jurisdictions surveyed, and the vast majority of the global pharmaceutical market; if China does pass its proposed test data exclusivity reform, a major emerging pharmaceutical market with a huge population will join this group.

On the other hand, a number of jurisdictions have implemented test data exclusivity in a manner that places significant limitations upon the right. In a few cases, this has been achieved by some mechanism that significantly reduces the effectiveness of test data exclusivity in practice; requiring global novelty for pharmaceutical products in the case of China,[157] and limiting test data exclusivity to the term of an

[157] China, Regulations for Implementation of the Drug Administration Law of the People's Republic of China (Promulgated by Decree No. 360 of the State Council of the People's Republic of China on August 4, 2002), Article 35.

associated patent in the case of Turkey.[158] Many drugs launched in China will not be new-to-the-world, and exclusivity that ends with a patent provides little protection that the patent itself did not already provide. While such measures will obviously significantly decrease the chances that test data exclusivity will adversely affect access to medicine in these jurisdictions, it is a precarious position because developed countries are likely to apply pressure to provide more effective protection. It is unlikely that this approach is open to any but the largest developing economies—and even these may be unable to sustain such an approach indefinitely.

However, a number of the jurisdictions surveyed have implemented measures that mitigate the costs that test data exclusivity imposes without undermining the logic of protecting submitted test data. Test data exclusivity is justified on the grounds of incentivising the research necessary to bring drugs to market; protection should therefore only be provided to submitted test data when the originator actually brings the product in question to market. As such, rules which require that the application for marketing approval of the originator product be made within a certain window after its first international approval to receive test data exclusivity, provisions which measure the term of protection from a foreign approval, or rules which require that a product actually be marketed in the jurisdiction to receive test data exclusivity are all in keeping with the fundamental logic of the intellectual property right. Applying market exclusivity, or a mixture of data exclusivity *per se* followed by a short period of market exclusivity, ensures that the *de jure* term of protection is close to the *de facto* term. Furthermore, having specific systems in place to permit test data exclusivity to be challenged helps ensure that only drugs and data intended to be protected actually receive protection. A system of publication and opposition, such as the one operated by Peru, adds an element of transparency to the system without preventing test data exclusivity from performing its function. Lastly, robust exceptions to test data exclusivity guard against the possibility of the intellectual property right damaging the public interest in exceptional circumstances. Specific exceptions for cases in which a compulsory license is issued or an abuse of competition law has taken place ensure that test data exclusivity does not undermine the exceptions already built into patent law. Wider exceptions relating to the general public interest guard against unforeseen circumstances.

For the vast majority of jurisdictions with test data exclusivity provisions, the ability to vary the terms of submitted test data protection is constrained to some extent at least by international obligations. However, the presence of well thought out limitations on and exceptions to test data exclusivity in some of the jurisdictions surveyed in this chapter demonstrate that such nuance can be added to national test data exclusivity laws, even when a jurisdiction has committed to test data exclusivity at the international level; these exceptions and limitations provide a model in how to better implement the protection of submitted test data.

---

[158] Turkey, Regulation on Authorization of Pharmaceutical Products for Human Use (2005), Article 9.

References

Balzano JC (2022) China. In: Kingham R (ed) The life sciences law review. Law Business Research Ltd, London, pp 70–91

Basheer S (2006) Protection of regulatory data under Article 39.3 of TRIPs: the Indian context. Intellectual Property Institute

Braithwaite J, Drahos P (2000) Global business regulation. Cambridge University Press, Cambridge

Correa C (2002) Protection of data submitted for the registration of pharmaceuticals: implementing the standards of the TRIPS agreement. South Centre, Geneva

Dutfield G (2008) Delivering drugs to the poor: will the TRIPS amendment help? Am J Law Med 34:107–124

EMA (2019) European Medicines Agency policy on publication of clinical data for medicinal products for human. EMA/144064/2019

European Commission (2004) Report to the Trade Barriers Regulation Committee – TBR proceedings concerning Turkish practices affecting trade in pharmaceutical products

European Commission (2006) Letter from the European Commission to Mr. Greg Perry, EGA-European Generic Medicines Association on the subject of Tamiflu application and data exclusivity in an emergency compulsory license situation

Gitter DM (2013) Biopharmaceuticals under the patient protection and affordable care act: determining the appropriate market and data exclusivity periods. Texas Intellect Prop Law J 21:213

Grabowski H (2008) Follow-on biologics: data exclusivity and the balance between innovation and competition. Nat Rev Drug Discov 7(6):479–488

Heled Y (2015) Regulatory competitive shelters. Ohio State Law J 76:299

Matthews D (2017) Exclusivity for biologics. In: Matthews D, Zech H (eds) Research handbook on intellectual property and the life sciences. Edward Elgar, Cheltenham, pp 104–121

NMPA (2018) Implementation measures for drug trial data protection (interim) (draft for comments)

Perehudoff K, 't Hoen EFM, Boulet P (2021) Overriding drug and medical technology patents for pandemic recovery: a legitimate move for high-income countries, too. BMJ Glob Health 6(4): e005518

Shaikh OH (2016) Access to medicine versus test data exclusivity: safeguarding flexibilities under international law. Springer, Berlin

Sharma A (2007) Data exclusivity with regard to clinical data. Indian J Law Technol 3:82

't Hoen EFM, Boulet P, Baker BK (2017) Data exclusivity exceptions and compulsory licensing to promote generic medicines in the European Union: a proposal for greater coherence in European pharmaceutical legislation. J Pharma Policy Pract 10(1):1–9

Torronteguy MAA, Ribas G, Avallone VHC (2022) Brazil. In: Kingham R (ed) The life sciences law review. Law Business Research Ltd, London, pp 54–70

Tridico A, Jacobstein J, Wall L (2014) Facilitating generic drug manufacturing: Bolar exemptions worldwide. WIPO Magazine 3:17–20

USTR (1995) 1995 Special 301 Report

USTR (2016) 2016 Special 301 Report

USTR (2017) 2017 Special 301 Report

USTR (2018) 2018 Special 301 Report

USTR (2019) 2019 Special 301 Report

Yu PK (2019) China's innovative turn and the changing pharmaceutical landscape. Univ Pacific Law Rev 51:593

Chapter 7
The Impact of Test Data Exclusivity on Abbreviated New Drug Applications in the United States

Abstract This chapter examines an aspect of the impact of test data exclusivity through an analysis of the first Abbreviated New Drug Applications (ANDAs) to reference new chemical entities which qualified for test data exclusivity in the US between 1999 and 2009. The findings of this analysis show that test data exclusivity would appear to have an impact on the date of first generic approval for about 8% of new chemical entities approved in the US in the period studied. In addition, test data exclusivity would also appear to have had an impact on delaying patent challenges made against originator pharmaceutical products.

7.1 Introduction

All of the debate over test data exclusivity discussed in this book rests on a central assumption—that, for better or worse, test data exclusivity rights have a real impact on the market entry of generic versions of originator drugs. If test data exclusivity did not prevent or delay the market entry of generics in some capacity, it could neither provide an incentive for research-based firms, as its proponents argue, nor restrict access to medicines, as its critics fear. Whether or not test data exclusivity rights have such an impact is not immediately obvious. In all of the jurisdictions discussed in this book, the term of protection offered by test data exclusivity rights is significantly shorter than the minimum 20-year term of protection offered by a patent, the primary means of obtaining a market monopoly over a pharmaceutical product. As Pugatch observed in 2004, it therefore seems logical to assume that for the majority of drugs, the patent term will fully subsume the test data exclusivity term.[1]

This chapter, along with Chap. 8, aims to shed light upon what impact test data exclusivity rights have in practice. Whereas Chap. 8 focuses on the impact of test data exclusivity rights on measures designed to promote public health, such as compulsory licensing, this chapter examines the impact that test data exclusivity

[1] Pugatch (2006), p. 118.

A. Buick, *Intellectual Property Rights in Pharmaceutical Test Data*,
https://doi.org/10.1007/978-3-031-29436-5_7

has upon the market entry of generic pharmaceuticals in the US. As this analysis shows, test data exclusivity rights may have played a role in delaying the market entry of generic versions of pharmaceuticals in a small but not insignificant number of cases. Furthermore, test data exclusivity rights appear to have played a role in delaying patent challenges to pharmaceutical products. It should be borne in mind that these conclusions are specific to the US; as discussed below, the impact on test data exclusivity on delaying first generic approval is likely to be larger, and its impact on patent challenges smaller, in other jurisdictions.

7.2 The Potential Impact of Test Data Exclusivity

The issue of the impact of test data exclusivity is intrinsically bound up with the relationship between test data exclusivity and pharmaceutical patents, as discussed in detail at Sect. 2.3.1.1. To recapitulate, the primary reason that test data exclusivity will have an impact on the market entry of generic products is because patent protection is for some reason absent. There are at least three scenarios in which this may be the case. Firstly, scenarios in which a pharmaceutical product was never protected from competition by a patent. Secondly, scenarios in which a pharmaceutical product was protected by a patent (or patents) but the patent term has expired. Thirdly, scenarios in which patent protection over a pharmaceutical product has been acquired but subsequently compromised in some way, such as if the validity of the patent has been challenged by a competitor or if the patent has been subject to a mechanism such as a compulsory license issued by a government. The analysis of this chapter focuses on the role that test data exclusivity may play regarding products which lack patent protection, products for which patent protection has expired, and products whose patent protection has been challenged; the issue of the impact of test data exclusivity on measures such as compulsory licensing is discussed in the next chapter.

7.3 The Impact of Test Data Exclusivity in the United States 1999–2009

There are several reasons to examine the impact of test data exclusivity in the US specifically. Firstly, the US is the world's largest pharmaceutical market and as such important for any discussion of the global pharmaceutical industry. In addition, the US was the first jurisdiction to adopt test data exclusivity laws for pharmaceuticals, and the regulatory situation has stayed largely the same since that time, at least regarding NCEs—as such, it seems reasonable to assume that the behaviour of pharmaceutical firms will have adapted to take test data exclusivity into account to a greater degree than those jurisdictions in which test data exclusivity is a more recent phenomenon. Perhaps most importantly, however, the US publishes a great deal of data relating to the approval of pharmaceutical products, and the quirks of its regulatory system (discussed in detail below) mean that meaningful conclusions regarding the impact of test data exclusivity can be drawn from them.

It is difficult to determine whether or not test data exclusivity has had an impact on the overall period of exclusivity enjoyed by a particular drug. The end result—the absence of generic competition—is the same regardless of whether this is because of patent protection, test data exclusivity or another form of exclusivity. The US FDA does provide information on the patents and other sources of exclusivity associated with a particular product in its 'Orange Book', the list of pharmaceuticals approved in the US, as discussed below.[2] However, determining whether these patents would actually prevent generic competition is problematic. As Aidan Hollis observes, because of the difficulties involved in evaluating which patents are relevant to which drugs, the FDA relies on the originator firms themselves to provide details of the patents to be listed.[3] The mere fact that a patent is listed in the Orange Book cannot be taken as definitive proof that it would block generic competition—indeed, debate over whether a particular listed patent will block a generic competitor frequently ends in litigation.

However, the FDA does make available information on the dates that Abbreviated New Drug Approvals (ANDAs) are submitted and approved. This information provides a guide for when test data exclusivity matters—or more accurately, when it does *not*. In the US, ANDAs cannot even be submitted to the FDA until the period of test data exclusivity which accrues to NCEs has expired; as such, if the application for the first generic competitor is submitted long after the expiration of test data exclusivity, it strongly suggests that test data exclusivity had little to no impact on the entry of generic competitors to the market. If the sponsor of the generic application did not submit their application until many years after the end of the test data exclusivity period, it is unlikely that they would have submitted their application for market authorisation any faster if there had been no test data exclusivity period at all. Furthermore, because the FDA will only grant full approval to an ANDA when all relevant patents and other exclusivities have ended, if a product submitted soon after the end of test data exclusivity is approved quickly it strongly suggests that there were no additional sources of exclusivity.

It is important to be aware of the limits of this method. Even if a generic application comes immediately after the end of test data exclusivity and is approved soon after, we cannot tell how much sooner the sponsor would have made an application in the absence of test data exclusivity—indeed, it may be the case that the generic applicant would not have made their application a single day sooner even if they could have done so. Furthermore, it is worth emphasising that market authorisation is not the same as market entry; there may be further delays before

[2] Hollis (2001), p. 14.

[3] Ibid.

the generic drug is actually competing with the originator product. Still, this provides a guide to how often test data exclusivity impacts generic market entry in the US.

7.3.1 The US Drug Approval System in Detail

In order to meaningfully interpret the data on generic drug approvals in the US in the period under study, it is necessary to understand the particulars of the US drug approval system. These are set out below.

7.3.1.1 Patent Law

The US allows for the patenting of products, processes and methods of manufacture, including those related to pharmaceuticals.[4] Once granted, the patent term lasts for 20 years (240 months) from the date of filing. Patent term extensions are available in the US; as part of the 'Patent Term Restoration' half of the Hatch-Waxman Act, patents over a product (or its use or manufacture) which requires regulatory approval can be extended; for pharmaceuticals, the period of extension is calculated as half of the testing time of the product (measured from when human trials began) plus the entire time spent in regulatory review. The extension is capped at 5 years (60 months) and the total patent term including extension cannot last for more than 14 years (168 months) after the regulatory review.

Even with patent term extensions, however, the 'effective' period of patent protection available to a new drug after its approval is considerably shorter. Research by Henry Grabowski and John Vernon found that the average period of effective patent protection (including extensions) for drugs approved between 1990 and 1995 was 11.7 years (140 months).[5] Research by C Scott Hempill and Bhaven Sampat looking at the later period of 2001–2010 found an extremely similar effective patent term of 12 years (144 months).[6] Still, even this reduced period of 'effective' protection significantly outlasts test data exclusivity in the US.

7.3.1.2 Market Authorisation

In order to gain market authorisation in the US, the sponsor of a 'new' drug must submit a New Drug Application (NDA) to the FDA.[7] The NDA must include a great deal of technical information on the drug in question, including the results of clinical

---

[4]USA, 35 USC § 101.

[5]Grabowski and Vernon (2000), p. 116.

[6]Hemphill and Sampat (2012), p. 330.

[7]USA, FDCA s505(b).

trials establishing the product's safety and efficacy.[8] Sponsors of NDAs are also required to submit information on patents associated with the pharmaceutical in question.[9] These are included in the Orange Book, along with details of other relevant exclusivities.[10]

Sponsors for generic products may submit an ANDA. In an ANDA, the sponsor is not required to submit their own evidence of safety and efficacy but instead relies on the data submitted by the 'Reference Listed Drug (RLD)' of which it is a bioequivalent copy.[11] Once test data exclusivity over the RLD expires, generic applicants can submit an abbreviated application which references it. However, the generic applicant must make one of four certifications regarding any patents associated with the RLD listed in the Orange Book. A paragraph I certification states that no such patents have been filed with the FDA; a paragraph II certification states that the listed patents have expired; a paragraph III certification states the date of expiration of the listed patents and explains that the generic product will not go on the market before that time; and a paragraph IV certification states that the listed patents are invalid, unenforceable or will not be infringed by the manufacture, use or sale of the drug product for which the ANDA is submitted.[12] If a paragraph IV certification is filed, the ANDA sponsor must notify the NDA/patent holder of this; if the NDA or patent holder files a patent infringement suit against the generic firm within 45 days, the FDA's approval of the generic product will be automatically stayed for 30 months, or until a court determines that there is no cause of action for patent infringement or invalidity.[13]

7.3.1.3 Test Data Exclusivity

Test data exclusivity for new chemical entities in the US is now codified as 21 USC § 355(c)(3)(f). This creates a qualification to the use of the abbreviated drug application discussed above; if a drug, no active ingredient of which has been previously approved in the US, is approved in an NDA, then an ANDA may not be submitted for 5 years (60 months) from the approval of the NDA. An exception is made if the drug in question has been subject to a successful invalidity or

[8]USA, 21 USC § 355.

[9]Ibid.

[10]Ibid.

[11]Other forms of authorisation also exist; so-called 505(b)(2) applications act as a hybrid NDA/ANDA, with the applicant relying partially on their own tests, but also partially on investigations which they did not carry out. This could be published literature, or it could be the FDA's finding of safety or efficacy of a previously approved drug. In addition, a 'petitioned ANDA' refers to an ANDA for a generic that differs in dosage form, route of administration, strength or (in the case of a combination product) active ingredient submitted under 505(j)(2)(C) and approved under 505(j).

[12]USA, 21 USC § 314.94(a)(12)(i)(A)(1)–(4).

[13]USA, 21 USC § 355 (c)(3)(c).

noninfringement judgment—in such a case, an application may be submitted after 4 years (48 months).

However, it should be noted that if a paragraph IV certification is submitted before 5 years of exclusivity have elapsed and an action for patent infringement is brought against the ANDA sponsor, the 30-month stay period can be extended such that it would last up to seven and a half years from the approval of the initial NDA; in other words, the remainder of the last year of the original 5-year test data exclusivity term can be added to the 30-month stay.[14]

In addition, the period of test data exclusivity can also be modified by paediatric exclusivity under the FDA Modernization Act of 1997.[15] This will extend the term of all listed patents, Hatch-Waxman data exclusivity, BPCIA exclusivity, and orphan drug exclusivity associated with the product by 6 months. As such, the test data exclusivity period for NCEs in the US can range between four years and five and a half years (48 and 66 months).

It should be noted that because ANDAs cannot even be accepted until the end of the test data exclusivity period, the time taken by the FDA to approve the product in question further extends the period of market monopoly enjoyed by the originator. The median approval time for an ANDA was 31 months in 2012, up from 16 months in 2003.[16]

7.3.1.4 Other Forms of Exclusivity

Aside from patent law and test data exclusivity for new chemical entities, the US also provides a number of other forms of exclusivity for pharmaceutical products.

The Hatch-Waxman Act also grants a 180-day (6 month) period of exclusivity to *generic* drugs when they are the first to file a substantially complete application that contains and lawfully maintains a paragraph IV certification alleging that a patent or patents related to the originator product are invalid, unenforceable or will not be infringed by the manufacture, use or sale of the drug product for which the ANDA is submitted.[17] In 1998, the FDA changed the rules regarding 180-day exclusivity to grant it to not only to those firms who won a court battle against the patent holder, but also those who reached a settlement with the patent owner as a result of a legal case.[18] As a consequence of this decision, paragraph IV certification substantially increased from 1998 onwards.

[14] USA, 21 USC § 355 (c)(3)(c).

[15] FDA Modernization Act of 1997.

[16] Shaikh (2016), p. 98. Accessed 27 February 2018. See also Boehm et al. (2013), pp. 297 and 306.

[17] USA, 21 USC § 355(j)(5)(B)(iv)(II).

[18] Grabowski et al. (2017), p. 34.

As discussed in previous chapters, the US grants 3 years (36 months) of *market* exclusivity for applications and supplements containing new clinical investigations essential to the approval of the application or supplement.[19]

The US grants 'orphan drug exclusivity' to orphan drugs under the Orphan Drug Act 1983. This creates an exclusivity term of 7 years (84 months) for treatments of rare diseases, although the FDA may approve treatments for the disease during the exclusivity period if the holder of the exclusivity cannot ensure the availability of sufficient quantities of the drug.[20] Details of orphan exclusivity were not collected for this analysis, but it should be borne in mind that where orphan exclusivity *is* granted, it automatically renders data exclusivity redundant by virtue of being both longer in duration and wider in scope.

7.3.2 Method

The FDA maintains lists of all 'new molecular entities' (NMEs) approved by the agency since 1999 on its website; these drugs contain an active moiety not previously approved by the FDA. Not all of these NMEs qualified for the 5-year period of test data exclusivity under the HWA; some are combination products which contain previously approved active ingredients (such as Kaletra, a combination of lopinavir and the previously approved ritonavir), while some are biologics approved via a Biologic License Application (BLA) rather than NDA. Excluding these products, a list of 239 previously unapproved drugs which would have qualified for test data exclusivity between 1999 and 2009 was created.

Details of the approval of generic versions of these drugs were then acquired from the FDA's website. 126 of the drugs which qualified for test data exclusivity between 1999 and 2009 had had at least one generic competitor approved by July 2019, when the data was collected. Data was gathered on the dates of submission and approval for the ANDA of the first generic competitor to be approved for these products; in cases in which multiple ANDAs were approved within a few days of each other, the ANDA with the most complete data was selected, and in cases where multiple ANDAs had complete data, the first to be submitted was selected. This data is presented in Appendix B.

Data on the date of submission was only available for 91 of the first approved ANDAs (72.2% of the total). It is not clear why data is missing for the remaining 35 ANDAs, but based on the time between the submission of the originator drug and the approval of the first ANDA for each group there appears to be little difference between them; this was 133.8 months for all the ANDAs, 134.2 months for those for which data on submission was available and 132.8 months for those for which data on submission was missing. These 91 ANDAs have therefore been treated as a

[19] USA, 21 USC § 355(c)(3)(f)(iii)–(iv).

[20] USA, 21 USC § 360cc(a)(2).

representative sample of all of the first approved ANDAs for the NCEs which qualified for test data exclusivity in this period.

The gathered data was used to determine which ANDAs had been submitted between 48 months (4 years) and 67 months (5 years and 7 months) from the date of approval of the NDA for the originator product and which therefore had been submitted either up to a year before the end of the 60 month test data exclusivity period (presumably because a paragraph IV certification had been filed) or within 7 months of the end of the 60 month test data exclusivity period. These ANDAs were then sorted into three categories; those approved within 36 months (3 years) of submission, those approved within 37–72 months (3–6 years) of submission and those approved 73 months or more (more than 6 years) from submission. Based on the assumption that test data exclusivity is most likely to have had an impact on the market entry of ANDAs both submitted soon after the end of the test data exclusivity period and approved soon after submission, this provides an estimate of the proportion of NCEs which qualified for test data exclusivity between 1999 and 2009 for which this exclusivity played a role in delayed the market entry of generic competition.

Because the only way an ANDA can be submitted sooner than 60 months from the approval of the RLD is if a paragraph IV certification has been made, this data also provides an insight into the role than test data exclusivity plays in delaying patent challenges.

7.3.3 *Findings*

Of the 91 first ANDAs for which information on submission data was available, 50 were submitted between 48 and 67 months of the approval of the RLD;[21] extrapolating this to all of the first ANDAs would mean that the ANDA for the first approved generic version of 69.23 NCEs (28.9%) which qualified for test data exclusivity between 1999 and 2009 was submitted close to the end of the test data exclusivity period (Table 7.1).

Interestingly, the majority of these ANDAs (34) were submitted between 48 and 60 months from the approval of the originator products, suggesting that a paragraph IV challenge had been made against one or more of the listed patents associated with the RLD. Extrapolating to all of the first ANDAs, this suggests that the ANDA for the first approved generic version of 57.08 or 19.7% of the NCEs which qualified for test data exclusivity between 1999 and 2009 was submitted prior to the end of the 'usual' 5-year term of test data exclusivity due to a paragraph IV challenge.

[21] The ANDA for the first approved generic of one drug, Razadyne (galantamine hydrobromide), was submitted 10 days before the end of the 48-month period from the approval of the originator NDA. This appears to have been an administrative fluke on the part of the FDA and has been recorded as being submitted 48 months after the approval of the originator product. No other ANDAs were submitted earlier than 48 months from the approval of the originator.

Table 7.1 First approved ANDAs submitted within 67 months of new drugs approved by the FDA 1999–2009 by time from submission to approval in months

	Number of ANDAs with complete data	Number of ANDAs, extrapolating to all first ANDAs	As a percentage of all NCEs which qualified for TDE 1999–2009
ANDAs submitted between 48 and 67 months from approval of RLD	50	69.23	28.90%
... which were approved within 36 months of submission	14	19.89	8.11%
... which were approved between 37 and 72 months of submission	21	29.08	12.17%
... which were approved over 72 months from submission	15	20.77	8.69%

On the assumption that test data exclusivity has no impact in cases when the first generic application is submitted a significant amount of time after the test data exclusivity period has ended, this suggests that test data exclusivity may have impacted the generic market entry for 28.9% at most of the new drugs which qualified for test data exclusivity in the period under analysis. However, it is doubtful that test data exclusivity played a significant role beyond the protection offered by patents and other forms of exclusivity in every single one of these cases. For those ANDAs submitted soon after the end of the test data exclusivity period, the median delay between the submission and approval was 49 months, significantly longer than the 16–31 month period it took to approve the median ANDA between 2003 and 2012; this implies that other forms of exclusivity continued to prevent the approval of these ANDAs in a significant number of cases.

Figure 7.1 shows a breakdown of the time in months between the submission and approval of the ANDAs submitted within 67 months of the originator product in the period surveyed; it is obviously much more likely that the market entry of those ANDAs approved very shortly after their submission was delayed by test data exclusivity than the market entry of those ANDAs approved 120+ months after submission. The ANDAs have been grouped into three categories; those approved within 36 months of their submission, for which it is likely that test data exclusivity impacted the market entry of the first generic competitor, those ANDAs approved between 37 and 72 months from submission, for which it is less likely that test data exclusivity delayed generic market entry, and those drugs approved more than 72 months from their submission, for which it is extremely unlikely that test data exclusivity delayed generic market entry. 14 ANDAs fall into the first category, 21 into the second category and 15 into the third category. Extrapolating to all of the first ANDAs, this would be 19.89 or 8.11%, 29.08 or 12.17% and 20.77 or 8.69% respectively of the NCEs which received test data exclusivity in the period under analysis.

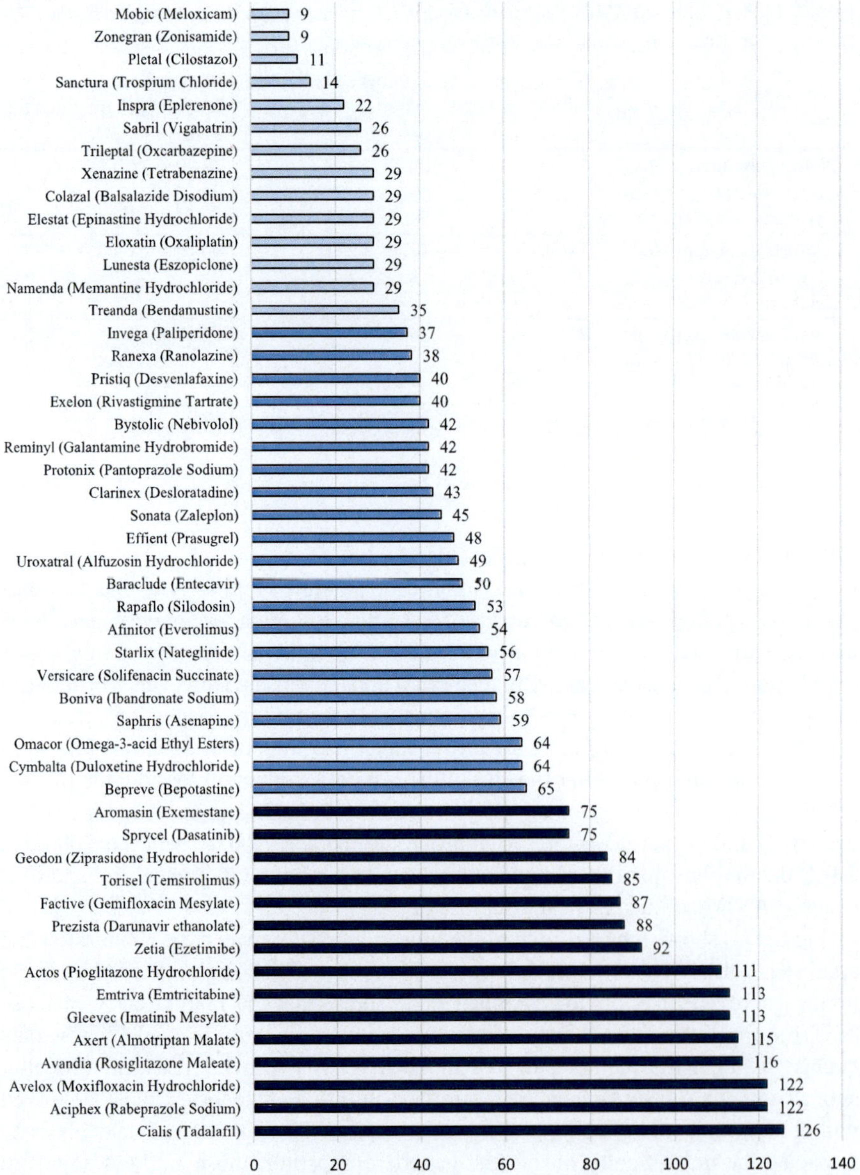

Fig. 7.1 Time in months from submission to approval for first approved ANDAs submitted within 67 months of new drugs approved by the FDA 1999–2009

7.3.4 Discussion

The 28.9% of NCEs for which the first ANDA to be approved was submitted soon after the expiration of test data exclusivity represents a 'ceiling' on the proportion of cases in which test data exclusivity is likely to have had an impact in the period analysed, because those ANDAs submitted many months or years after the expiration of test data exclusivity are unlikely to have been delayed by the presence of such an exclusivity period. The 8.11% of NCEs for which the first ANDA to be approved was both submitted between 48 and 67 months after the expiration of test data exclusivity and approved within 36 months of submission represents the proportion of NCEs in the period analysed for which test data exclusivity is most likely to have had an impact on the market entry of generic competitors. This is a small but nonetheless significant proportion, especially considering that many originator products never see the launch of a generic competitor.

It is also significant to note the relatively high proportion of NCEs which qualified for test data exclusivity for the application for which the first approved generic competitor was submitted *before* the end of the 'usual' 5-year (60 month) test data exclusivity period—almost 20%. Indeed, the majority of first approved ANDAs filed soon after the end of the test data exclusivity period were filed before the usual end of the test data exclusivity period (34 out of 50, or 64% of the first approved ANDAs filed close to the end of test data exclusivity). As noted above, these 'early' ANDA submissions are presumably the result of paragraph IV certifications regarding some or all of the listed patents for the RLD because a paragraph IV certification reduces the test data exclusivity term from 5 years (60 months) to 4 years (48 months). Indeed, for those ANDAs submitted sooner than 60 months from the approval of the reference drug it is impossible that patent protection expired before the end of the test data exclusivity period because if this had been the case, there would have been no listed patents to make a paragraph IV certification against. It is worth noting that the majority of these ANDAs submitted before the usual end of the test data exclusivity term were only approved long after submission—over 10 years afterwards in some cases. This may be the result of the fact that even successful patent challenges can take years, although it also reflects the fact that the 180-day exclusivity period is lucrative enough to incentivise generic firms to make patent challenges even in cases where there is a low probability of success.[22] An important impact of test data exclusivity in the US is therefore the delay of challenges to the validity of the patents associated with the pharmaceutical in question.

It seems highly probable that the position outside of the US will be quite different, given the unique position of the US pharmaceutical market and the peculiarities of its regulatory system. On the one hand, pharmaceutical products are typically launched in the US before they are launched in other markets; as such, it might be expected that patent protection expiring before test data exclusivity would be more common outside of the US, especially in those jurisdictions in which patent term extensions

[22] Grabowski et al. (2017), p. 34.

are not available. Pharmaceuticals are also more likely to be heavily patented in the US compared to other jurisdictions, given the value of its pharmaceutical market—but also more likely to be challenged, both as a result of the value of the market to which the applicant stands to gain access, as well as the incentives provided to challenging pharmaceutical patents.

In addition, it should also be noted that while the US has a fairly typical test data exclusivity term of 5 years, many jurisdictions have longer terms—in some cases considerably so. The term of test data exclusivity in Europe lasts between 120 to 132 months from the originator drug's approval (although generic applications can be submitted from 96 months onwards); 27.6% of the NCEs which qualified for test data exclusivity between 1999 and 2009 in the US had their first generic competitor approved within 132 months of the reference drug's approval and would therefore have been impacted if the US had a test data exclusivity term similar to that of the EU. Even amongst those jurisdictions in which test data exclusivity is 5 years, as in the US, virtually all lack a mechanism like paragraph IV certification to reduce the test data exclusivity term.

7.4 Conclusion

The analysis of this chapter suggests that in the US at least, test data exclusivity has an impact on the date of approval for the first generic competitor for a small but significant proportion of new chemical entities, and a much larger impact on delaying patent challenges to pharmaceutical products. *A priori*, the impact of test data exclusivity on delaying first generic approval is likely to be larger outside of the US, while its impact on patent challenges is likely to be smaller; this is the result of a number of factors, including the fact that other (largely developed) countries provide a longer exclusivity term than the US, that drugs typically launch later in the patent term in non-US markets, that drugs are less likely to be patented outside of the US (especially in developing countries), and that the size of the US pharmaceutical market and the regulatory incentives it provides make patent challenges more likely. This is concerning because, as was observed in Chap. 6, test data exclusivity laws show a high degree of similarity; if the impact of test data exclusivity rights in the US is likely to be significantly different to the impact of test data exclusivity rights in other jurisdictions, the widespread modelling of the US approach to the protection of submitted test data may be poorly adapted to local conditions in many instances.

References

Boehm G, Yao L, Han L, Zheng Q (2013) Development of the generic drug industry in the US after the Hatch-Waxman Act of 1984. Acta Pharm Sin B 3(5):297–311

Grabowski H, Vernon JM (2000) Effective patent life in pharmaceuticals. Int J Technol Manag 19(1-2):98–120

Grabowski H, Brain C, Taub A, Guha R (2017) Pharmaceutical patent challenges: company strategies and litigation outcomes. Am J Health Econ 3(1):33–59

Hemphill CS, Sampat BN (2012) Evergreening, patent challenges, and effective market life in pharmaceuticals. J Health Econ 31(2):327–339

Hollis A (2001) Closing the FDA's Orange Book. Regulation 24(4):14–17

Pugatch M (2006) Intellectual property, data exclusivity, innovation and market access. In: Roffe P, Tansey G, Vivas-Eugui D (eds) Negotiating health: intellectual property and access to medicine. Earthscan, London, pp 97–132

Shaikh OH (2016) Access to medicine versus test data exclusivity: safeguarding flexibilities under international law. Springer, Berlin

Chapter 8
The Impact of Test Data Exclusivity on Measures for the Protection of Public Health

Abstract This chapter considers how test data exclusivity has impacted measures which are intended to protect public health such as compulsory licensing. It begins by examining the general relationship between test data exclusivity and the use of compulsory licensing since the signing of the TRIPS Agreement, before turning to consider the role of test data exclusivity in the context of the response to the COVID-19 pandemic specifically.

The analysis of this chapter shows that while there is evidence that test data exclusivity may have a chilling effect on the use of compulsory licensing, there are no known direct examples of test data exclusivity actively frustrating the use of measures intended to protect public health in the post-TRIPS period. This should not be taken as evidence that there is no tension between test data exclusivity and measures to protect public health, however. The fact remains that the test data exclusivity laws of many jurisdictions do not provide for the suspension or waiver of the protection of submitted test data; if greater use of the flexibilities in intellectual property law intended to promote public health is to be made in future, test data exclusivity laws must be amended to facilitate this.

8.1 Introduction

As discussed at Sect. 2.4.1.2, one major concern that has been raised regarding test data exclusivity is that such rights may prevent the effective use of public health safeguards within the intellectual property system, in particular compulsory licensing, because it would not be possible to approve pharmaceutical products produced under such public health measures through an abbreviated drug approval if test data exclusivity protection could not be suspended.[1] Indeed, it has been suggested that such a desire to frustrate the use of such public health measures with regards to pharmaceutical products may lie behind the proliferation of test data exclusivity

[1] See, for example, Correa (2002), Chandler (2020), and Lokuge et al. (2006).

A. Buick, *Intellectual Property Rights in Pharmaceutical Test Data*,
https://doi.org/10.1007/978-3-031-29436-5_8

provisions in free trade agreements.[2] This issue has received renewed attention in light of the response to the COVID-19 pandemic.

8.2 Test Data Exclusivity and Measures for the Protection of Public Health

It has always been unlikely that Article 39.3 itself prohibits the use of submitted test data in order to facilitate a compulsory license, as discussed at Sect. 4.4.3.1; the TRIPS Agreement is entirely silent on the issue, suggestions that the compulsory licensing of confidential information be prohibited were rejected during the Uruguay Round, and the 2022 Ministerial Decision on the TRIPS Agreement has now acknowledged that Article 39.3 would not prevent the rapid approval of a COVID-19 vaccine produced under the Decision. Furthermore, as was discussed in Chap. 5, no trade agreement explicitly prohibits the use of submitted test data in a compulsory licensing scenario, and a number contain provisions specifying that the signatories may take actions to safeguard public health in line with the TRIPS Agreement and Doha Declaration which suggests that exceptions to test data protection will be permissible as long as they are compliant with TRIPS.[3]

However, as noted in Chap. 6, while a few jurisdictions, such as Malaysia, Chile and Vietnam, provide comprehensive provisions enabling the suspension of test data exclusivity in certain circumstances, the test data exclusivity laws of most jurisdictions contain no provisions that would permit the use of protected submitted test data in emergency situations.[4] As previously noted, the European Commission infamously acknowledged in 2006 that as a consequence of the lack of such flexibilities in the EU legislation on test data exclusivity, a compulsory license issued over a pharmaceutical product protected by test data exclusivity within the EU could not receive marketing approval without the permission of the right holder.[5]

The following sections consider what impact test data exclusivity has had on such public health measures in the post-TRIPS period, firstly by considering the role of test data exclusivity in 'episodes' of compulsory licensing since the signing of TRIPS, and secondly by examining the role of test data exclusivity in the response to the COVID-19 pandemic in particular.

---

[2] Abbott (2004).

[3] For example, USMCA (2018) Articles 20.6(b) and 20.48(3) and the Trade Agreement between the EU and Peru and Colombia (2012) Article 197(2).

[4] Vietnam; Chile Law No 19.039, Article 91; Malaysia, Directive on Data Exclusivity (2010) Article 4.7.

[5] European Commission (2006). As observed by 't Hoen et al. (2017), the EU has enacted an exception to test data exclusivity for the purposes of approving pharmaceutical products approved for export under Article 31*bis* of TRIPS.

8.2.1 *Compulsory Licensing of Pharmaceuticals and Test Data Exclusivity Post-TRIPS*

Considering the relationship between test data exclusivity and compulsory licensing first requires a consideration of the general use of compulsory licenses since the signing of the TRIPS Agreement. The 'use' of compulsory licencing must be understood as extending beyond situations in which such licenses have actually been issued; for example, the Brazilian government famously used the *threat* of issuing a compulsory license to negotiate substantial discounts on a number of patented pharmaceuticals between 2001 and 2009 (ultimately issuing a compulsory license in 2007 over the antiretroviral efavirenz when price negotiations fell through).[6] Compulsory licensing 'episodes' thus also include situations in which a compulsory license was threatened or considered by a government in addition to those scenarios in which such a license was actually deployed.[7]

Even under this broad definition, however, the compulsory licensing of pharmaceutical products has been uncommon in the post-TRIPS period. For example, in an examination of the period 1995–2012, 't Hoen identified 24 occasions on which compulsory licenses were issued with regard to pharmaceutical products, 51 examples of government use of pharmaceutical patents and 9 compulsory licenses very nearly issued regarding a pharmaceutical product; this is fewer than five compulsory licensing 'episodes' per year worldwide.[8] A range of non-exclusive suggestions have been made as to why compulsory licensing remains so infrequent, including fear of retaliation from developed countries and research-based pharmaceutical firms, lack of domestic capacity to produce pharmaceutical products, the development of alternative methods of increasing access to patented medicines such as voluntary licenses and patent pools,[9] the high price of active ingredients even when patent protection is removed, and the fact that patents over pharmaceuticals are relatively uncommon in many developing jurisdictions.[10]

It is apparent that test data exclusivity cannot have had any impact in most of the limited number of compulsory licensing episodes which have occurred in the post-TRIPS period. Very few of the countries which have made use of compulsory licences since 1995 have test data exclusivity laws, or at least did not have such laws at the time the compulsory license was issued. This is in part a reflection of the fact that most compulsory licensing activity post-TRIPS has been in developing countries, and most developing countries have either never had test data exclusivity laws or adopted them only recently, meaning that any compulsory licenses are likely to have been issued before the country began protecting submitted test data.

---

[6] 't Hoen (2016), p. 55.

[7] Beall and Kuhn (2012), p. 3.

[8] 't Hoen (2016), p. 57.

[9] Beall and Kuhn (2012), pp. 2–6.

[10] Attaran and Gillespie-White (2001), p. 1889.

Even when focusing solely on compulsory licensing episodes in jurisdictions which had test data exclusivity laws at the relevant time, it is difficult to point to a clear example of test data exclusivity provisions interfering with a compulsory license in the post-TRIPS period. In some compulsory licensing episodes, the possibility of test data exclusivity frustrating the license does not seem to have been given any contemporary discussion. This appears to have been the case when the US and Canada considered issuing compulsory licenses with regards to ciprofloxacin hydroxide during the post-9/11 anthrax scare,[11] as well as when the Taiwanese government issued a compulsory license over a patent covering the antiviral oseltamivir in the context of the spread of avian influenza in 2005.[12] In all of these cases, no pharmaceuticals were ever actually produced under compulsory license, which may explain the absence of discussion around the practicalities of test data exclusivity protection (it is of course also possible that the products in question had never been protected by test data exclusivity, or that the term of protection had expired).

In others, the particular specifics of the situation have meant that there was never a possibility of test data exclusivity frustrating the use of a compulsory license. This was the case regarding compulsory licenses over pharmaceutical products issued by both Italy and Germany in the context of competition law; Italy over imipenem/cilastatin in 2005,[13] sumatriptan in 2006[14] and finasteride in 2007,[15] Germany over raltegravir in 2017.[16] Both the imipenem/cilastatin and sumatriptan licenses were granted with the primary purpose of allowing the drugs to be manufactured in Italy but then exported to other European markets where patent protection had already expired;[17] and in the German case, the beneficiary of the license was also the originator of the product, meaning it had no need to make use of an abbreviated approval process.[18]

Test data exclusivity was similarly not an issue due to the specific circumstances of the collaboration between Canada and Rwanda to supply TriAvir, an HIV medication, to the latter country in 2007–2008.[19] This partnership was the first (and so far only) use of the so-called 'Paragraph 6 solution',[20] the mechanism

[11] See generally Mullin (2002).

[12] Liu (2014), p. 79.

[13] KEI (2014), p. 2.

[14] Ibid.

[15] Ibid.

[16] KEI, German Federal Supreme Court Affirms Compulsory License on HIV Drug (13 July 2012); https://www.keionline.org/23403. Accessed 26 January 2023.

[17] AGCM (2005).

[18] KEI, German Federal Supreme Court Affirms Compulsory License on HIV Drug (13 July 2012); https://www.keionline.org/23403. Accessed 26 January 2023.

[19] WTO, *Notification under Paragraph 2(a) of the Decision of 30 August 2003 on the Implementation of Paragraph 6 of the Doha Declaration on the TRIPS Agreement and Public Health*, Doc. IP/N/9/RWA/1 (19 July 2007).

[20] WTO, *Amendment of the TRIPS Agreement* WT/L/641 (8 December 2005).

introduced by the WTO following the Doha Declaration which permits the waiver of the requirements under Article 31(f) in order for a member to produce pharmaceuticals under compulsory license for the purpose of exporting them to a country with insufficient or no manufacturing capacity for the product in question.[21] The Canada-Rwanda episode has been generally considered a failure in terms of promoting access to medicine.[22] This was not, however, a failure that test data exclusivity contributed to; as the drug wasn't intended to be sold on the Canadian market (not least because the Canadian patents remained in force) there was no requirement that the drug be approved in Canada, while Rwanda, like most LDCs, did not (and does not) have test data exclusivity laws.

This is not to suggest that the issue of test data exclusivity has not had any impact on compulsory licensing, however. The contrasting experiences of the Malaysian and Romanian governments regarding the licensing of sofosbuvir, a treatment for Hepatitis C, suggest that test data exclusivity laws may have a chilling effect on the use of compulsory licensing. The Malaysian government issued a compulsory license for sofosbuvir in 2017;[23] while the test data exclusivity term for sofosbuvir (marketed as Sovaldi) was still in effect in Malaysia at the time, this did not pose an issue because, as discussed at Sect. 6.4.6, the Malaysian law on test data exclusivity specifies that protection does not apply in cases where a compulsory license has been issued over the associated drug.[24] A few weeks prior to the issuance of the Malaysian compulsory license, Gilead, which holds the rights to sofosbuvir, had announced the extension of its voluntary licensing programme for sofosbuvir to Malaysia, a decision that appears to have been made in order to pre-empt the compulsory license issued by the Malaysian government.[25] Correspondence between representatives of Gilead and the USTR during negotiations with the Malaysian government in the run up to the decision to issue a compulsory license shows that Gilead had sought to rely on test data exclusivity as well as Article 39.3 of the TRIPS agreement in order to render the proposed compulsory license ineffective;[26] as such, the fact that test data exclusivity cannot actually be used to frustrate a compulsory license in Malaysia

---

[21] The Paragraph 6 Solution became the first ever amendment to a WTO agreement to take effect in 2017, following its acceptance by two thirds of WTO members; WTO, WTO IP rules amended to ease poor countries' access to affordable medicines; https://www.wto.org/english/news_e/news17_e/trip_23jan17_e.htm. Accessed 26 January 2023.

[22] See further Amollo (2009).

[23] Health Policy Watch, Malaysia Inclusion In Gilead Voluntary Licence—A Product Of Compulsory Licence Pressure (24 August 2017); https://healthpolicy-watch.news/malaysia-inclusion-gilead-voluntary-licence-product-compulsory-licence-pressure/. Accessed 26 January 2023.

[24] Malaysia, Directive on Data Exclusivity (Directive No. 2 of 2011) Article 5.

[25] Health Policy Watch, Malaysia Inclusion In Gilead Voluntary Licence—A Product Of Compulsory Licence Pressure (24 August 2017); https://healthpolicy-watch.news/malaysia-inclusion-gilead-voluntary-licence-product-compulsory-licence-pressure/. Accessed 26 January 2023.

[26] See further KEI, Communications between Gilead and USTR regarding Malaysia compulsory license on HCV patents, 2017 to May 2018 (28 November 2018); https://www.keionline.org/29257. Accessed 26 January 2023.

would appear to have been instrumental in securing an outcome in the Malaysian government's favour. This can be contrasted with the experience of Romania; the Romanian government had considered issuing a compulsory license for sofosbuvir in 2016—however, the absence of any mechanism to circumvent test data exclusivity in the EU meant that such a license would have been ineffectual given that the full test data exclusivity term associated with sofosbuvir in the EU does not expire until 2024.[27] No compulsory license was issued by the Romanian government, and Gilead has not extended its voluntary license for sofosbuvir to Romania.[28]

8.2.2 *Test Data Exclusivity and the Response to COVID-19*

As perhaps the most significant public health crises of the twenty-first century thus far, the COVID-19 pandemic has drawn widespread attention to the debate around the relationship between intellectual property rights and access to medicine. As even the governments of high-income countries struggled to ensure adequate supplies of materials necessary to respond to the pandemic, commentators and political leaders began to take seriously the possibility that test data exclusivity rights might frustrate or complicate attempts to suspend, waive or otherwise abrogate patents connected to the prevention or treatment of COVID-19.[29] These concerns focused on two particular responses to the pandemic—the proposed waiver of certain sections of the TRIPS Agreement, and the use of compulsory licenses by national governments.

8.2.2.1 Test Data Exclusivity and the Proposed TRIPS Waiver

On 2 October 2020, 7 months after the WHO had declared COVID-19 to be a global pandemic, the WTO published a joint submission by India and South Africa which proposed the waiver of certain provisions of the TRIPS Agreement in order to prevent, contain and treat COVID-19.[30] The proposed waiver would have suspended the obligations of WTO members to implement or apply certain aspects of Part II of the TRIPS agreement in relation to the prevention, containment or treatment of COVID-19 for a limited but open-ended period of time; these parts were Sections 1 (copyright and related rights), 4 (industrial designs), 5 (patents) and 7 (undisclosed information). Proponents of the waiver argued that the existing flexibilities within the TRIPS agreement, such as those contained within Article 31, were not sufficient

---

[27] 't Hoen (2022), pp. 191–192.

[28] MSF (2020), p. 23.

[29] Perehudoff et al. (2021), p. 2.

[30] WTO, *Waiver from Certain Provisions of the TRIPS Agreement for the Prevention, Containment and Treatment of COVID-19, Communication from India and South Africa*, IP/C/W/669 (2 October 2020).

to address a health crisis of the magnitude of the COVID-19 pandemic due to the considerable complexity and practical difficulties of issuing even a single compulsory license.[31] Furthermore, the proposed waiver would have covered intellectual property rights other than patents including trade secrets and, most significantly for the purposes of this book, submitted test data.

The inclusion of submitted test data within the scope of the waiver proved to be a contentious point during negotiations. While, as previously noted, the argument that the requirements of Article 39.3 could block a compulsory license by preventing the approval of a pharmaceutical product produced under license has always been weak, developing nations pointed to the fact that Article 39.3 has historically been invoked by the US and other developed countries to criticise WTO members which make use of TRIPS flexibilities such as compulsory licenses. As such, it was argued that including Section 7 of TRIPS within the scope of any waiver would provide governments with 'legal certainty' regarding what was permissible in addressing the pandemic.[32]

The proposed waiver quickly found support from developing countries,[33] although there was predictable opposition from many developed countries, including the US. However, the US changed its position in May 2021, announcing that while the US Government believed strongly in intellectual property protection, it would support the waiver of those protections for COVID-19 vaccines.[34] Shortly after this announcement, India, South Africa and over 60 co-sponsors submitted a revised waiver proposal that clarified the range of subject matter covered by the proposal as well as providing that the waiver would remain in force for 'at least three years', after which the General Council would determine whether the waiver should be ended or continued.[35] Other developed countries continued to oppose the waiver; in particular, the European Commission argued that the existing flexibilities within the TRIPS Agreement were adequate to address intellectual property barriers to combatting the pandemic.[36] However, negotiations between the US, EU, India and South Africa

[31] WTO, *Waiver from Certain Provisions of the TRIPS Agreement for the Prevention, Containment and Treatment of COVID-19—Response to Questions, Communication from Bolivia, Eswatini, India, Kenya, Mozambique, Mongolia, Pakistan, South Africa, Venezuela, and Zimbabwe*, IP/C/W/672 (15 January 2021).

[32] Ibid, p. 24.

[33] WTO, TRIPS Council to Continue to discuss temporary IP waiver, revised proposal expected in May, (30 April 2021); www.wto.org/english/news_e/news21_e/trip_30apr21_e.htm. Accessed 26 January 2023.

[34] USTR, Statement from Ambassador Katherine Tai on the Covid-19 Trips Waiver (5 May 2021); https://ustr.gov/about-us/policy-offices/press-office/press-releases/2021/may/statement-ambassador-katherine-tai-covid-19-trips-waiver. Accessed 26 January 2023.

[35] WTO, *Waiver from Certain Provisions of the TRIPS Agreement for the Prevention, Containment and Treatment of COVID-19, Communication from the African Group, Bolivia, Egypt, Eswatini, Fiji, India, Indonesia, Kenya, LDC Group, Maldives, Mozambique, Mongolia, Namibia, Pakistan, South Africa, Vanuatu, Venezuela and Zimbabwe*, IP/C/W/669/Rev.1 (21 May 2021).

[36] European Commission, Opening statement by Executive Vice-President Valdis Dombrovskis at the European Parliament Plenary Debate on the Global Covid-19 Challenge (19 May 2021); https://

produced a compromise version of the waiver proposal in May 2022.[37] This document then formed the basis for the 'Ministerial Decision on the TRIPS Agreement' adopted by the WTO's 12th Ministerial Conference in June 2022.[38]

This final Ministerial Decision differs significantly from the original and revised proposals. An in-depth discussion of the Ministerial Decision is beyond the scope of this book. It should be noted, however, that the Ministerial Decision has been heavily criticised for falling far short of the original proposal, and has been described as a limited exception to which eases restrictions on compulsory licensing for export in certain circumstances as opposed to a waiver of any aspects of the TRIPS Agreement.[39] Rather than suspending Sections 1, 4, 5 and 7 in relation to a broad category of products and technologies for the prevention, treatment or containment of COVID-19, it instead permits eligible members of the WTO to limit the rights under Article 28.1 of the TRIPS Agreement (which specifies the rights conferred by patents) by authorising 'the use of the subject matter of a patent required for the production and supply of COVID-19 vaccines without the consent of the right holder to the extent necessary to address the COVID-19 pandemic.'[40] The Decision also contains a commitment for members to decide on its possible extension to the production and supply of COVID-19 diagnostics and therapeutics; at time of writing, the initial deadline for this decision has been extended but no decision has been made.[41] 'Eligible members' are defined as 'all developing country Members', although developing country members with 'existing capacity to manufacture COVID-19 vaccines' are encouraged to 'make a binding commitment not to avail themselves of this Decision.'[42] The Decision also contains a number of clarifications, perhaps most significantly including that eligible members may waive the requirement in Article 31(f) that a compulsory license be predominantly to supply the domestic market.[43]

The Ministerial Decision discusses Article 39.3 at Paragraph 4, which states that it is 'understood that Article 39.3 of the Agreement does not prevent an eligible Member from enabling the rapid approval for use of a COVID-19 vaccine.'[44] As discussed at Sect. 4.4.3.1, this appears to clarify that Article 39.3 is not an

ec.europa.eu/commission/commissioners/2019-2024/dombrovskis/announcements/opening-statement-executive-vice-president-valdis-dombrovskis-europeanparliament-plenary-debate_en. Accessed 26 January 2023.

[37] WTO, *Council for Trade Related Aspects of Intellectual Property Rights, Communication from the Chairperson on TRIPS COVID-19*, WTO/IP/C/W/688 (3 May 2018).

[38] WTO, *Ministerial Decision on the TRIPS Agreement, Ministerial Conference, 12th Session*, WT/MIN(22)/30, 22 June 2022.

[39] Mercurio and Upreti (2022,), p. 6.

[40] WTO, *Ministerial Decision on the TRIPS Agreement, Ministerial Conference, 12th Session*, WT/MIN(22)/30, 22 June 2022, para 1.

[41] South Centre (2023).

[42] Ibid, footnote 1.

[43] Ibid, para 3(b).

[44] Ibid, para 4.

impediment to the effective use of compulsory licenses with regards to pharmaceutical products.[45]

8.2.2.2 Compulsory Licensing During the COVID-19 Pandemic

While the June 2022 Decision provides welcome clarification to Article 39.3, this did not come into force until over 2 years into the pandemic. Furthermore, the test data exclusivity provisions in national legislation that have proliferated since the signing of the TRIPS Agreement have always presented a much more significant potential impediment to the compulsory licensing of pharmaceuticals given that many of these lack any mechanism to suspend test data exclusivity. As a number of governments, including those of Canada, Australia, Chile and Germany, moved to facilitate the issuance of compulsory licenses early in the pandemic,[46] some commentators feared that a clash between the use of compulsory licensing and inflexible test data exclusivity laws of the sort highlighted by the Terberger letter was now likely.[47]

Amongst the few compulsory licenses used during the COVID-19 pandemic were those issued by the governments of Hungary (over remdesivir);[48] Israel (over lopinavir/ritonavir);[49] Russia (over remdesivir);[50] and Ecuador (over raltegravir).[51] It is not clear what role, if any, test data exclusivity played in these cases; while all four countries have test data exclusivity laws, only Ecuador's law contains explicit provision permitting the use of submitted test data in emergency situations.[52] If test data exclusivity created complications regarding the Hungarian, Israeli and Russian compulsory licenses, these would appear to have gone unreported.

Beyond these small number of cases, there has been little use of compulsory licensing as a response to COVID-19. In 2021 Bolivia notified the TRIPS Council of its intention to import COVID-19 vaccines from Biolyse, a Canadian company, if the

---

[45] Mercurio and Upreti (2022), p. 7.

[46] Perehudoff et al. (2021), p. 2.

[47] See, for example, Chandler (2020).

[48] Kluwer Patent Blog, Russia: First "public security" Compulsory License (4 March 2021); http://patentblog.kluweriplaw.com/2021/03/04/russia-first-public-security-compulsory-license/. Accessed 26 January 2023.

[49] KEI, Israel issues compulsory license to allow the government to import generic versions of Kaletra (23 March 2020); https://www.keionline.org/32503. Accessed 26 January 2023.

[50] KEI, Hungarian compulsory license for remdesivir raises a stir with BIO, PhRMA and the US Chamber of Commerce (8 March 2021); https://www.keionline.org/35558. Accessed 26 January 2023.

[51] KEI, Ecuador grants compulsory license over HIV drug raltegravir (4 March 2021); https://www.keionline.org/35509. Accessed 26 January 2023.

[52] Ecuador, Organic Code of the Social Economy of Knowledge, Creativity and Innovation Article 509.

Canadian government would grant them a compulsory license under the system in Article 31*bis* of the TRIPS Agreement,[53] and Antigua and Barbuda also notified the WTO of its intent to make use of the Article 31*bis* system in May 2021, although it did not indicate a potential partner country.[54] However, as of early 2023 no compulsory licenses have been issued in either of these cases.

There are a number of possible reasons that compulsory licensing did not play a larger role in the response to COVID-19. The Ministerial Decision was only adopted over 2 years after the beginning of the pandemic and was considerably more limited in scope than the waiver originally proposed in October 2020; this has led commentators to brand it 'too little, too late.'[55] Others have suggested that more important causes of the shortages of medicines during the pandemic were limited supplies of raw materials, lack of production capacity and the complexity of the manufacturing processes involved, which compulsory licensing would not have addressed.[56] Others still have pointed to intellectual property rights beyond patents and test data exclusivity, such as industrial know-how and trade secrets involved in the manufacturing process, which would be difficult to force firms to share.[57] It seems clear, however, that test data exclusivity was not the main limiting factor, or even a particularly significant factor, regarding the use of compulsory licensing in response to COVID-19. While there has been a considerable discussion over the potential of test data exclusivity to thwart the use of compulsory licenses within academic circles, the issue has received little mainstream attention. There do not appear to be any examples of proposed compulsory licenses during the pandemic in which test data exclusivity issues became a serious concern, let alone compulsory licenses that were granted but subsequently thwarted by test data exclusivity. Furthermore, there has not been a significant use of compulsory licenses in response to the pandemic even amongst those jurisdictions that either have public health exceptions to test data exclusivity, such as Malaysia and Chile, or indeed do not provide test data exclusivity at all, such as India.

8.2.3 The Impact of Test Data Exclusivity on Measures for the Protection of Public Health

As the above analysis shows, while the differing experiences of Malaysia and Romania suggest that test data exclusivity rights may have a chilling effect on the use of compulsory licenses, there is little direct evidence of test data exclusivity undermining measures to protect public health in the post-TRIPS period. Certainly,

[53] WTO, *Notification Under the Amended TRIPS Agreement* (11 May 2021) IP/N/9/BOL/1.

[54] WTO, *Notification Under the Amended TRIPS Agreement* (17 May 2021) IP/N/8/ATG/1.

[55] See, for example, Ranjan and Gour (2022).

[56] Hilty et al. (2021), p. 2.

[57] McMahon (2020), p. 338.

there do not appear to be any examples of the most dramatic scenario envisaged by commentators, i.e. one in which a compulsory license is granted but the generic products produced under the license cannot be approved through an abbreviated approval pathway. Even the COVID-19 pandemic, exactly the sort of global public health crisis that many commentators feared would exposed the potential of test data exclusivity to frustrate measures designed to protect public health, has not produced an obvious example of such a clash.

None of this is to suggest that the potential of test data exclusivity to undermine measures designed to safeguard public health is a non-issue, however. As the USTR correspondence regarding the Malaysian compulsory license shows, test data exclusivity rights are viewed as a mechanism to prevent unauthorised use of patented subject matter—while difficult to prove, it is logical to assume that similar arguments have been made regarding other potential compulsory licenses. Furthermore, the absence of direct clashes between test data exclusivity and the use of compulsory licenses is at least partially a result of the fact that the compulsory licensing of pharmaceutical products has been so uncommon in the post-TRIPS period, especially amongst the high income and upper middle income countries most likely to provide test data exclusivity. Test data exclusivity may not be the main limiting factor preventing the use of compulsory licensing and other public health measures with regards to pharmaceutical products—but alongside international political pressure, the possible inadequacy of domestic manufacturing infrastructure, the need to engage in potentially lengthy negotiations with the right holder, legal challenges, and others, it is one of an overlapping network of factors that would need to be overcome in order to make effective use of a compulsory license in many circumstances. In this sense, the relationship between test data exclusivity and measures for safeguarding public health is not dissimilar to the role of test data exclusivity in the context of access to medicines more generally; while test data exclusivity is not the sole or even the main cause of inadequate access to medicines, it is part of a system of interlinking and overlapping legal rights that, together, keep the costs of medicines high and make efforts to reduce those costs exceptionally difficult.

8.3 Reconciling Test Data Exclusivity and Measures for the Protection of Public Health

The absence of direct clashes between test data exclusivity and measures to protect public health does not mean that governments should be complacent regarding the issue. All disasters are theoretical until they are not, as the regulatory failings behind the elixir sulfanilamide and thalidomide tragedies discussed in Chap. 3 show. In the aftermath of the COVID-19 pandemic, it is abundantly clear that major public health crises can and will occur, even in developed countries. It is quite obviously in the interests of the vast majority of parties that test data exclusivity not prevent the supply of life-saving medications in the event of a public health disaster, regardless of one's view as to whether test data exclusivity is justified in general terms.

Governments which have committed to providing test data exclusivity rights should enact legislation making it clear that such rights will be automatically suspended if a compulsory license is issued regarding an associated pharmaceutical product, or if it is necessary to do so in order to protect public health. The automatic nature of such an exception obviates the need to seek a separate permission to enable the compulsory license to be effective, both speeding the process in an emergency and removing another possible avenue of obstruction for those opposed to the license. A further broadly drafted exception to allow the government to act in the public interest is also important in order to cover other unexpected ways that test data exclusivity might need to be limited other than the grant of a compulsory license over a pharmaceutical product during a public health emergency. This is exactly the approach taken by the Malaysian law on test data exclusivity,[58] and one which appears to have enabled the Malaysian government to make effective use of compulsory licensing, as discussed above.

Consideration should also be given to reconciling test data exclusivity with the Paragraph 6 System now set out at Article 31*bis* of TRIPS. If a pharmaceutical product remains subject to test data exclusivity in both the exporting and importing member, it could potentially undermine the use of Article 31*bis*. As previously noted, the EU's instrument for implementing the 30 August 2003 Decision of the WTO, the 'EU Regulation on compulsory licensing of patents for the manufacture of pharmaceutical products for export to countries with public health problems outside the EU', states at Article 18 that applicants for compulsory licenses for pharmaceutical products may make reference to originator products, and that the 'protection period' (test data exclusivity) set out in Article 6 of Directive 2001/83/EC shall not apply in such a case.[59] Even if not extended to drugs produced under compulsory license within the EU, as 't Hoen, Boulet and Baker have argued they should be,[60] such provisions minimise the risk of test data exclusivity undermining the Paragraph 6 System, if indeed it is used again, and other jurisdictions with the capacity to produce pharmaceutical products for export should consider adopting similar provisions.

---

[58] Malaysia, Directive on Data Exclusivity (2011), Article 5.

[59] Council Regulation (EC) 816/2006 on compulsory licensing of patents relating to the manufacture of pharmaceutical products for export to countries with public health problems [2006] Article 18(2).

[60] 't Hoen et al. (2017), p. 23.

8.4 Conclusion

An analysis of national experiences of the use of public health measures since the signing of TRIPS reveals that there do not appear to have been any cases in which test data exclusivity has directly frustrated the use of a compulsory license or similar measure, even after the COVID-19 pandemic. This does not, however, suggest that the risks of a conflict between test data exclusivity rights and the use of public health flexibilities is not real. The absence of direct conflicts between test data exclusivity rights and compulsory licensing is in part a reflection of how rarely compulsory licenses have been used in the post-TRIPS era. Furthermore, as the experience of the Malaysian government's compulsory licensing of sofosbuvir shows, test data exclusivity rights have been used as a rhetorical tactic against the use of public health flexibilities. The contrasting experience of the Romanian government regarding its attempt to issue a compulsory license over the same product hints at the chilling effect test data exclusivity may be having behind closed doors.

Test data exclusivity rights may not be the main reason that public health flexibilities have been used so rarely since the signing of the TRIPS Agreement, but they are one of a number of factors that must be over come if such flexibilities are to be used more frequently. The COVID-19 pandemic has demonstrated the importance of preparing for public health crises before the fact. The approach of countries such as Malaysia to building comprehensive safeguards into national test data exclusivity laws provides a model to other jurisdictions as to how this might be done.

References

Abbott FM (2004) The Doha Declaration on the TRIPS Agreement and Public Health and the contradictory trend in bilateral and regional free trade agreements. Quaker United Nations Office (QUNO), Occasional Paper 14

AGCM (2005) Press release, pharmaceuticals: antitrust obliges Merck to license manufacture of the antibiotic Imipenem Cilastatin

Amollo R (2009) Revisiting the TRIPS regime: Rwanda-Canadian ARV drug deal tests the WTO General Council Decision. Afr J Int Comp Law 17:240

Attaran A, Gillespie-White L (2001) Do patents for antiretroviral drugs constrain access to AIDS treatment in Africa? JAMA 286(15):1886–1189

Beall R, Kuhn R (2012) Trends in compulsory licensing of pharmaceuticals since the Doha Declaration: a database analysis. PLoS Med 9(1):e1001154

Chandler DC (2020) Uh-Oh we are in trouble! Compulsory licences v data exclusivity in the EU: one more challenge to overcome in the race to find a COVID-19 vaccine? Eur Intellect Prop Rev 42(9):539–547

Correa C (2002) Protection of data submitted for the registration of pharmaceuticals: implementing the standards of the TRIPS agreement. South Centre, Geneva

European Commission (2006) Letter from the European Commission to Mr. Greg Perry, EGA-European Generic Medicines Association on the subject of Tamiflu application and data exclusivity in an emergency compulsory license situation

Hilty R, Batista PHD, Carls S, Kim D, Lamping M, Slowinski PR (2021) COVID-19 and the role of intellectual property: position statement of the Max Planck Institute for Innovation and

Competition of 7 May 2021. Max Planck Institute for Innovation & Competition Research Paper No. 21-13

KEI (2014) KEI research note: recent European Union compulsory licenses

Liu KC (2014) Compulsory licence and government use in Taiwan: a regress. In: Hilty R, Liu KC (eds) Compulsory licensing: practical experiences and ways forward. Springer, Berlin, pp 79–93

Lokuge B, Drahos P, Neville W (2006) Pandemics, antiviral stockpiles and biosecurity in Australia: what about the generic option? Med J Aust 184(1):16–20

McMahon A (2020) Patents, access to health and COVID-19-the role of compulsory and government-use licensing in Ireland. North Ireland Leg Q 71:331

Mercurio B, Upreti P (2022) From necessity to flexibility: a reflection on the negotiations for a TRIPS waiver for Covid-19 vaccines and treatments. World Trade Rev 21(5):633–649

MSF (2020) Voluntary licenses and access to medicines: Médecins Sans Frontières technical briefing document

Mullin TF (2002) AIDS, anthrax, and compulsory licensing: has the United States learned anything-a comment on recent decisions on the international intellectual property rights of pharmaceutical patents. ILSA J Int Comp Law 9:185

Perehudoff K, 't Hoen EFM, Boulet P (2021) Overriding drug and medical technology patents for pandemic recovery: a legitimate move for high-income countries, too. BMJ Glob Health 6(4): e005518

Ranjan P, Gour P (2022) The TRIPS waiver decision at the World Trade Organization: too little too late! Asian J Int Law, 1–12

South Centre (2023) South Centre Statement on the extension of the TRIPS waiver for diagnostics and therapeutics for COVID-19

't Hoen EFM (2016) Private patents and public health: changing intellectual property rules for access to medicines. Health Action International, Amsterdam

't Hoen EFM (2022) Protection of clinical test data and public health: a proposal to end the stronghold of data exclusivity. In: Correa C, Hilty RM (eds) Access to medicines and vaccines. Springer, Cham, pp 183–200

't Hoen EFM, Boulet P, Baker BK (2017) Data exclusivity exceptions and compulsory licensing to promote generic medicines in the European Union: a proposal for greater coherence in European pharmaceutical legislation. J Pharm Policy Pract 10(1):1–9

Chapter 9
Conclusion

Abstract This final chapter first summarises the major findings of this book before moving to discuss some of the implications of those findings. Finally, it offers a few concluding remarks on the book as a whole.

9.1 Findings of This Book

In only a few decades, test data exclusivity has gone from a politically expedient last-minute addition to a reform of the US system of pharmaceutical regulation to near ubiquity amongst the legal systems of states with significant pharmaceutical markets. This exceptionally rapid globalisation has been contingent on a very particular set of historical circumstances and actors. Test data exclusivity might have remained another quirk of the US regulatory system if not for the fact that this approach was modelled by the EC immediately prior to the GATT Uruguay Round; this, coupled with the fact that Japan had also developed a system with superficial similarities to test data exclusivity (although based on quite different policy goals), meant that the major centres of the research-based pharmaceutical industry were able to establish the principle that submitted test data should be protected in Article 39.3 of TRIPS, even if they were not able to establish exactly how (and against what) submitted test data should be protected.

It is not initially obvious what impact Article 39.3 has had on the globalisation of test data exclusivity post-TRIPS; the article remains deeply ambiguous, there have been no meaningful attempts to enforce one particular interpretation through the WTO's dispute settlement process, and states have mostly adopted test data exclusivity rights as a result of post-TRIPS trade negotiations. This book has argued, however, that Article 39.3 has played an important role in the globalisation of test data exclusivity beyond simply establishing the principle that submitted test data should be protected. The uncertain nature of Article 39.3 has made developing an original model for the protection of submitted test data in conformity with TRIPS a politically costly and uncertain venture, and indeed no such alternative model other than to offer submitted test data protection against 'misappropriation' alone has emerged. As a result, when states are pressured to meet their obligations to protect

A. Buick, *Intellectual Property Rights in Pharmaceutical Test Data*,
https://doi.org/10.1007/978-3-031-29436-5_9

test data from unfair commercial use during trade negotiations with developed countries, they are incentivised to accept the model suggested by the other party, which is almost invariably test data exclusivity.

This may also explain the fact that test data exclusivity provisions in national laws exhibit a high degree of similarity (even beyond what is required in the relevant international obligations). However, these textually similar test data exclusivity provisions are likely to have a significantly different impact between jurisdictions as a result of the differing political, economic, social, legal and epidemiological conditions in these jurisdictions.

In the US, test data exclusivity provisions seem likely to have delayed the market entry of a small but significant number of generic pharmaceuticals, as well as delaying a number of patent challenges (an impact of test data exclusivity that has been underappreciated in the literature, and may warrant further investigation). Furthermore, while there has not been a dramatic example of a conflict between test data exclusivity rights and the use of a measure intended to promote public health, such as a compulsory license, there is reason to believe that test data exclusivity has had a chilling effect on the use of such measures in at least some cases. Test data exclusivity is far from the main barrier to more equitable access to medicines; however, it is a component of a complex legal and political framework that contributes to high pharmaceutical prices and impedes measures to make medicines more widely available.

9.2 Implications for the Future

Whatever the merits of test data exclusivity, it would now appear that absent some fundamental restructuring of the current trade order and the network of trade agreements that have proliferated since the 1990s, it will remain a feature of most significant pharmaceutical markets. However, there are also opportunities to reform the protection of submitted pharmaceutical test data that do not exist for other intellectual property rights because the absence of detailed global-level obligations regarding the protection of submitted test data leave governments with wide discretion here.

While the vast majority of jurisdictions with a significant pharmaceutical market now have test data exclusivity laws, many countries still do not. In the absence of the emergence of an alternative, it seems likely that members of this group of countries will continue to adopt test data exclusivity laws when pressured to meet their Article 39.3 obligations in trade negotiations. As an alternative, those states without test data exclusivity rights but which also have significant regulatory capacity, such as Argentina, Brazil, India and South Africa, could cooperate to develop and implement a different means of protecting submitted test data; as other countries with less regulatory capacity develop further and become more integrated into the global economy, this would provide an alternative means to comply with Article 39.3. However, such coordination would be difficult. Furthermore, even states with larger economies which have ignored Article 39.3 for years have made commitments to provide test data exclusivity, as the example of the EFTA-Indonesia FTA demonstrates.

Other states might adapt test data exclusivity rights in a manner that better promotes access to medicines; this is the case even for many states that have signed trade agreements with test data exclusivity provisions, as these are often vague and permit many flexibilities. Most jurisdictions with test data exclusivity provisions do not have measures in place to prevent such exclusivity rights undermining measures intended to protect public health such as the use of compulsory licenses. Even on the assumption that test data exclusivity plays an important role in incentivising drug development, undermining efforts to relieve a public health crisis is quite obviously not in the interests of society as a whole. As such, the exceptions to test data exclusivity for reasons of the public interest provided by jurisdictions such as Malaysia should provide a model for other jurisdictions in reconciling test data exclusivity and compulsory licensing.[1]

There are other checks and balances which could also be incorporated into national laws on the protection of submitted test data. Some jurisdictions, including Vietnam and Peru, have systems in place to oppose the grant of test data exclusivity or challenge its validity.[2] While the impact of these systems in practice is a question for future research, such a provision at least provides a mechanism to review cases in which protection may have been granted improperly. Perhaps more significantly, measuring the term of test data exclusivity protection from the date of approval in a developed country, as Peru and Malaysia both do, has a significant impact on the term of test data exclusivity while also acting as an incentive to bring new drugs to market in a timely manner.[3]

The inclusion of checks and balances to test data exclusivity is important because the impact of even superficially similar test data exclusivity provisions is likely to differ between jurisdictions. For example, while the analysis in Chap. 7 concluded that test data exclusivity provisions delayed the market entry of a small but significant number of generic pharmaceutical products, and delayed a larger number of patent challenges, in the US between 1999 and 2009, identical test data exclusivity provisions would have a very different impact in other countries, where both patents and patent challenges are less common. Even within developed countries, the soaring prices of medicines and the increased healthcare burdens of an aging population may provide cause to reassess the balance between access to medicine and test data exclusivity rights, as well as other intellectual property rights in pharmaceuticals; the 2019 manifesto of the UK's Labour Party, for example,

---

[1] Malaysia, Regulation 29 of the Control of Drugs and Cosmetics Regulations 1984, 4.7.

[2] Peru, Regulation on Legislative Decree No. 1072 on the Protection of Test Data and Other Undisclosed Data Relating to Pharmaceuticals (approved by Supreme Decree No. 002-2009-SA) (2009), Article 7–8; Vietnam, Circular No 17/2011/TT-BNNPTNT 2011, Article 11, 14.

[3] Peru, Legislative Decree 1072 of 2008, Article 3; Malaysia, Directive on Data Exclusivity (2011), Article 4.6.

promised to exclude provisions on regulatory exclusivities, including test data exclusivity, from future trade deals, and to move away from the EU's approach to the protection of submitted test data.[4]

While most of the debate over test data exclusivity has thus far been focused on data submitted with regards to small molecule drugs, there is likely to be a greater focus on test data submitted with regards to biologics in future as biologic drugs come to represent an increasingly valuable part of the pharmaceutical industry. The TPP and USMCA both demonstrate a desire by elements within the US government to take a more aggressive stance regarding biologic test data exclusivity; however, the ultimate removal of the provisions on test data exclusivity from both those agreements as a result of domestic US political pressure also hints at the decline in America's influence in matters of regulatory globalisation. While the EU and EFTA states have been more active than the US in the globalisation of test data exclusivity in the past decade, their negotiating power is significantly lower.

This speaks to a final point; since the Uruguay Round, developed countries led by the US have pushed one particular approach to the protection of submitted test data on the rest of the world. This reflects the wider domination of geopolitics by the US and its allies since the end of the Cold War. It may be that the rest of the twenty-first century will witness a move away from the established world order that has predominated since the 1990s to a more multipolar world. China in particular is likely to play a leading role in such a multipolar order—if this is the case, the decision of the Chinese government regarding the proposed reforms to its laws on test data exclusivity and its subsequent approach to the protection of submitted test data in future negotiations with economic partners will be key.[5]

9.3 Concluding Remarks

As the economist Thomas Piketty has observed, the notion of what can be owned as property is not an immutable concept, and instead reflects the state of development and the prevailing social relations of a given society.[6] The existence of intellectual property rights in submitted pharmaceutical test data is, of course, no exception. Indeed, it is difficult to think of a form of property more contingent on (geo)political and social relations than test data exclusivity.

The globalisation of test data exclusivity has been so thorough amongst jurisdictions with significant pharmaceutical markets that the chance to implement an alternative regime for the protection of submitted test data has passed for many countries. Given that most jurisdictions with significant pharmaceutical markets now have test data exclusivity laws of some variety, it may be that the future of the

[4] Labour Party (2019).

[5] See further Yu (2019).

[6] Piketty (2014), p. 40.

globalisation of test data exclusivity focuses on the ratcheting up of standards of exclusivity protection such as by extending protection to biologics. However, there is another possibility. A number of qualifications and adaptations to test data exclusivity rights that support access to medicines have emerged; as the COVID-19 pandemic ends and governments around the world consider how to prepare for the next public health crisis, lessons can and should be learned from these approaches. The story of intellectual property rights in submitted test data over the last three decades has been the story of the globalisation of measures to protect the investment of pharmaceutical companies; it is the hope of the author that the story in the coming decades will be one of the globalisation of measures to protect the health and lives of human beings.

References

Labour Party (2019) Medicines for the many

Piketty T (2014) Capital in the twenty-first century. Harvard University Press, Cambridge

Yu PK (2019) China's innovative turn and the changing pharmaceutical landscape. Univ Pacific Law Rev 51:5

Appendix A: The Following Tables A1, A2 and A3 Contain the Data Used at Sect. 6.4.3.1 for the Purposes of Calculating the Impact of Measuring the Test Data Exclusivity Term from the Date of a Drug's Approval in a Foreign Jurisdiction

A. Buick, *Intellectual Property Rights in Pharmaceutical Test Data*,
https://doi.org/10.1007/978-3-031-29436-5

Table A1 Effective length of test data exclusivity period for NCEs granted test data exclusivity protection in Peru between 22 February 2010 and 07 June 2018

Name of drug	Registration date in reference country	Registration date in Peru	End of test data exclusivity in Peru	Length of exclusivity period in Peru in months
Xarelto (Rivaroxaban)	15 September 2008	22 February 2010	15 September 2013	42
Multaq (Dronedarona)	01 July 2009	22 February 2010	01 July 2014	52
Ecalta (Anidulafungina)	17 February 2006	13 April 2010	17 February 2011	10
Effient (Prasugrel)	25 February 2009	26 April 2010	25 February 2014	45
Yondelis (Trabectedina)	17 September 2007	26 June 2010	17 September 2012	26
Onglyza (Saxagliptina)	31 July 2009	30 June 2010	31 July 2014	49
Resolor (Prucaloprida)	15 October 2009	02 June 2011	15 October 2014	40
Jevtana (Cabazitaxel)	17 June 2010	16 June 2011	17 June 2015	48
Pazopanib (Votrient)	19 October 2009	21 July 2011	19 October 2014	38
Revolade (Eltrombopag)	20 November 2008	26 July 2011	20 November 2013	27
Priligy (Dapoxetina)	06 February 2009	03 August 2011	06 February 2014	30
Brilinta (Ticagrelor)	03 December 2010	15 November 2011	03 December 2015	48
Gilenya (Fingolimod)	21 September 2010	07 December 2011	21 September 2015	45
Brinavess (Vernakalant)	01 September 2010	20 April 2012	01 September 2015	40
Eliquis (Apixaban)	18 May 2011	20 August 2012	18 May 2016	44
Edurant (Rilpivirina)	20 May 2011	04 September 2012	20 May 2016	44
Tayenta (Linagliptina)	02 May 2011	13 September 2012	02 May 2016	43
Xalkori (Crizotinib)	26 August 2011	23 October 2012	26 August 2016	46
Zytga (Abiraterona)	28 April 2011	12 April 2013	28 April 2016	36
Jakavi (Ruxolitinib)	16 November 2011	31 May 2013	16 November 2016	41
Onbrize (Indacaterol)	30 November 2009	15 July 2013	30 November 2014	16

(continued)

Table A1 (continued)

Name of drug	Registration date in reference country	Registration date in Peru	End of test data exclusivity in Peru	Length of exclusivity period in Peru in months
Xeljanz (Tofacitinib)	06 November 2012	25 July 2013	06 November 2017	51
Inlyta (Axitinib)	27 January 2012	11 October 2013	27 January 2017	39
Stivarga (Regorafenib)	27 September 2012	28 October 2013	27 September 2017	46
Signifor (Pasireotida)	24 April 2012	17 February 2014	24 April 2017	38
Invokana (Canagliflozina)	29 March 2013	10 March 2014	29 March 2018	48
Giotrif (Afatinib)	12 July 2013	27 June 2014	12 July 2018	48
Lyxumia (Lixisenatide)	01 February 2013	17 July 2014	01 February 2018	42
Brintellix (Vortioxetina)	30 September 2013	29 October 2014	30 September 2018	47
Sovriad (Simeprevir)	27 September 2013	01 December 2014	27 September 2018	45
Sirturo (Bedaquilina)	28 December 2012	13 December 2014	28 December 2017	36
Imbruvica (Ibrutinib)	12 February 2014	17 March 2015	12 February 2019	46
Jardiance (Empagliflozina)	30 April 2014	25 March 2015	30 April 2019	49
Xtandi (Enzalutamida)	31 August 2012	13 April 2015	31 August 2017	28
Forxiga (Dapagliflozina)	12 November 2012	23 June 2015	12 November 2017	28
Striverdi (Olodaterol)	11 June 2013	17 July 2015	11 June 2018	34
Tivicay (Dolutegravir)	12 August 2013	04 December 2015	12 August 2018	32
Sunvepra (Asunaprevir)	04 July 2014	21 December 2015	04 July 2019	42
Daklinza (Daclatasvir)	04 July 2014	21 December 2015	04 July 2019	42
Adempas (Riociguat)	19 September 2013	21 January 2016	19 September 2018	31
Vargatef (Nintedanib)	15 October 2014	29 February 2016	15 October 2019	43
Anoro Ellipta (Umeclidinio + Vilanterol)	18 December 2013	02 May 2016	18 December 2018	31
Sovaldi (Sofosbuvir)	06 December 2013	09 May 2016	06 December 2018	30

(continued)

Table A1 (continued)

Name of drug	Registration date in reference country	Registration date in Peru	End of test data exclusivity in Peru	Length of exclusivity period in Peru in months
Ibrance (Palbociclib)	03 February 2015	10 May 2016	03 February 2020	44
Cerdelga (Eliglustat)	19 August 2014	30 June 2016	19 August 2019	37
Cotellic (Cobimetinib)	24 August 2015	30 June 2016	24 August 2020	49
Zykadia (Ceritinib)	29 April 2014	18 August 2016	29 April 2019	32
Venclexta (Venetoclax)	11 April 2016	06 April 2017	11 April 2021	48
Lynparza (Olaparib)	16 December 2016	06 April 2017	16 December 2021	56
Zepatier (Grazoprevir+ Elbasvir)	16 April 2016	28 June 2017	16 April 2021	45
Tafinlar (Dabrafenib)	29 May 2013	26 September 2017	29 May 2018	8
Ninlaro (Ixazomib)	20 November 2015	28 September 2017	20 November 2020	37
Aleneca (Alecfinib)	11 December 2015	13 December 2017	11 December 2020	35
Tagrisso (Osermertinib)	13 November 2015	22 March 2018	13 November 2020	31
Olumiant (Baricitinib)	13 February 2017	02 May 2018	13 February 2022	45
Maviret (Glecaprevir +Pibrentasbir)	26 July 2017	15 May 2018	26 July 2022	50
Zevetera (Ceftobiprol)	20 November 2013	07 June 2018	20 November 2018	5
Cresemba (Isavuconazol)	06 March 2015	07 June 2018	06 March 2020	20

Table A2 Effective length of test data exclusivity period for NCEs granted test data exclusivity protection in Malaysia between 21 September 2012 and 04 April 2019

Name of drug	Registration date in reference country	Registration date in Malaysia	End of Test Data Exclusivity in Malaysia	Length of exclusivity period in Malaysia in months
Gilenya (fingolimod hydrochloride)	21 September 2010	19 January 2012	21 September 2015	44
Victrelis (boceprevir)	13 May 2011	29 March 2012	13 May 2016	49
Halaven (Erbulin mesylate)	15 November 2010	27 September 2012	15 November 2015	37
Xalkori (crizotinib)	26 September 2011	27 September 2012	26 September 2016	47
Zinforo/Teflaro (Ceftaroline fosamil)	29 October 2010	29 November 2012	29 October 2015	35
Jakavi (Ruxolitinib phosphate)	16 November 2011	28 February 2013	16 November 2016	44
Stivarga (Regorafenib monohydrate)	27 September 2012	27 June 2013	27 September 2017	51
Inlyta (Axitinib)	27 January 2012	06 November 2013	27 January 2017	38
Forxiga (Dapagliflozin Propanediol)	12 November 2012	23 January 2014	12 November 2017	45
Fycompa (Perampanel)	23 July 2012	27 March 2014	23 July 2017	39
Xofigo (Radium-223 Dichloride)	15 May 2013	09 May 2014	15 May 2018	48
Xeljanz (Tofacitinib citrate)	06 November 2012	24 July 2014	06 November 2017	39
Adempas (Riociguat)	08 October 2013	24 November 2014	08 October 2018	46
Brintellix (Vortioxetine hydrobromide)	30 September 2013	30 April 2015	30 September 2018	41
Tecfidera (Dimethyl fumarate)	27 March 2013	20 August 2015	27 March 2018	31
Sovaldi (Sofosbuvir)	06 December 2013	28 September 2015	06 December 2018	38
Jardiance (Empagliflozin)	30 April 2014	22 December 2015	30 April 2019	40
Entresto (Sacubitril/ valsartan)	07 July 2015	22 December 2015	07 July 2020	54
Zykadia (Ceritinib)	29 April 2014	21 January 2016	29 April 2019	39
Opsumit (Macitentan)	18 October 2013	07 June 2016	18 October 2018	28

(continued)

Table A2 (continued)

Name of drug	Registration date in reference country	Registration date in Malaysia	End of Test Data Exclusivity in Malaysia	Length of exclusivity period in Malaysia in months
OFEV (Nintedanib esilate)	15 October 2014	07 June 2016	15 October 2019	40
Ibrance (Palbociclib)	03 February 2015	07 June 2016	03 February 2020	43
Lynparza (Olaparib)	16 December 2014	30 June 2016	16 December 2019	41
Zerbaxa (Ceftolozane sulphate)	19 December 2014	22 December 2016	19 December 2019	35
Farydak (Panobinostat lactate anhydrous)	24 February 2015	24 February 2017	24 February 2020	36
Tagrisso (Osimertinib mesylate)	13 November 2015	28 April 2017	13 November 2020	42
Duaklir Genuair (aclidinium bromide)	19 November 2014	03 October 2017	19 November 2019	25
Kryxana (Ribociclib succinate)	13 March 2017	02 April 2018	13 March 2022	47
Uptravi (Selexipag)	21 December 2015	28 August 2018	21 December 2020	27
Lusefi (Luseogliflozin hydrate)	24 March 2014	04 December 2018	24 March 2019	3
Epclusa (Velpatasvir and sofosbuvir, TDE granted for Velpatasvir only)	28 June 2016	23 January 2019	28 June 2021	29
Rydapt (Midostaurin)	28 April 2017	04 April 2019	28 April 2022	36

Table A3 Effective length of test data exclusivity period for new indications granted test data exclusivity protection in Malaysia between 28 June 2012 and 15 November 2019

Name of drug	Registration date in reference country	Registration date in Malaysia	End of Test Data Exclusivity in Malaysia	Length of exclusivity period in Malaysia in months
Onglyza (Saxagliptin hydrochloride)	16 December 2011	28 June 2012	16 December 2014	29
Xarelto (rivaroxaban)	02 November 2012	28 March 2013	02 November 2015	31
Stivarga (Regorafenib monohydrate)	25 February 2013	23 January 2014	25 February 2016	25
Jardiance (Empagliflozin)	02 December 2016	27 November 2017	02 December 2019	24
Giotrif (Afatinib Dimaleate)	15 April 2016	28 February 2018	15 April 2019	13
Xalkori (Crizotinib)	11 March 2016	31 May 2018	11 March 2019	9
Zykadia (Ceritinib)	26 May 2017	28 August 2018	26 May 2020	20
Tagrisso (Osimertinib)	18 April 2018	15 November 2018	18 April 2021	29

Appendix B: The Following Table A4 Contains the Data Used in Chap. 7 for the Purposes of Calculating the Impact of Test Data Exclusivity on the Date of Approval of the First Generic Version of Pharmaceutical Products First Approved in the US Between 1999 and 2000

A. Buick, *Intellectual Property Rights in Pharmaceutical Test Data*,
https://doi.org/10.1007/978-3-031-29436-5

Table A4 Table showing the key dates for NDAs which qualified for test data exclusivity in the US between 1999 and 2009 and which had been the reference listed drug for at least one ANDA by July 2019, and the first of those ANDAs to have been approved

Name of drug	NDA	NDA approval date	ANDA	ANDA submission date	ANDA approval date	NDA approval to ANDA submission, months	NDA approval to ANDA approval, months	ANDA submission to approval, months
Pletal (Cilostazol)	N020863	15-Jan-99	A077019	19-Dec-03	23-Nov-04	59	70	11
Ferrlecit (Sodium Ferric Gluconate Complex)	N020955	18-Feb-99	A078215	21-Mar-06	31-Mar-11	85	145	60
Avandia (Rosiglitazone Maleate)	N021071	25-May-99	A076747	25-May-03	25-Jan-13	48	164	116
Hectorol (Doxercalciferol)	N020862	09-Jun-99	A091101	25-Nov-08	30-Aug-13	113	170	57
Zaditor (Ketotifen Fumarate)	N021066	02-Jul-99	A077354	Unknown	09-May-06	N/A	N/A	N/A
Actos (Pioglitazone Hydrochloride)	N021073	15-Jul-99	A076798	15-Jul-03	26-Oct-12	48	159	111
Antagon (Ganirelix Acetate)	N021057	29-Jul-99	A204246	Unknown	30-Nov-18	N/A	N/A	N/A
Temodar (Temozolomide)	N021029	11-Aug-99	A078879	19-Mar-07	01-Mar-10	91	126	35
Sonata (Zaleplon)	N020859	13-Aug-99	A077237	13-Aug-04	06-Jun-08	60	105	45
Aciphex (Rabeprazole Sodium)	N020973	19-Aug-99	A076822	19-Aug-03	08-Nov-13	48	170	122
Ellence (Epirubicin Hydrochloride)	N050778	15-Sep-99	A065289	Unknown	27-Jun-07	N/A	N/A	N/A

Rapamune (Sirolimus)	N021083	15-Sep-99	A201676	Unknown	08-Jan-14	N/A	N/A	N/A
Tikosync (Dofetilide)	N020931	01-Oct-99	A207058	Unknown	06-Jun-16	N/A	N/A	N/A
Comtan (Entacapone)	N020796	19-Oct-99	A078941	Unknown	16-Aug-12	N/A	N/A	N/A
Aromasin (Exemestane)	N020753	21-Oct-99	A077431	08-Dec-04	01-Apr-11	61	137	75
Tamiflu (Oseltamivir Phosphate)	N021087	27-Oct-99	A202595	Unknown	08-Mar-16	N/A	N/A	N/A
Keppra (Levetiracetam)	N021035	30-Nov-99	A076919	Unknown	04-Nov-18	N/A	N/A	N/A
Avelox (Moxifloxacin Hydrochloride)	N021085	10-Dec-99	A076938	10-Dec-03	04-Mar-14	48	170	122
Tequin (Gatifloxacin)	N021061	17-Dec-99	A079084	Unknown	19-Aug-11	N/A	N/A	N/A
Precedex (Dexmedetomidine Hydrochloride)	N021038	17-Dec-99	A202881	Unknown	18-Aug-14	N/A	N/A	N/A
INOmax (Nitric Oxide)	N020845	23-Dec-99	A207141	20-May-14	02-Oct-18	172	225	52
Targretin (Bexarotene)	N021055	29-Dec-99	A203174	03-Jun-11	12-Aug-14	137	175	38
Evoxac (Cevimeline Hydrochloride)	N020989	11-Jan-00	A091260	27-Feb-09	25-Aug-11	109	139	29
Trileptal (Oxcarbazepine)	N021014	14-Jan-00	A077794	08-Jul-05	10-Sep-07	65	91	26
Protonix (Pantoprazole Sodium)	N020987	02-Feb-00	A077056	02-Feb-04	02-Aug-07	48	90	42

(continued)

Table A4 (continued)

Name of drug	NDA	NDA approval date	ANDA	ANDA submission date	ANDA approval date	NDA approval to ANDA submission, months	NDA approval to ANDA approval, months	ANDA submission to approval, months
Lotronex (Alosetron Hydrochloride)	N021107	09-Feb-00	A200652	14-Oct-09	04-May-15	116	182	66
Zonegran (Zonisamide)	N020789	27-Mar-00	A077647	18-Mar-05	22-Dec-05	59	68	9
Mobic (Meloxicam)	N020938	13-Apr-00	A077921	12-Oct-05	19-Jul-06	65	75	9
Zyvox (Linezolid)	N021130	18-Apr-00	A200222	18-Aug-05	31-Aug-09	64	112	48
Exelon (Rivastigmine Tartrate)	N020823	21-Apr-00	A077131	21-Apr-04	22-Aug-07	48	88	40
Welchol (Colesevelam Hydrochloride)	N021176	26-May-00	A091600	01-Jul-09	16-May-18	109	215	106
Acova (Argatroban)	N020883	30-Jun-00	A091665	Unknown	30-Jun-14	N/A	N/A	N/A
Colazal (Balsalazide Disodium)	N020610	18-Jul-00	A077807	18-Jul-05	28-Dec-07	60	89	29
Abreva (Docosanol)	N020941	25-Jul-00	A208754	23-Dec-15	19-Nov-18	184	219	34
Trisenox (Arsenic Trioxide)	N021248	25-Sep-00	A208231	11-Aug-15	31-Aug-18	178	215	36
Mifeprex (Mifepristone)	N020687	28-Sep-00	A091178	03-Feb-09	11-Apr-19	100	222	122
Angiomax (Bivalirudin)	N020873	15-Dec-00	A090811	15-Aug-08	14-Jul-15	92	174	82

Starlix (Nateglinide)	N021204	22-Dec-00	A077463	22-Dec-04	09-Sep-09	48	104	56
Cancidas (Caspofungin Acetate)	N021227	26-Jan-01	A207092	02-May-14	29-Sep-17	159	200	40
Geodon (Ziprasidone Hydrochloride)	N020825	05-Feb-01	A077565	07-Feb-05	02-Mar-12	48	132	84
Reminyl (Galantamine Hydrobromide)	N021169	28-Feb-01	A077603	18-Feb-05	28-Aug-08	47	90	42
Travatan (Travoprost)	N021257	16-Mar-01	A091340	Unknown	01-Mar-13	N/A	N/A	N/A
Lumigan (Bimatopros)	N021275	16-Mar-01	A201894	Unknown	01-Dec-14	N/A	N/A	N/A
Axert (Almotriptan Malate)	N021001	07-May-01	A078027	07-Dec-05	07-Jul-15	55	170	115
Gleevec (Imatinib Mesylate)	N021335	10-May-01	A078340	16-Jun-06	03-Dec-15	61	174	113
Zometa (Zoledronic Acid)	N021223	20-Aug-01	A090018	Unknown	04-Mar-13	N/A	N/A	N/A
Viread (Tenofovir Disoproxil Fumarate)	N021356	26-Oct-01	A091612	01-Jul-09	26-Jan-18	92	195	102
Frova (Frovatriptan Succinate)	N021006	08-Nov-01	A202931	Unknown	28-Aug-14	N/A	N/A	N/A
Avodart (Dutasteride)	N021319	20-Nov-01	A090095	26-Oct-07	21-Dec-10	71	109	37
Tracleer (Bosentan)	N021290	20-Nov-01	A205699	20-Mar-13	26-Apr-19	136	209	73
Invanz (Ertapenem Sodium)	N021337	21-Nov-01	A208790	10-Dec-15	16-Apr-18	168	196	28

(continued)

Table A4 (continued)

Name of drug	NDA	NDA approval date	ANDA	ANDA submission date	ANDA approval date	NDA approval to ANDA submission, months	NDA approval to ANDA approval, months	ANDA submission to approval, months
Arixtra (Fondaparinux Sodium)	N021345	07-Dec-01	A091316	09-Mar-09	11-Jul-11	87	115	28
Elidel (Pimecrolimus)	N021302	13-Dec-01	A209345	19-Dec-16	27-Dec-18	180	204	24
Clarinex (Desloratadine)	N021165	21-Dec-01	A078357	21-Jun-06	19-Feb-10	54	97	43
Faslodex (Fulvestrant)	N021344	25-Apr-02	A210044	28-Dec-16	04-Mar-19	176	202	26
Benicar (Olmesartan Medoxomil)	N021286	25-Apr-02	A078276	Unknown	26-Oct-16	N/A	N/A	N/A
Remodulin (Treprostinil Sodium)	N021272	21-May-02	A203649	02-Dec-11	30-Nov-17	114	186	71
Vfend (Voriconazole)	N021266	24-May-02	A090547	14-Apr-08	22-Apr-10	70	94	24
Xyrem (Sodium Oxybate)	N021196	17-Jul-02	A202090	08-Jul-10	17-Jan-17	95	174	78
Eloxatin (Oxaliplatin)	N021492	09-Aug-02	A078813	09-Feb-07	07-Aug-09	54	83	29
Hepsera (Adefovir Dipivoxil)	N021449	20-Sep-02	A202051	07-Jun-10	29-Aug-13	92	131	38
Inspra (Eplerenone)	N021437	27-Sep-02	A078482	27-Sep-06	30-Jul-08	48	70	22
Zetia (Ezetimibe)	N021445	25-Oct-02	A078560	25-Oct-07	26-Jun-15	60	152	92

Abilify (Aripiprazole)	N021436	15-Nov-02	A202102	18-Jun-10	28-Apr-15	91	149	58
Strattera (Atomoxetine Hydrochloride)	N021411	26-Nov-02	A079017	Unknown	16-Sep-10	N/A	N/A	N/A
Relpax (Eletriptan Hydrobromide)	N021016	26-Dec-02	A206409	31-Oct-13	16-Jun-17	130	173	43
Emend (Aprepitant)	N021549	26-Mar-03	A090999	31-Oct-08	24-Sep-12	67	113	46
Factive (Gemifloxacin Mesylate)	N021158	04-Apr-03	A090466	04-Mar-08	15-Jun-15	59	146	87
Boniva (Ibandronate Sodium)	N021455	16-May-03	A078995	16-May-07	19-Mar-12	48	106	58
Uroxatral (Alfuzosin Hydrochloride)	N021287	12-Jun-03	A079014	12-Jun-07	18-Jul-11	48	97	49
Reyataz (Atazanavir sulfate)	N021567	20-Jun-03	A091673	20-Jul-09	22-Apr-14	73	130	57
Emtriva (Emtricitabine)	N021500	02-Jul-03	A091168	30-Jan-09	02-Jul-18	66	180	113
Aloxi (Palonosetron Hydrochloride)	N021372	25-Jul-03	A202521	03-Dec-10	13-Oct-15	88	146	58
Zavesca (Miglustat)	N021348	31-Jul-03	A208342	04-Jan-16	17-Apr-18	149	176	27
Crestor (Rosuvastatin Calcium)	N021366	12-Aug-03	A079167	Unknown	19-Jul-16	N/A	N/A	N/A
Levitra (Vardenafil Hydrochloride)	N021400	19-Aug-03	A091347	Unknown	03-May-12	N/A	N/A	N/A
Cubicin (Daptomycin)	N021572	12-Sep-03	A202857	31-Mar-11	12-Sep-14	90	132	41

(continued)

Table A4 (continued)

Name of drug	NDA	NDA approval date	ANDA	ANDA submission date	ANDA approval date	NDA approval to ANDA submission, months	NDA approval to ANDA approval, months	ANDA submission to approval, months
Namenda (Memantine Hydrochloride)	N021487	16-Oct-03	A090048	16-Oct-07	14-Apr-10	48	77	29
Elestat (Epinastine Hydrochloride)	N021565	16-Oct-03	A090870	10-Oct-08	14-Mar-11	59	88	29
Cialis (Tadalafil)	N021368	21-Nov-03	A090141	21-Nov-07	22-May-18	48	174	126
Sensipar (Cinacalcet Hydrochloride)	N021688	08-Mar-04	A206125	30-Aug-13	08-Mar-18	113	168	54
Tindamax (Tinidazole)	N021618	17-May-04	A201172	Unknown	30-Apr-12	N/A	N/A	N/A
Vidaza (Azacitidine)	N050794	19-May-04	A201537	29-Mar-10	16-Sep-13	70	111	41
Sanctura (Trospium Chloride)	N021595	28-May-04	A091575	28-May-09	13-Aug-10	60	74	14
Campral (Acamprosate Calcium)	N021431	29-Jul-04	A202229	13-Sep-10	16-Jul-13	73	107	34
Cymbalta (Duloxetine Hydrochloride)	N021427	03-Aug-04	A090774	04-Aug-08	11-Dec-13	48	112	64
Fosrenol (Lanthanum Carbonate)	N021468	26-Oct-04	A090978	Unknown	11-Aug-17	N/A	N/A	N/A
Omacor (Omega-3-acid Ethyl Esters)	N021654	10-Nov-04	A091028	10-Nov-08	07-Apr-14	48	112	64
Tarceva (Erlotinib Hydrochloride)	N021743	18-Nov-04	A091002	Unknown	11-Jun-14	N/A	N/A	N/A

VESIcare (Solifenacin Succinate)	N021518	19-Nov-04	A091464	09-Apr-09	04-Feb-14	52	110	57
Lunesta (Eszopiclone)	N021476	15-Dec-04	A091169	15-Dec-08	23-May-11	48	77	29
Enablex (Darifenacin Hydrobromide)	N021513	22-Dec-04	A091190	Unknown	13-Mar-15	N/A	N/A	N/A
Clolar (Clofarabine)	N021673	28-Dec-04	A204029	23-Feb-12	09-May-17	85	148	62
Lyrica (Pregabalin)	N021446	30-Dec-04	A091219	Unknown	19-Jul-19	N/A	N/A	N/A
Mycamine (Micafungin Sodium)	N021506	16-Mar-05	A207344	16-Jun-14	17-May-19	111	170	59
Baraclude (Entecavir)	N021797	29-Mar-05	A202122	14-Jun-10	26-Aug-14	62	112	50
Tygacil (Tigecycline)	N021821	15-Jun-05	A091620	Unknown	27-May-15	N/A	N/A	N/A
Rozerem (Ramelteon)	N021782	22-Jul-05	A091610	Unknown	19-Aug-15	N/A	N/A	N/A
Exjade (Deferasirox)	N021882	02-Nov-05	A203560	28-Oct-11	26-Jan-16	71	122	50
Ranexa (Ranolazine)	N021526	27-Jan-06	A201046	17-May-10	20-Jul-13	51	89	38
Dacogen (Decitabine)	N021790	02-May-06	A203131	Unknown	11-Jul-13	N/A	N/A	N/A
Azilect (Rasagiline mesylate)	N021641	16-May-06	A201823	Unknown	07-Jan-13	N/A	N/A	N/A
Prezista (Darunavir ethanolate)	N021976	23-Jun-06	A202118	23-Jun-10	21-Nov-17	48	136	88

(continued)

Table A4 (continued)

Name of drug	NDA	NDA approval date	ANDA	ANDA submission date	ANDA approval date	NDA approval to ANDA submission, months	NDA approval to ANDA approval, months	ANDA submission to approval, months
Sprycel (Dasatinib)	N021986	28-Jun-06	A202103	28-Jun-10	06-Oct-16	48	123	75
Invega (Paliperidone)	N021999	19-Dec-06	A202645	19-Jun-12	03-Aug-15	66	103	37
Tekturna (Aliskiren hemifumarate)	N021985	05-Mar-07	A206665	13-Dec-13	22-Mar-19	81	144	63
Torisel (Temsirolimus)	N022088	30-May-07	A203153	31-May-11	30-Jul-18	48	134	85
Letairis (Ambrisentan)	N022081	15-Jun-07	A208252	09-Feb-15	28-Mar-19	91	141	49
Ammonia N13 (Ammonia)	N022119	23-Aug-07	A203543	Unknown	14-Dec-12	N/A	N/A	N/A
Kuvan (Sapropterin dihydrochloride)	N022181	13-Dec-07	A207200	05-Jun-14	10-May-19	77	136	59
Bystolic (Nebivolol)	N021742	17-Dec-07	A203741	17-Dec-11	24-Jun-15	48	90	42
Pristiq (Desvenlafaxine succinate)	N021992	29-Feb-08	A204003	29-Feb-12	29-Jun-15	48	88	40
Treanda (bendamustine hydrochloride)	N022249	20-Mar-08	A205574	04-Jun-13	19-May-16	62	97	35
Xenazine (Tetrabenazine)	N021894	15-Aug-08	A206129	30-Aug-13	03-Feb-16	60	89	29
Rapaflo (Silodosin)	N022206	08-Oct-08	A204726	09-Oct-12	31-Mar-17	48	101	53

Toviaz (Fesoterodine fumarate)	N22030	31-Oct-08	A204827	Unknown	10-Dec-15	N/A	N/A	N/A
Banzel (Rufinamide)	N021911	14-Nov-08	A204988	Unknown	16-May-16	N/A	N/A	N/A
Savella (Milnacipran hcl)	N022256	14-Jan-09	A205071	Unknown	27-Jan-16	N/A	N/A	N/A
Uloric (Febuxostat)	N021856	13-Feb-09	A205421	Unknown	01-Jun-19	N/A	N/A	N/A
Afinator (Everolimus)	N022334	30-Mar-09	A206133	30-Sep-13	12-Apr-18	54	108	54
Fanapt (Iloperidone)	N022192	06-May-09	A207231	Unknown	28-Nov-16	N/A	N/A	N/A
Effient (Prasugrel)	N022307	10-Jul-09	A205927	10-Jul-13	12-Jul-17	48	96	48
Livalo (Fitavastatin)	N022363	03-Aug-09	A206015	Unknown	20-Dec-16	N/A	N/A	N/A
Saphris (Asenapine)	N022117	13-Aug-09	A206107	13-Aug-13	17-Jul-18	48	107	59
Sabril (Vigabatrin)	N020427	21-Aug-09	A208218	23-Feb-15	27-Apr-17	66	92	26
Bepreve (Bepotastine besilate)	N022288	08-Sep-09	A206066	09-Sep-13	05-Mar-19	48	113	65